STRAIGHT AHEAD

The Memoirs of a Mississippi Governor

STRAIGHT AHEAD

*The Memoirs
of a
Mississippi Governor*

―――――――

BILL WALLER

QUAIL RIDGE PRESS

Library of Congress Cataloging-in-Publication Data

Waller, Bill, 1926-
    Straight ahead : the memoirs of a Mississippi governor / Bill Waller. – 1st ed.
        p. cm.
    Includes index.
    ISBN-13: 978-1-934193-04-4
    ISBN-10: 1-934193-04-6
        1. Waller, Bill, 1926- 2. Governors–Mississippi–Biography. 3. Mississippi–Politics and
    government–1951- 4. Lawyers–Mississippi–Jackson–Biography. 5. Jackson (Miss.)–Biography.
    6. Lafayette County (Miss.)–Biography. I. Title.
    F345.3.W35A3 2007
    976.2'063--dc22   2007002089

Manufactured in the United States of America
First Edition

Design by Cynthia Clark

On the cover: Bill Waller entering the Hinds County courthouse during the trial of Byron De La Beckwith in January 1964. Courtesy AP Images

QUAIL RIDGE PRESS
P. O. Box 123 • Brandon, MS 39047
1-800-343-1583 • info@quailridge.com • www.quailridge.com

This book is dedicated to
Carroll Overton Waller
Joy, our beloved departed daughter
Bill, Jr., Bob, Eddie, Don
my fourteen grandchildren
Percy and Myrtle Waller
and
Miss Emma Winter Waller

Contents

Preface

When I first ran for governor in 1967 Mississippi's political system had been virtually unchanged since the horse and buggy days of the late nineteenth century. The Constitution of 1890 did not allow the governor to succeed himself and strictly limited the authority of the executive branch of state government. Political power was vested in the legislature, whose members were not term-limited, and through the years a small group of powerful legislators assumed control of state government. When the Speaker of the House died in 1966, he had been in the legislature for half a century, and Speaker for a quarter of a century. The legislature, in combination with the social and business leadership of the state, formed a ruling elite that determined public policy and perpetuated the racial traditions that had been in place since Reconstruction. At both the state and local level a network of "good old boys" protected the status quo and convinced the voters to resist any change in the system. Mississippi was standing still.

All of this began to change in the early 1960s with the murder of Medgar Evers and the prosecution of Byron De La Beckwith. I ran for governor in 1967 because I wanted to help move Mississippi out of the horse and buggy age into the modern era. During that campaign I promised if I were elected governor my administration would be about the future, not the past. After the integration of the public school system and other public facilities, the voters were looking for new leaders who were not identified with the old political machine. In the 1971 campaign I offered them a viable alternative to the old guard that had held Mississippi back for so many years. The people of Mississippi elected me governor, and I endeavored to fulfill my solemn promise to them.

It is now thirty years since I left office, and I am approaching eighty years of age. The privilege of serving the people of Mississippi as their governor is one of the great experiences in my life. It seemed appropriate to me that I should recall those years in a formal way, so I began accumulating the details of my administration, and in the process I expanded the project into a book of memoirs.

Mississippi has had sixty-three governors since its admission to statehood in 1817. As I began writing these memoirs, I was surprised to learn that there are biographies of only ten Mississippi governors. I was even more surprised to learn that I would be one of only two governors to publish a book of memoirs. Governor Henry Stuart Foote, who served from 1852 to 1854, published A Casket of Reminiscences in 1874. A biographical sketch of all sixty-three governors can be found at Mississippi HistoryNow, an online publication of the Mississippi Historical Society.

During the long process of writing these memoirs I became indebted to many people who graciously shared their knowledge and time, and I want to thank them. In the early stages of the book Bob Pittman, a distinguished journalist and long-time president of the Mississippi Economic Council, and a friend of many years, conducted interviews with several members of my staff and gathered information about my administration at the Mississippi Department of Archives and History. Elbert Hilliard, Director of the Department of Archives and History, his successor Hank Holmes and his fine staff, in particular Anne Webster, head of Reference Services, were helpful in the process of collecting information and locating photographs that were taken during my administration.

For their many contributions I want to thank my brother Don Waller, Dr. Milton Baxter, Judge W. O. "Chet" Dillard, Insurance Commissioner George Dale, John H. Fox, III, Paul Fugate, Bobby Chain, Chief Justice Edwin Pittman, Charles McKellar, Wayne Edwards, Dr. Robert Robinson, and Terry Whittington.

I also want to thank Professor Dennis Mitchell of Mississippi

State University-Meridian, Professor Bill Baker of Mississippi College, Professor Chester Morgan of Delta State University, Charles McKellar, my former press secretary, and Jack Mayfield of Oxford for reading all or parts of the manuscript and for making many helpful suggestions. I want to express my special appreciation to Brenda Eagles of Oxford for copy editing the manuscript.

Bill Waller, Jr., and Professor David G. Sansing of The University of Mississippi worked closely with me in writing the final draft and I thank them both.

Finally, I want to express my appreciation to Barney McKee and Cyndi Clark for designing the book and guiding it through the process of publication.

CHAPTER 1

The Inauguration

"It's Time for a Change"

1971 CAMPAIGN SLOGAN

A festive crowd of more than 5,000 gathered on the south lawn of the New Capitol for my inauguration. It was the largest inauguration in the state's history and the first to be broadcast live on statewide television. Jackson officials estimated that 75,000 lined Capitol Street for the inaugural parade, which took more than two hours to pass the reviewing stand in front of the Governor's Mansion.

James O. Eastland, Mississippi's senior United States Senator who supported me in the campaign and attended my inauguration, told me it was the biggest one he had ever seen. To give you some idea of just how senior he was, "Big Jim" Eastland was elected to the Senate when I was in junior high school. Now, on January 18, 1972, I was about to become Mississippi's fifty-sixth governor. Though I had no way of knowing it on the day of my inauguration, several years later Senator Eastland would again play a major role in my political future, in a way that neither of us could have anticipated.

As the crowd assembled on the capitol grounds, a band played martial music and jet planes streaked across the southern sky leaving red, white and blue plumes in their wake. Thousands of my most dedicated and loyal supporters, people who had believed in me and shared my goals for Mississippi, had come to Jackson to celebrate the long, hard-fought victory. Some had been with me since my first governor's campaign in 1967, and for most of them it was their first inauguration. A few of them went all the way back to my campaigns for district attorney in the 1950s. I wanted them, and my boyhood friends and family, to savor that moment with me.

My Lafayette County second grade teacher, Mrs. Tommy Hale, drove down from Pontotoc to attend my inauguration. She admitted to a reporter that she never dreamed I would be governor of Mississippi, but voted for me and thought I would make a good one. Her approval was a source of special pride to me.

It was a happy occasion, as those kinds of ceremonies always are, and I was enjoying it but I was getting restless. I was ready to take the oath of office, to be the governor of Mississippi, to go to work, to make all the appointments I would have to make, to meet with the legislature, and to lay out my agenda. As I had said during the campaign, it was time to start moving Mississippi "Straight Ahead."

I have been in a hurry all my life. I knew that I would have only four years, and there was so much to do. In 1972 Mississippi governors could not succeed themselves. A succession bill was introduced every year during my four years in office, and I supported the bill. But it did not pass because the old guard wanted to keep the governor weak.

I entered the governor's office with no illusions. I knew that under Mississippi's antiquated constitution the office was largely a ceremonial position. The legislature held the real power. But I was determined to use all the power and authority at my disposal to make Mississippi better, and I wanted to make its people proud to be Mississippians. I would use the power of appointment carefully and judiciously. If I could not change the state with new laws, I would change it with new and progressive leaders.

As I was waiting on the platform on the front steps of Mississippi's grand state Capitol, thinking about all of these things, looking over that huge crowd and the platform dignitaries, I glanced at my wife Carroll who was sitting next to me and thought of how important she had always been to me, what an asset she had been in all my campaigns, especially in the 1971 race. Carroll is the best campaigner I have ever known. She has a natural appeal to people, she is so authentic and positive, and people are drawn to her and trust her implicitly. Some said, maybe only half-jokingly, that she ought to be running for governor and that I should be campaigning for her.

Sitting next to Carroll were our five children, Bill, Jr., who was twenty years old and a Mississippi State University student; Joy, who was eighteen, and the three younger boys, Bob, Eddie, and Don, who were fourteen, eleven, and seven. They had enjoyed the hectic pace of the campaign and had traveled all across Mississippi during the summer months of 1971.

In his infinite wisdom the Good Lord does not allow us to know the future, and on that day of celebration there was no foreboding of the grief that would be caused by the tragic demise of our daughter Joy ten years later.

On that day of pomp and ceremony almost everyone noticed the young people at the inauguration. Louise Hardy of Jackson and Bill, Jr., had enlisted thousands of young Mississippians into our campaign. After the election I appointed a large number of Youth Colonels and authorized them to wear blue wind-breakers with a special emblem of the state flag encircled by the words, "Governor's Staff 1972-1976." Young people had played an important role in my campaign, and I wanted to recognize them. In addition to the traditional inaugural ball, we held a special ball for young people at the old Heidelberg Hotel, which was attended by more than two thousand young men and women from all across the state.

On inauguration day I could see scattered throughout the crowd a number of black Mississippians, most of whom were probably attending their first inauguration. They had supported me during the campaign and wanted to serve their state, and I was determined to give them an opportunity to do so. Their futures, and the well-being of their children, were tied to the future of Mississippi.

I wish there had been more, but I was glad to see those who did come, especially after my long, hard campaign against Charles Evers, the independent candidate and older brother of Medgar Evers, the slain civil rights leader. From the beginning of my campaign in the spring of 1971, I pledged to all Mississippians—black and white, rich and poor, young and old, rural and urban—that no one would be left out of my administration. We were all Mississippians and by working together we could change the state and make it a better place for everyone.

Although I have never been one to stand on formality or resort to sentimentality, it was a source of great satisfaction to me that my father, Percy Andreth Waller, attended the inaugural ceremony and saw his oldest son take the oath of office as governor of the state of Mississippi. My mother, Myrtle Ora Gatewood Waller, had passed away nearly a decade earlier, but all of my family was proud to have our stepmother, Emma Winter Waller, share that special day with my father. Also present was my beloved mother-in-law, Edith Watkins Overton. Members of my immediate family, including my sister Mildred and brother Don, were with us on the inaugural platform.

It was not until long after I left home and had my own family, that I realized that the most enduring lesson I learned from my mother and father was the importance of family and continuity. I was not just one individual trying to make a life for myself, but I was part of a long family tradition. The heritage I received from my father, which he had received from his father and his father's father, I was bound to pass on to my children.

When at last I heard Governor John Bell Williams begin his introduction, I reached over and took Carroll's hand. She was holding the Watkins family Bible that belonged to her grandfather, a Southern Baptist Missionary. On that Bible I would pledge to do my duty as governor of the state of Mississippi.

I was anxious to get to work.

CHAPTER 2

A Journey of a Thousand Years

*From the meadows of Normandy to the
farmlands of Lafayette County.*

Like most southerners, I am proud of my heritage. I know the
names of my grandfather and my great-grandfather. I know
the wars my ancestors fought in, when they came to America,
when they left Virginia and moved down to South Carolina and
out to Kentucky and Tennessee and finally into Mississippi. I
know where they bought land, cleared it and farmed it, what professions they followed, and the churches they belonged to. Family
genealogists have traced the Waller lineage back across ten cen-
turies, and two proud family traditions have marked that journey
of a thousand years. One is faith, and the other is law.

The Waller family of the American South is descended from
Allured d' Waller who migrated from Normandy to Nottingham,
England. The first Waller who came to America was John Waller,
Jr., the son of Dr. John Waller and nephew of the poet Edmund
Waller. He settled in Gloucester County, Virginia, and was

described as "a wild young fellow" who had fallen into some kind of trouble. Waller genealogists have not identified precisely what that trouble was.

Soon after arriving in America, John Waller married Mary Key. Their son Benjamin was a prominent lawyer and chief judge of the Court of Admiralty. John Waller's grandsonWilliam Waller was also a member of the Virginia bar in the mid 1750s, and another grandson, the Reverend John Waller, was a Baptist minister in Spotsylvania, Virginia. In those early years the Waller heritage of Baptist faith and the practice of law was clearly marked.

Near Fredericksburg, Virginia, in 1768, the Reverend John Waller and two other ministers, Lewis Craig and James Chiles, were arrested by the sheriff and carried before the local magistrate. The young ministers were charged with disturbing the peace and ordered to report to the court two days later. At the hearing before the magistrate the sheriff testified, "These men are great disturbers of the peace. They can meet no man on the road but that they must ram a text of the scripture down his throat."

According to the court records, the Reverend Waller presented the ministers' defense "so ingeniously" that the judges "were puzzled to know what to do with them." They offered the ministers a plea bargain: they could go free if they would agree not to preach in the county for at least one year and a day.

The young ministers declined the offer and went to jail. As they walked through the streets of Fredericksburg from the courthouse to the jail house, the pastors sang the popular hymn, "Broad is the Road that Leads to Death." They appealed their conviction to the governor, who soon released them from jail and cleared them of all charges.

During America's war for independence the Reverend John Waller joined the revolution and provided beef and other supplies to George Washington's army. Waller later migrated to South Carolina and died at Abbeville in 1802. His grandson Addison was born in Abbeville, South Carolina, in 1801 and later moved to Abbeville, Mississippi, a community about fifteen miles from Burgess where I was born. Families from Abbeville, South Carolina, named their new home in Mississippi for the community they left behind. Mary Ann "Mollie" McGehee, Addison's daughter, was born in Abbeville, Mississippi, in 1849 and married Benjamin Sneed in 1869. Mollie, who was probably the first Waller born in Lafayette County, died at Lafayette Springs, in 1924.

Another branch of the Waller family, which included Dr. Benjamin Smith Waller, moved from Virginia to Kentucky. He later moved to Clinton, Mississippi, with his brother William Mikell Waller. Soon after settling in Mississippi, William M. Waller married Clara Longino, the sister of Governor Andrew Longino, Mississippi's thirty-fifth governor and the state's first governor of the twentieth century. Their daughter Mae Batson was a member of the faculty at Mississippi Woman's College in Hattiesburg, a Baptist institution of higher learning now known as William Carey University.

My great-great-grandfather, Ralph Lowe Waller, whose middle name I bear, was born in Kentucky in 1804. At the age of twenty-six he moved with his wife Sarah and their children to Henry County, in west Tennessee. When the Chickasaw Indian territory in north Mississippi was opened to white settlers in 1836, my great-great-grandfather bought a 640-acre section for $6,600 from Jesse Low and Andrew Carothers. He built a home at College Hill, eight miles north of Oxford, and by the 1860s he was raising crops and cattle on 420 of his 640 acres. With his ten slaves he raised wheat, rye, cotton, peas, beans, and potatoes. In addition to his row crops, he raised fifty hogs, forty-eight head of cattle, and eight horses.

Shortly after Ralph Lowe Waller moved to Lafayette County the Ebenezer Presbyterian Church, the first Presbyterian church in the county, was organized in his home on November 1, 1836. The name of the church was later changed to College Hill Presbyterian Church, where William Faulkner would be married many years later.

At a camp ground revival meeting in Lafayette County my great-great-grandfather was converted to the Baptist faith. One of his first works as a Baptist was to help build the Clear Creek Baptist Church, the church I would join many years later.

Two of Ralph Lowe Waller's sons were killed in the Civil War. James A. and John W. Waller joined Company F of the 19th Mississippi Infantry Regiment and served for a short time under the command of Colonel L.Q.C. Lamar. When they died, James was thirty-two years old and John was twenty-one.

Ralph Lowe Waller's third son, Ralph Young Waller, was born in 1852 and was too young to serve in the Confederate army. He married Kate Ayles of Lafayette County and they had six sons. One of their sons was Morgan Lowe Waller, the father of my father, Percy Andreth Waller.

My family had at last completed its journey of a thousand years, from Normandy to the New World and, finally, to the Old South and Lafayette County, Mississippi.

CHAPTER 3

My Lafayette County Boyhood

"Bill wasn't very good at farming, especially the plowing."
—DON WALLER

Lafayette County has produced two Mississippi governors. Lee Russell, who served from 1920 to 1924, is the other one. But our rank in the county's history is far below that of William Faulkner, Mississippi's only Nobel Laureate, and L.Q.C. Lamar, Mississippi's only U.S. Supreme Court Justice. There are many others of great fame and fortune identifed with the county, including Secretary of the Interior Jacob Thompson, legendary Ole Miss coach Johnny Vaught, and best selling novelist John Grisham. Like all of them, I am proud of my Lafayette County heritage and have always called it home.

When I was growing up in Lafayette County almost ninety percent of Mississippi's population was rural and about eighty percent were farmers. My grandfather Morgan Lowe Waller and five other Waller boys of his generation owned farmland in Lafayette County. My grandfather married Lillie May Murphy, who also grew up in Lafayette County. They had one daughter and four sons. One of those sons was my father, Percy Andreth Waller. The Burgess community has been sometimes jokingly called "Wallerville" because there were so many of us out there.

My grandfather Morgan Waller was prosperous for that time and place. The children in the countryside thought he must have been a rich man, measuring his wealth by the Coca-Colas he kept on his front porch. He usually had a whole case, and sometimes two cases. Back then Cokes were packaged in a wooden case that contained twenty-four six-ounce bottles. And you had to pay a deposit for the real glass bottle. Naturally, he was a favorite among his grandchildren and their friends. If you wanted a Coke, you could always go to his house and get one, but you had to wait for him to invite you to help yourself.

I do not remember seeing my grandfather work in the fields. He was a farmer but he had field hands who did most of the work. He was also a kind and generous man. I remember him giving food to neighbors who were in need, or anyone, even those who just happened to be passing through the community.

Born on July 7, 1899, my father was the fourth generation of his family to own farmland in Lafayette County. If he had lived in a more promising time, he might have studied the law. He often expressed an interest in the law, but that opportunity never came to him. After he finished high school, he enrolled at Mississippi College, a Baptist liberal arts college in Clinton. To pay his college expenses my father, who was the proud owner of a second-hand Model-T Ford, operated a taxi service during the two years he was at Mississippi College. He made two runs a day from Clinton to Jackson providing round trip service to the male students at Mississippi College and the young ladies of Hillman College. Unfortunately, his Model-T taxi broke down and his collegiate education came to an end.

I think my father went to Mississippi College rather than Ole Miss for two reasons. He thought his taxi service could pay his college expenses and that would be preferable to living on the farm while attending Ole Miss. Second, my father might have gone to Mississippi College because he aspired to be a Baptist minister. I do know that his Baptist faith was one of the most important things in his life.

My mother, Myrtle Ora Gatewood, was born on January 17, 1898, in the Lillian community near Hillsboro, which was the county seat of Scott County before the Civil War. She was the oldest of ten children born to Levy and Mildred Gatewood. One of her brothers, Henry Gatewood, moved to Burgess in the early 1930s and married my father's only sister, May Waller. Henry Gatewood worked on my grandfather's farm and had four daughters, Mary Agnes, Imogene, Francis, and Joyce, who were my double first cousins.

Donna Gatewood, one of my mother's younger sisters, also moved to Burgess. She married Joseph Shipp who owned a general merchandise store located on Highway 6, a new state highway that bypassed the village of Burgess.

After my mother graduated from high school in the early 1920s a family friend invited her to come live with them in Burgess and teach in the county school. In those days a high school diploma qualified her to teach in the public schools. After a brief courtship she and my father were married, and they purchased some farmland between Burgess and the Clear Creek Baptist Church.

Most of their crop land was located along Clear Creek, which meandered through a deep water swamp. My father used a floating dredge mounted on a small barge to channel the creek straight enough and deep enough to drain the swamp. As soon as he had drained and cleared the land, he started plowing it, numerous roots and stumps notwithstanding. The "new ground," as it was called, was still full of stumps and roots when I got old enough to plow. We burned the huge piles of stumps and other debris in the fields in the winter time.

My mother and father set up housekeeping in a three room shotgun house. In that household, on Waller land, I was born October 21, 1926. I was known in the community as William Lowe, not Bill or William, always as William Lowe. Bill Evans, an older neighbor who peddled meat from a horse-drawn wagon, for some reason always called me "Bill High." My birth came two years after the birth of my sister Mildred, known affectionately as "Millie." My brother Don was born six years later.

As the oldest child in her large family my mother felt a sense of responsibility for her younger siblings and usually hosted the Gatewood family reunions. She would also have members of her family as house guests in Lafayette County for several days at a time. Because my mother wanted us to know our maternal grandparents, in the summer after the crops were laid by she would take Millie, Don, and me to Scott County to visit our Gatewood grandparents. On those trips, someone would drive us to the Illinois Central depot in Batesville, which was about eighteen miles west of Burgess.

At Batesville we would catch the "City of New Orleans" down to Jackson. When we passed through Jackson I did not think that I would ever live in that great big town, but I knew I was not going to live in Burgess the rest of my life. At Jackson we transferred to the Vicksburg and Meridian Railroad for the final forty miles east to Forest, the new county seat of Scott County. It was always an exciting trip for me as a young boy to ride in those fancy coaches and to hear the sound of those huge locomotives. Sometimes we ate lunch in the dining car, which was really special. But most of the time mother packed a lunch.

My grandfather, William Levy Gatewood, would always meet us at the depot in Forest. He was over six feet tall and his personal trademarks were his bright yellow suspenders and a large white mustache, which almost always showed traces of tobacco stains.

My mother's brothers and sisters often joined us for those family get-togethers at the old Gatewood home place. Roger, the youngest of ten Gatewood children and about eight years older than I was, stilléd lived at home and I especially enjoyed visiting him. Those summer trips meant a lot to us because we got to spend long, leisurely visits with our Gatewood grandparents and their family.

I also have fond memories of visiting my cousins, William Edward and Ralph Metcalf, who lived in the Delta. To a boy from the hills of Lafayette County, the flat land of the Delta was a strange sight. One of my mother's sisters, Teresa Gatewood Metcalf, lived in Cleveland. Her family had some financial difficulty because of her husband's illness, and I remember several times filling up the back seat of our 1933 black Chevrolet with flour and corn meal, canned goods, and other food. There was always a big sack of potatoes. I remember that because I had to sit on that sack of potatoes all the way to Cleveland, and I will never forget how happy they were to see us coming, and bringing all that food. Years later Aunt Teresa, William Edward, and Ralph, and their wives Bonita and Dolly, were loyal supporters in all my political campaigns.

My father's two hundred acre farm was virtually self-sufficient and provided a full range of food products, including pork, beef, chickens, eggs, dairy products, and vegetables from a large family garden. We also kept a herd of about twenty-five to thirty Jersey milk cows and about the same number of beef cattle. Like most working farms of that time the Waller farmland was divided into pastures and row crops and subdivided into plots of varying sizes that were worked by tenants who lived in small wooden shotgun houses. At the turn of the century the federal census classified about half of the farm families in Lafayette County as tenants.

When I was growing up I did not regard us as being poor or deprived. Although we lived in a three-room shotgun house without running water or electricity, as children we thought of ourselves as being well off because some of our neighbors were worse off than we were. Our shotgun house consisted of three rooms in a straight line under a single roof. There was no hallway in the house, and if you walked in the front door you passed through all three rooms to get out the back door. It was like most other houses in the neighborhood, and not much different from the unpainted tenant houses that stood in nearby fields.

According to an old family story one of my mother's cousins, Erma Gatewood Ginn and her husband Earl, came up from Tylertown to visit her Waller kinfolks. She was a home demonstration agent in Walthall County in southwest Mississippi and was unfamiliar with the gullied terrain of Lafayette County. During her stay Erma became concerned about her cousin and her family. When cousin Erma and Earl left our place to go back home, they drove about a half mile down the road. Worried that we could never make a living off such poor land, they pulled off the county road and said a prayer for Myrtle and Percy Waller, and their three little children.

In 1937, when I was eleven years old and Mississippi was slowly emerging from the depression, my father built a three bedroom house with indoor plumbing. It was a fine house by the standards of that day, but a grand house in the eyes of his children. I did not realize that we had been living in a shack until we moved into that big, brand new house. In the neighborly tradition of that time and place Charlie Faust, a cousin and a fine carpenter, built our house.

In keeping with my father's code of saving and using everything possible, when our new home was built the old shotgun house was rolled on logs across the road and converted into a barn. The old barn is now grayed and weathered. But it was to this old barn that my father would take his two sons when the rains came. He was not one to waste either time or resources. On those rainy days inside the barn we would straighten-out bent and crooked nails so they could be used again. We would also roll-up barbed wire that had been stripped from old fences so it could be used on new fences.

My boyhood home now sits on a green hillside on County Road 313, shaded by two pecan trees and a grand old oak. Four brick pillars and four rocking chairs are spread evenly across the front porch, a silent reminder of my mother and father and their neighbors who spent many spring and summer evenings on that porch. The old house is empty now, but my brother Don keeps the house in good repair and sees that the grass is always cut.

Don and my father eventually formed a partnership, and Don convinced him to modernize his farm equipment and to accept new technology. In the 1960s, Don moved our grandparents' house, which he and his wife Patsy had been living in, across the road and built a new house on the site of the old Waller home place. Don is a successful farmer and continues to produce cotton and timber on some of the land our father acquired in the 1920s.

We lived in our new house only a year or two before the Rural Electrification Administration brought electric power to the Burgess community. We no longer had to read or study by coal oil lamps, though some of my fondest memories of my mother are her helping me with my school work by the light of an oil lamp.

Then came the telephone. I do not recall how many of our neighbors, or which ones, were on our party line. But I do remember that our telephone was three long and two short rings. I practiced using the telephone by calling my grandfather, whose house was about a mile down the road from ours.

One of the big events of my boyhood was the construction of a flood control project in north Mississippi by the U.S. Corps of Engineers in the late 1930s. The initial phase of that project was the construction of a dam on the Tallahatchie River that created Sardis Lake, a huge flood control reservoir. Clear Creek flowed across our land and emptied into the reservoir. After the creation of Sardis Lake, Clear Creek stopped flowing and backed up on our land and filled the channel that my father had dredged when he first bought the farm. For the Waller boys and our cousins and neighbors, the old channel became one of our favorite swimming holes and the best fishing pond in the Burgess community. My mother loved to fish, and when Clear Creek overflowed during the spring rains, fish were everywhere. I probably got my love for fishing from my mother. Neighborhood fish fries at our house became a regular spring festival.

Another important site during my boyhood was Maybelle's Lake, which was about five miles down the road from our house. Like most of my contemporaries who went to Clear Creek Baptist Church, I was baptized in Maybelle's Lake in 1936 at the age of ten. The lake was named for its owner, Mrs. Mike Williams, who was known affectionately by her friends and neighbors as Maybelle.

Maybelle's Lake was clean and clear, and spring fed, making it one of the most beautiful spots in north Mississippi. An unusual thing about Maybelle's Lake was its sandy beach. In an area like Lafayette County, which had been subjected to erosion for many years, most natural lake beds are mud rather than sand. The lake was a popular gathering place for the community's teenagers. In the summers we would ride our horses to Maybelle's Lake on Saturday and Sunday afternoon to swim. The lake was only about five acres, but to us it was as big and wonderful as an ocean.

One Saturday afternoon I was tussling with a friend and my senior class ring slipped off my finger. It got buried in the sand and I could not find it. About ten years later the Reverend Roy Hewlett, an itinerant preacher who always raked the sandy bed of Maybelle's Lake when he passed through our community, found my ring and returned it to me.

Growing up on a small working farm was a good life, but it was not an easy life. Before we went to school in the morning we milked about twenty-five or thirty cows. Years later I would refer to this enterprise as our "hand-operated dairy." When we came home in the afternoon we took our school clothes off, put our work clothes back on, and worked in the fields until it was time to round up the cows for milking.

I really did not take to farming. Don and my boyhood friend Gayle Crowe tell me that I was not very good at it, especially the plowing. My father thought I was stubborn and hard-headed. He said I would argue with a fence post and predicted that I would become a lawyer.

While my mother and father attached a great deal of importance to hard work and diligence, they placed an even higher premium on education. They were determined that we would get the best education possible in our community. I never made the honor roll, and I had to work hard to get through college and law school. I was a "Gentleman C Student," and I have told many young people over the years that if I could make it, they could too.

The year I started high school, Lafayette County closed the school at Burgess. High school students in the western part of Lafayette County were bused to a school in the Black Jack community in Panola County. I went to Black Jack High School for only one year because my father did not think I was getting a good enough education. He arranged for me to be transferred to University High School in Oxford. School buses were going up and down the same county road in opposite directions. You could go west to the schools in Panola County or east to the schools in Oxford. My father put my sister Millie and me on the bus that went to Oxford.

During my sophomore year in high school my life took a significant turn following a hunting accident that nearly cost me my life. I got a double-barreled shotgun for Christmas and during the holidays about ten of us went bird hunting. I carried my new shotgun and soon into the hunt I shot a quail, but a stray dog that had been following us jumped on the bird. I swung my shotgun at the dog and knocked him away, but the gun discharged and I was hit in my right thigh. Two black men who were in our hunting party picked me up, carried me to the road, stopped a passing automobile, and asked the driver to take me to Dr. Andrew Sims' office in Oxford.

Odell Shorter, one of the black men, probably saved my life and he remained a close friend for the rest of his life. Odell was at least a third or fourth generation sharecropper who worked for my father. Years later I came back to Lafayette County and represented Odell on a murder charge. In 1970 he was involved in a barroom fight and killed a bystander. I convinced the jury that the death of the bystander was manslaughter, rather than first-degree murder. The Mississippi Supreme Court in *Shorter vs. State*, 257 So. 2d 236 (Miss. 1972), upheld the conviction and a fifteen year sentence.

Dr. Sims told me that the gunshot severely damaged my thigh bone and it would take some time for the wound to heal, but there was no permanent damage. I was confined to my bed for more than six months, and actually had to learn how to walk again. To this day I still have about twenty pellets in my leg.

Because my mother wanted me to be near the doctor during my recovery, I lived with Uncle Robert and Aunt Jessie Waller and my cousins James and Louise during the spring semester of 1942. Uncle Robert had an apartment above his store on North Lamar, which was one block off the Square and across the street from the Dr. Sims' office. Aunt Jessie's eighty-two year old mother, Mrs. Gayle Wells, also lived with them. Mrs. Wells took care of me and was both my counselor and my nurse.

The accident happened when I was in the tenth grade, and I did not go to school the spring semester of that year. Two University High School teachers came to the apartment several days a week and "home schooled" me for the rest of that year. They kept me from getting behind the other students, and I graduated with my class from University High School in 1944. I have never forgotten the comity in Uncle Robert's household and the encouragement I received from my Oxford teachers.

My Lafayette County boyhood was an idyllic time in my life, and I knew little about the world beyond Burgess. Gayle Crowe, perhaps my closest boyhood friend, still lives within a stone's throw of where we grew up. Burgess boys did the same things other country boys did. We played ball, hunted rabbits, bream fished, helped neighbors kill hogs, and rode horses.

My cousin Howard Waller, William "Cracker Jack" Evans,

Gayle Crowe and his brother Hugh, several other boys and I had a Sunday afternoon riding club. We would have let anyone who had a horse and wanted to ride with us in the club, but two or three of the big boys decided who could ride with us and who could not ride. If they did not let you in the club, you did not get in. That riding club experience was my first encounter with ringleaders, and for much of the rest of my life I would be battling the ruling elites.

Family Photographs

The high school senior class picture of my mother, Myrtle Gatewood Waller

The school house at Burgess where I attended grade school

My brother, Don, my father, Percy, and I in front of my grandfather's house

With my father, Percy, and stepmother, Emma Winter Waller, in front of the Waller home place soon after I announced for governor in 1967

The Waller Home Place

Getting some good advice from my father in 1971

A 1967 family photograph with Carroll, Joy, 13; Bob, 8; Bill Jr., 15; (seated) Eddie, 6; Don, 4

An inaugural day family photograph

An inaugural
day photograph
with my sister
Mildred
Burtschell, my
father, and my
brother Don

Reviewing the inaugural parade in front of the Mansion with
Governor and Mrs. Williams

Joy painted this mural of the Governor's Mansion on an attic wall
and the boys signed their names

A family photograph circa 1980

Our family
picture taken
November 25, 2006
1st Row:
Emma Carroll,
Dannie, Jeannie,
William, III
2nd Row:
Bill, Carroll, Robert,
Charlotte, Bill, Jr.,
Clayton
3rd Row:
Don, Yonnie, Don,
Maggie, Joy,
Margaret, Bob
4th Row:
Eddie, Bae, Lucy,
Anne Overton,
Millie, Ava Burton,
Madeline

PHOTO BY DARYLL
STEGALL

CHAPTER 4

In A Hurry

"Get up early, work all day, do right by your neighbor, get as much
education as you can and live by the precepts of the Christian faith."

—Percy Andreth Waller

During my junior year at University High School in 1943, I
enrolled in a program called "Diversified Occupations." This
was an after school work program that allowed me to leave school
early in the afternoon to go to a part-time job. The program was
a great benefit to the students and to our families who needed the
extra income. The local businesses also needed the additional
workers with so many men and women away at war. In addition
to on-the-job training I also received academic credit for my work
experience. I was sixteen years old and was still having problems
with my leg injury, but I needed to work.

I got a part-time job at the Douglas Funeral Home. Oscar
Douglas also owned several other businesses, so he did not spend
a lot of time at the funeral home. But he did teach me how to

drive the flower truck. My job was to load the flowers that had been on display at the church or the funeral home into the truck, race ahead of the funeral procession to the cemetery, and arrange the flowers at the burial site.

Mr. Douglas gradually gave me added responsibilities, and I began working on Saturdays. Many of his customers came by the funeral home when they came to town on Saturdays to make a payment on their burial policy, which was about fifty cents a month for a $500 policy.

Mr. Douglas was a kind man, and he and his wife were very generous to me. They were always trying to give me something and to make sure that I had everything a sixteen-year-old boy needed. When I graduated from high school, with two years of training and experience at the Douglas Funeral Home, my mother encouraged me to consider a career as a funeral home director, and I did consider it. I wanted to own my own business. I just did not know what kind.

But there was something else I had to do first. In 1944 the war was still going on and I wanted to serve my country. I tried to enlist in the Army Air Corps but did not pass the physical examination because of my leg injury. After being rejected by the Army Air Corps, my life took on more of a sense of urgency. I was young and in a hurry, anxious to get off the farm and to get my military service behind me, anxious to get an education and get on with my life. The day after high school graduation I packed a bag and hitchhiked to Memphis. I did not have a job, but I had a letter of recommendation from Oscar Douglas.

My sister Millie was living in Memphis where she had started her distinguished banking career at Union Planter's Bank and I stayed with her until I found a job. She and her husband John H. Burtschell supported me throughout my career and were active in all my campaigns.

When I got to Memphis I tried one more time to join the Army Air Corps but was rejected again for the same reason as before. After I could not get into the military service, I enrolled at Memphis State College, which is now the University of Memphis. I also got a job at the J.W. Norris Funeral Home, an old and respected establishment that provided funeral services for many of the prominent families in Memphis.

I went to Memphis State rather than Ole Miss because the social climate and the Greek system at The University of Mississippi was not a friendly environment for the sons of Mississippi farmers. Most of them went to Mississippi State College in Starkville. Ole Miss just did not have much appeal to me as an undergraduate. More important, I knew I could work my way through Memphis State, and I was not sure that I could at Ole Miss. The Douglas Funeral Home in Oxford might have two or three funerals a month. In Memphis, the funeral homes might have two or three a day. My mother also influenced my decision to go to Memphis. She wanted me to get additional training in the funeral home business.

I did not have an automobile so I used the Memphis public transportation system, which coordinated its bus runs to accommodate college students throughout the metropolitan area. During my college days in Memphis I rode a city bus from my dormitory room at the funeral home to the campus. My father would have gladly paid my college expenses, but like many other Mississippi farmers in the 1940s, he did not have the money.

Funeral homes in Memphis maintained a staff twenty-four hours a day and employed college students who were available for work shifts at different hours of the day and night. A free room in the funeral home dormitory made the job even more attractive to me. When I worked at the Norris Funeral Home there were students from the University of Tennessee School of Dentistry and the Southern College of Optometry also living in the dormitory.

I arranged my classes in the morning so I could leave the campus at noon and be at work by one o'clock, work an eight-hour shift, and then take calls during the evening from my dorm room. The funeral home kept a staff on hand twenty-four hours a day because it provided ambulance services, and someone had to answer the emergency calls and drive the ambulances to the sites where they were needed. If you answered an emergency call and there had been a fatality, the family would usually ask the funeral home to provide the burial services.

I had a couple of wrecks speeding through traffic in an ambulance, but they were not serious. One night I drove to the scene of an accident on Third Street in downtown Memphis. I stopped on a hill, put the ambulance in neutral, and put on the emergency brake. The brake failed, and the ambulance rolled down the hill and crashed into a police car

During my three years in Memphis I worked for three different funeral homes. I worked year-round, almost every day, including Saturdays and Sundays, and I was also taking a full load of classes at Memphis State College. At that point in my life, without a car and a decent wardrobe, that paycheck was almost as important to me as a college degree.

One of my responsibilities at the Norris Funeral Home was to greet the friends of the family and escort them to the parlor where the family members were. Visitors came to the front door of that old and stately mansion on Union Avenue, and I would answer the bell and open the ornate, stained glass doors. Every person I met was a stranger and most were older than I was. From that experience I learned how important it was to greet people and to call them by their name.

I also worked at the Cosmopolitan Funeral Home and the Thompson Funeral Home in the downtown area. The other funeral homes paid me more, but I eventually went back to work for Norris. I was working there when I graduated from Memphis State. I considered a career in the funeral home business but eventually decided against it. My brother Don and his wife Patsy, who served a long and distinguished tenure as Lafayette County Chancery Clerk, established Waller Funeral Home in Oxford in 1979.

When I had a free weekend, which was about once a month, I usually hitchhiked back home to Oxford. My mother and father were proud of me and always made my coming home something special. I do not remember ever having a cross word with my parents. My father was the finest man I ever knew.

In addition to the steady income, my employment at the funeral homes in Memphis had an additional benefit. The funeral homes owned several automobiles and the owners would let me use them when I was off duty, or when I had someone covering for me. I was in the Alpha Tau Omega fraternity, went to football games, and did all the things most other undergraduates did. I do not think I missed out on anything during my college days at Memphis State. I coordinated my class schedule and my workload to make enough money to pay my expenses and still take the classes I needed to graduate in three years.

After graduating from Memphis State I decided that the study of law would provide a good background for banking or insurance or any other business that I might want to pursue. I enrolled at The University of Mississippi School of Law because I intended to stay in Mississippi, and a law degree from Ole Miss just made good sense.

Bramlett Roberts, an Oxford attorney that I worked for when I was in law school, greatly influenced my decision to practice law rather than go into business. Mr. Roberts had a general law practice and was one of Oxford's leading and most respected attorneys. In my second year of law school Mr. Roberts invited me to spend some time in his office and learn the practical aspects of legal work. He told me that he had an extra office that I could use. As it turned out, the office was a small room just large enough for a desk and a couple of chairs. My cousin Durley Jones, who had a retail produce market about three blocks down the street, loaned me a desk and an old chair. I borrowed those, found a couple of outdated side chairs, and I had me a law office.

When I was not in class I would sit in that office waiting for someone to avail themselves of my services. Eventually, Mr. Roberts allowed me to read his files and do some legal research, and then I started going to court with him. Judge Herbert Holmes, the chancellor of the Third Chancery Court District, held regular terms of court in the eleven counties in his district,

which included Lafayette County. Between terms he held court
in his hometown of Senatobia. Mr. Roberts and I made a number
of trips to Senatobia when the judge was not holding court in
Lafayette County.

Judge Taylor McElroy of Oxford and a distant cousin, was the
circuit judge for the Third District. Armis Hawkins, a friend and
law school classmate, would later serve as the district attorney of
this district. In 1980 Armis was elected to the Mississippi
Supreme Court.

My duties with Mr. Roberts increased during the brief period I
was associated with him, and by the time I graduated from law
school I was interviewing witnesses and prospective clients. From
the moment Mr. Roberts showed me that empty office I knew
that I would practice law.

The time I spent with Mr. Roberts was an invaluable intern-
ship for me, almost as important as my formal legal education in
the law school. One of the most important things I learned while
working with Mr. Roberts, and I learned this early in my association with him, was that a lawyer should not practice in his hometown. I had been in Mr. Roberts' office only a short time when my
relatives and friends started coming in to see me. They would
come in late in the afternoon, knowing I would be there, and
bring me their legal problems. They knew that I would not charge
them for my services.

If I stayed in Oxford I would get to practice a lot of law, but I
would not get paid for a lot of the law that I practiced. Mr.
Roberts and other local attorneys told me that Oxford was over-
crowded with attorneys and there was not much money to be
made in Oxford. There were fourteen or fifteen lawyers in Oxford
then, and there were eight or nine lawyers on the law faculty at
the University. At that time Oxford was a small university town
with a population of less than four thousand.

I was impatient to finish the study of law so I could begin the
practice of law. I looked forward to contending for my clients in
the courtroom. I knew early in my legal education that I wanted

to be a "fist fight" lawyer and to litigate, so I suffered through family law, contracts, torts, and several other such courses to get there.

All of my law professors were men of scholarly bearing, and the courses I took were useful to me, but the one professor that I remember with the most affection and admiration was my constitutional law professor, Judge Noah "Soggy" Sweat. Judge Sweat taught the course with all the drama and flair for which he was well known. He was a great raconteur and gave life and vitality to a nearly two hundred year-old document that is the foundation of our law. Like most of his students I was enthralled as he related the United States Constitution to everyday life in this country.

In law school I had no preference for the type of law I wanted to practice, except that I wanted to be in the courtroom and to try cases. My motivation was to try lawsuits of any type that were honorable and for which I could receive just compensation. I believed I was born to be a litigator.

Like many of my classmates at Ole Miss, I worked my way through law school. I was a dormitory manager, which meant I got a free room. I was also an assistant law librarian which earned me $67 a month, and I got $30 a month for picking up and delivering laundry in the dormitory.

Mr. Roberts did not pay me anything, but the practical experience I got from working with him was worth a fortune, and as I neared graduation I began to think about where I wanted to practice, and I was in a hurry. I finished a four-year college course at Memphis State in three years, and a three-year law course at Ole Miss in two and a half.

I wanted to find the right town or city to practice law, so I studied census reports, population trends, and compared economic indicators. I must have studied twenty-five towns and cities throughout the state. I never considered any place outside the state because I was determined to remain in Mississippi. Eventually, I narrowed my search to Natchez, Laurel, and Jackson.

All three of these cities showed signs of economic expansion in the 1950s. Natchez and Laurel were attractive because they were

centers of considerable oil and gas activity and had large manufacturing operations. The International Paper and Armstrong
Rubber companies were located in Natchez, and the Masonite
Corporation was in Laurel. Both towns had a number of oil well
service units.

Although both of the south Mississippi communities were
appealing, I was leaning toward Jackson. In addition to being the
state capital, Jackson was also the home of many significant
Mississippi-based enterprises, including the state's two largest
banks, the largest savings and loan company, the two largest
home-owned insurance companies, and major retail and whole-
sale operations. I knew that if I came to Jackson I would establish
my own firm rather than associate with one of the large Jackson
firms. Most of them were tied to the city's business and banking
structure, and it seemed to me that there were not enough lawyers
who focused on the legal problems of individual citizens. That
was one of the reasons I eventually located in Jackson.

As I was nearing my decision to move to the state capital, my
father and I made a trip to Jackson in January 1950 and called on
Ross Barnett, one of my father's Mississippi College classmates.
Ross Barnett would become Mississippi's fifty-third governor and
would attend my inauguration as the state's fifty-sixth governor.
When my father told him that I would soon be graduating from
the Ole Miss law school and might come to Jackson, Barnett said,
"We will be glad to have him. I will help him any way I can." I
was not sure what he meant by that. I hoped he meant that if he
had more clients than he could handle he would refer some of
them to me.

The visit with Ross Barnett was not the deciding factor in my
decision to locate in Jackson, but it was a reassuring gesture on his
part, and I appreciated it. After my father and I returned to
Oxford I decided to establish my legal practice and raise my family in Jackson, where I have remained for the past half-century.

CHAPTER 5

Capitol Street Lawyer

"We will be glad to have him. I will help him any way I can."

—Ross Barnett

In February 1950 I arrived in the capital city of the state of Mississippi with high hopes and $400 of borrowed money. It had been a long journey and I was grateful to all those who had helped me along the way. As many of my forebears had done, I joined a Baptist Church and began the practice of law.

My law office was on the second floor in a building next to the old Jitney Jungle grocery store on East Capitol Street, just a block or so from Mississippi's historic Governor's Mansion. I actually had two small rooms that were partitioned by a makeshift plywood wall. The building's owner, Ben Wakefield, advertised the office space for $40 a month, but he agreed to cut the rent in half to help this young lawyer get started. I had won my first pleading.

Mr. Wakefield told me about some second-hand oak furniture that might be available at a reasonable price. When I went to the store to look at the furniture, the owner Dorsey Barefield showed me a handsome desk, an executive chair, and two side chairs. He told me the furniture had belonged to Senator Theodore Bilbo, who had died just a couple of years earlier. After he agreed to a substantial discount, I purchased the furniture.

As a teenager I had heard Senator Bilbo speak on one of his many visits to Oxford. Bilbo had also served two terms as governor. After I was elected governor and we were restoring the Mansion, and trying to secure the property of former governors, I thought about that furniture and wished I had kept the desk. But as a young lawyer more concerned about the future than the past, I was just glad to have some decent furniture for my office. Carefully guarding my $400 capital, I paid only $35 for the Bilbo furniture. After moving the furniture into the office and putting up a $25 deposit on a telephone, I was ready for business.

I had to find a place to live as near my office as possible because I did not have an automobile and I would be walking to work. Fortunately, I found a boardinghouse on North Street about ten blocks from the office. I paid ten dollars a week for a room in an old white clapboard house, which I shared with two or three other men. The ten dollars a week included a bed, but no linens, and three meals a day, except on Sunday.

Although I was the only lawyer in the boarding house, there were two other lawyers in my office building on East Capitol Street. Lee Agnew, who had been practicing for about ten years, and his partner, Bill Slaymaker, a World War II veteran, had an office down the hall and we became good friends. Slaymaker was from Brookhaven and had lost a leg in combat. These two older and more experienced lawyers took an interest in me and helped me get started. The three of us took our morning and afternoon coffee breaks together. Like clock work every day, Monday through Friday, the three of us would leave our offices at ten o'clock in the morning and three o'clock in the afternoon, walk down Capitol Street to the Belmont Café, drink coffee, and talk about the law.

On one of those occasions Bill Slaymaker mentioned to me that a woman from Shreveport had a sister in Jackson who had recently died and needed someone to settle her estate. Slaymaker apparently had a conflict of interest and could not represent the woman. He asked me if I would be interested. I took the case immediately. It was one of my first cases.

The lady from Shreveport was cordial and pleasant to work with and my introduction to the practice of law was a good experience. Unfortunately, I can not say the same for all of the clients I have had since then. The estate included a limited number of collectibles, a small bank account, a few other items, and a four-door 1947 Chrysler sedan.

When I finished the work on the estate I charged the woman $500. She thought the fee was reasonable, but she did not have enough money to pay me. She offered me the Chrysler in lieu of the fee and I gladly accepted it. I was only a few months into my practice, and I owned my own car. The car was probably worth only about $150, but I was glad to get it.

I may have drawn a will or a deed for someone before I met the lady from Shreveport, but I did not have a lot of traffic coming through the door. I sat there, day after day, wondering how I could attract more clients. My father was always promoting me among his friends and acquaintances. A few former Oxford and Lafayette County natives who were living in Jackson came to see me, and I also began to get a number of referrals from Ross Barnett. My office was across the street from his, and on occasion he would call or have his secretary call to tell me he was sending over a prospective client. I never turned anyone down.

It is fascinating how you build a law practice. No two days are alike. New challenges and new opportunities come every time the phone rings, every time someone walks through the door, and every time you open the mail. I learned early in my legal career that a successful law practice is built one client at a time. If you have a man in your office who is in trouble, or maybe a son or someone else in his family needs legal counsel, and you are successful in your legal work for them, you will soon find his neighbor in your office.

I also quickly realized that the outcome of a lawsuit or any legal dispute could influence a family's happiness and success for years. The cardinal principle of my law practice has always been to make my clients feel that their case was as important to me as it was to them. Ordinary citizens are often bewildered when they find themselves caught up in what we call the "thickets of the law." I always tried to assure every client that I understood his plight and that we would resolve his problems in the best way we possibly could.

I was not becoming financially independent by any means, but I never had to borrow money to keep my office open. I never became discouraged, even while living in that boardinghouse with two or three other men in the same room, or having to take all my meals there because I could not afford to eat in a nice restaurant. I was impatient, perhaps, but never discouraged. I was always upbeat and knew I was going to make it. I was not going to let down all the people who had believed in me and helped me along the way.

Having practiced law in Jackson for more than a half century, I am now representing the third generation of families that I had as clients during the early years of my practice. It is not unusual for someone to walk into my office and say, "My grandfather used to tell me how you represented him and how much you helped him. I need some legal advice and I was hoping you could help me."

But like all lawyers, I have had clients who really do not appreciate what you have done for them and do not understand how the law works. That is especially true in estate settlements and divorces when there is not enough money for everyone and someone gets left out. Family members end up angry with each other, and especially angry at the lawyer. Once a family is split over a legal issue, especially when there is not enough money to support two or more households, it is difficult to reach a reconciliation. Still, with the family problems and other legal issues I have dealt with through the years, I have never had a single regret about my decision to practice law. I never come to work, even now, that I am not excited.

After a few months in my East Capitol Street office, I was financially able to move into the Plaza Building, which was a block off Capitol Street and a block closer to the new state Capitol. I shared an office with an older attorney, J. Arthur Sullivan, and we divided the office expenses, which included a full time secretary.

Meanwhile, the Selective Service Board decided to review my medical deferment. Ten months after I opened my law office in Jackson I was drafted into the Army. The United States was in an escalating military conflict in Korea. Several Mississippi National Guard units, including the 31st Infantry (Dixie) Division, had been activated and some of those units were already in Korea. Now the Army needed more men, and my name was added to the list.

I loved my country and had already volunteered for military service twice but had been rejected. I was almost twenty-four years old, had finished college and law school, was trying to get started as a lawyer, was married, and starting a family. I did not think the Korean conflict constituted a national emergency and was not happy about being drafted.

The United States Army offered me what seemed to be fifteen different deals. They offered me a commission if I would serve three years. I did not take any offers for a commission because it would have lengthened my term of service. I was anxious to get in, do my duty, get out, and return to my law practice. I went to Fort Chaffee, Arkansas, for basic training.

My captain and company commander in basic training was a lawyer from Muskogee, Oklahoma, and a ranking member in the Mormon Church. We became friends because of our common background as attorneys. He was a member of the Army Reserve, forty-five or fifty years old, and he was also unhappy about being called up. He and I complained every day about being there. He appointed me the company clerk and I made it through basic training.

After basic training, most of my buddies were shipped off to Korea, but I was sent to the school for the Army's Counter Intelligence Corps at Fort Holabird, Maryland. I spent most of my time in Baltimore with the Counter Intelligence Corps, wrote an investigative manual, taught some classes, lived in a three-story family housing unit, worked in military facilities that seemed more like an office building, and did not have to wear a uniform. I held the rank of sergeant but we did not display our ranks because that was a part of the intelligence deception strategy. Occasionally we would have a parade and I had to dress in full uniform for that, but generally those of us in the Counter Intelligence Corps did not wear uniforms.

While I was at Fort Holabird the Army again offered me a commission if I would sign up for another three years, but I was not interested. I just wanted to complete my term and get back to my career. I thought I was just wasting time. I stayed at Fort Holabird for about sixteen months of the twenty-two months I was in the Army, but that was not the end of my military career. I was required to serve four years in the active Army Reserve after I was discharged. The reserve did not interfere with my law practice, and I was never required to go to summer camp. However, I did attend special military classes at the Jackson Air Base. Purser Hewitt, the editor of the *Clarion-Ledger*, was our commander, holding the rank of colonel, and by which title he was always addressed. We had a great unit and all of us enjoyed the association.

When I was discharged from the Army on November 30, 1953, I returned immediately to Jackson. I made the rounds in the Plaza Building, shook hands with all the other lawyers and contacted my former clients to let them know I was back. I wanted them to know that I had not just disappeared, that I had been away in military service, and that I was ready to resume my practice.

During the early years of my career, I was never interested in joining a large firm. I gave it some thought but decided that I would do better on my own. I was not easy to get along with and never have been. Hugh Lipscomb and Henry Barksdale, who had a growing defense firm, offered me a position, but my side—the plaintiff's side—was much more exciting and remunerative.

In all my years in the law I have worked ten to twelve hours a day, and sometimes on Saturdays and Sundays. Maybe I am eccentric about work habits, but I do not enjoy being around people who do not have a similar drive and are not dedicated and committed.

Rather than specializing in one particular aspect of law, I had a general law practice that involved many different kinds of cases, and my clients ranged from large corporations to private citizens. In representing people from all walks of life you are rewarded, in addition to financial compensation, with the satisfaction of knowing that you are helping your fellow man. You are helping people who might not otherwise get help, and their gratitude is part of your reward.

My office schedule was not always voluntary. As a solo practitioner I sometimes had to be secretary as well as lawyer. I also had to work odd hours to keep the schedule required by the courts, and to diligently represent the interests of my clients. Arbitrary deadlines are involuntarily imposed by rules of law, by courts, and by the various emergency petitions I sometimes had to file.

Soon after I came to Jackson I joined the First Baptist Church, which was about eight blocks from my boardinghouse. A week or so after I joined the church I met Carroll Overton, and we were married a few months later. Although our meeting was by chance, I am convinced that it was providential, and a sign that the Good Lord was looking out for me. For all these years she has been a mother and a role model for our children, and she has given me the freedom to pursue my career and accepted my work habits without complaint. Now my wife of more than fifty years, Carroll has been an indispensable part of whatever success I have enjoyed.

CHAPTER 6

The Family Circle

Joy remains a loving member of our family circle.

Carroll and I were instantly attracted to each other and our love has grown deeper and stronger over the last fifty-six years. Carroll says she was attracted to me because I was always just who I was, and there was no pretense about me. I do not stand on ceremony and never have. She also realized that I was driven, and though she was not sure where we might wind up, she wanted to make the journey with me.

I was attracted to her at first by her beauty and charm. But as I got to know Carroll better, I loved and admired her for her character, integrity, and authenticity. We were both members of the First Baptist Church and we shared a common belief and a commitment to live our lives in accord with the faith of our forebears.

After admiring Carroll from afar I decided, especially after she smiled at me several times when she was singing in the choir, to ask her if I could take her to a church social at the home of Reid Moore, the Minister of Music. Actually, I do not remember whether I asked her for a date or if we just agreed to go to the party together. I do remember, unfortunately, that I did not have a car, and the house where the party was being held was too far for us to walk.

When I told Carroll that I could not pick her up, she said we could borrow her brother's car. So I walked the two blocks from my boarding house to Carroll's house, and we drove from there to the party. It was a late afternoon and early evening party with about twenty young adults from the church spending the evening together.

Carroll had grown up in Jackson, and after graduating from Central High School she enrolled at Mississippi College. Her grandfather, A.C. Watkins, was a long-time Baptist missionary to Mexico and a member of the Mississippi College faculty. Carroll was popular and attractive, and I was lucky that some young Baptist preacher did not get her before I did.

The Waller family's association with Mississippi College has been long and rewarding. In recognition of her dedicated service and support for her alma mater, Mississippi College awarded Carroll an honorary Doctor of Letters in 1974. Our daughter Joy attended Mississippi College, and our son Bob received both his undergraduate and law degrees from Mississippi College. Bob later served as the national president of the Mississippi College Alumni Association. Our grandson, William Lowe Waller, III, M.D., was president of the student body and graduated *summa cum laude*.

Some historians have given me credit for bringing about some significant changes in Mississippi. But there were some changes that I had nothing to do with, and I am not sure they are for the better. Dress codes and personal conduct, among both young and old, are not what they used to be. I remember as a twenty-three year old unmarried Capitol Street lawyer admiring Carroll and the other Mississippi College girls when they came to shop in downtown Jackson at Kennington's Department Store, the Emporium, and McRae's. I thought of my father and his taxi service that brought women students from Hillman College to Jackson for their shopping excursions. There was no mistaking the young ladies from Mississippi College. They wore hats and high heels, gloves and dresses, and acted like ladies. Carroll was a physical education major at Mississippi College, but in those days of innocence, she could not walk from her dormitory to the gymnasium in shorts unless they were covered by a raincoat.

After Carroll graduated from Mississippi College, she joined her mother in the family business. Mrs. Overton owned a boutique called The House of Overton, which was located in one of the nineteenth century mansions that lined North State Street. In the 1950s North State Street was a stretch of U.S. Highway 51, which ran from New Orleans through Jackson to Memphis, northward into Kentucky through Illinois and into Minnesota on its way northward to the shores of Lake Superior. Mrs. Overton liked to say that The House of Overton was on the main line of Mid-America.

Dr. and Mrs. Overton were active members of the First Baptist Church. Mrs. Overton taught a women's Sunday School class and led a weekly Bible study in her home on Tuesday evenings. In the winter of 1945, Dr. and Mrs. Overton traveled to Chicago to invite the leaders of the Youth for Christ organization to come to Jackson and start a Youth for Christ program in Mississippi. While they were in Chicago they met the charismatic young minister who had just been hired to conduct Youth for Christ rallies throughout the United States and Canada. The Overtons met him for the first time when they were ushered into his small office. His name was Billy Graham. The Overtons invited Billy Graham to Jackson to establish a Youth for Christ organization. Seven years later Billy Graham came back to Jackson for a ten-day crusade, which I attended along with thousands of others.

When I met Carroll she was working with her mother in The House of Overton. We started seeing each other on a regular basis in late March and after saving enough money I offered her an engagement ring in August. We were married on November 11, 1950. In March 1951, just four months after we were married, Carroll and I were shocked when I received an induction notice and was ordered to report to the United States Army base at Fort Chaffee, Arkansas.

Carroll stayed in Jackson while I was in basic training, but joined me at Fort Chaffee in the late spring of 1951, just in time for one of the worst snow storms in Arkansas history. While we were stationed in Arkansas, Carroll learned that she was expecting our first child. At first she did not know what was wrong. She thought she was terribly ill with a virus or something that just would not go away. When she finally realized what it was, she went back to Jackson for the birth of our first son, William Lowe Waller, Jr., on February 9, 1952. While Carroll was in Jackson, I was transferred to Fort Holabird, near Baltimore, Maryland.

After our first son was born, Carroll joined me in Baltimore. We lived in a third floor apartment, and in those days there was no such thing as a housekeeper or a babysitter, so Carroll would put Bill, Jr., in the laundry basket and walk down three flights of stairs to do the family laundry, then back up to the apartment. I never heard her complain. She was always happy and cheerful, and she made our home a special place, no matter where it was.

As soon as I was discharged, we came back home to Jackson, and I started rebuilding my law practice. Carroll supplemented our meager income by taking a position as a physical education instructor at Belhaven College, a Presbyterian liberal arts college a few blocks from Dr. Overton's home, where we were living at the time. Carroll and I later rented an apartment in the Belhaven neighborhood, and on January 8, 1954, our daughter Gloria Joy was born.

With two children under school age, Carroll decided that the children needed her at home more than the family needed the additional income. Although she gave up her teaching position at Belhaven, Carroll continued her volunteer work at the First Baptist Church and at her alma mater, Mississippi College. Over the next several years our family circle widened considerably with the addition of three more sons. The births of Robert Overton Waller on April 23, 1958, Edward Charles Waller on October 17,

1960, and Donald Eugene Waller on November 11, 1962, completed our family circle.

Carroll and I wanted our children to grow up as normal and
healthy as possible and to get to know their extended families,
especially their grandparents. We made it possible for them to
spend time with Carroll's parents in Jackson and with the Wallers
in Burgess. Bill, Jr., did yard work for his grandfather Overton on
Saturdays. This was no small undertaking as three yards were
involved—the residence on Bellevue Place, the dress shop on
North State Street, and the clinic on North Street.

During the Christmas holidays and the summer months Bill,
Jr., would spend time with his grandfather Waller in Lafayette
County killing hogs, making sausage, and working in the potato
patch. He is fond of telling the story of spending all one morning
digging potatoes and then going with his grandfather Waller in
the afternoon to peddle the potatoes to the Ole Miss cafeteria.
Maybe that is why he decided to go to Mississippi State.

My children never complained about my work ethic, except
when I applied it to them, like when we went fishing. I always fig-
ured if I took a day off to take my children fishing, we ought to
fish all day. Eventually, I realized that after three or four hours of
fishing they were ready to go home. What they enjoyed more
than fishing was swimming and water skiing, so I sold my small
aluminum fishing boat and bought them a sixteen foot boat with
a thirty-five horse power motor.

Growing up in a city as they did, it was hard for my sons to
enjoy the outdoors as I had in Burgess. So I encouraged them to
join the Boy Scouts and to participate in all the opportunities
that scouting offered. All four of my sons joined Scout Troop
Number 8, which was sponsored by the First Baptist Church.
Three of them attained the rank of Eagle Scout, and Bob was a
Life Scout. This is one of our family traditions that has been carried on by my grandsons. William Lowe Waller, III, and Clayton
also attained the rank of Eagle Scout. At this writing, my other

two grandsons, Robert, Jr., just finished his first year of Boy Scouts, and Don, Jr., has not reached scouting age.

I did not encourage my sons to enter law practice, but I did not discourage them from it either. Although some people enjoy making jokes and castigating lawyers, it is an honorable profession, and I am proud that two of my sons have practiced law with me. When Bill, Jr., was fifteen and old enough to drive he started coming to my office. He said he wanted to help clean up the office and keep things straight, but he was really there because he wanted to read law books and legal papers. From the time he was ten or eleven years old, he was always interested in the law. When he was a senior in high school I asked him if he wanted an appointment to West Point. He said he was going to get a college degree, join the National Guard, and then go to law school.

After receiving his undergraduate degree from Mississippi State University, Bill, Jr., earned his law degree from the University of Mississippi and became a member of my firm in the spring of 1977. He practiced law with me for nearly twenty years before his election to the Mississippi Supreme Court in 1996. He had seven opponents in his first campaign. Carroll and I enjoyed campaigning for him, as he had done for me. He was elected in the runoff against long-time Chancery Judge and sitting Appeals Court Judge Billy Bridges of Rankin County. Bill, Jr., was reelected in 2004, with only one opponent. He is now a presiding judge, and holds the second-ranking position in seniority on the nine-member court.

Our son Bob, who is a graduate of Mississippi College and the Mississippi College School of Law, is also a member of my firm. Eddie and Don, our two youngest sons, are graduates of The University of Mississippi, where they majored in business. Don is currently enrolled in graduate school at Mississippi College where he is studying marriage and family counseling. Both Bob and Eddie have served in the Mississippi National Guard and are veterans of Desert Storm. As I am writing these memoirs in the spring of 2006, Eddie, who holds the rank of major, recently returned from a combat tour in Iraq with the Mississippi National Guard. All of my sons and their families have settled in northeast Jackson near my home on West Cheryl Drive.

Carroll and I followed the scriptural injunction to "bring up your children in the nurture and admonition of the Lord," and we encouraged them to participate in the activities of our church. All of them, as their spiritual understanding matured, were baptized and became members of Jackson's First Baptist Church.

Tragically, our family circle was broken in March 1981. Our daughter Joy was a gifted artist. She attended Mississippi University for Women and Mississippi College, and after graduating from the Pratt Institute in New York, Joy became a graphic designer in The University of Mississippi's Department of Publications. She had been battling depression for some time, and was at last overwhelmed by it and took her own life. Her cousin Andy Waller, a member of the Oxford Police Department, found her body.

Although Joy's time as an artist was short, her work was both prolific and promising. We recently converted the interior of our home into the "Joy Waller Art Gallery." Carroll and I wanted our family and friends to become acquainted with her work and her creativity. I know my ten granddaughters will carry on Joy's spirit and creativity. Bill, Jr.'s, daughter, Jeannie, has taken Joy's originality and energy in a different direction. A *summa cum laude* English graduate of Mississippi State University, she is now pursuing a master's degree in journalism at The University of Mississippi.

We continue to mourn the death of our beautiful and gifted child. Bob's oldest daughter who is now twelve bears her name "Joy" as a living memorial to our beloved daughter. She is also gifted in language and literature and a straight "A" student at First Presbyterian Day School. Although Joy's death came at the age of twenty-seven, her lasting impression and influence on our extended family continues.

CHAPTER 7

Call To Public Service

*"Bill Waller has been running for governor
since he was a senior in high school."*

—JOHN H. FOX, III

After I had established my law practice and married and started a family, I knew that Jackson was the right place for me and my family, and I began to see things in Mississippi not as they were, but as they ought to be and someday could be. I wanted to help make Mississippi a better place for all of its citizens, black and white, rich and poor. The barrier between the "haves" and the "have nots" was a wall that could only be removed through better education, good jobs, and more business opportunities. It rankled me from an early age that Mississippi was last in almost every measurable category. I had known many people who did not have the opportunities to fulfill their goals and ambitions, and I began to realize that there were reasons why good, hard working men and women sometimes could not get ahead. Things did not have to be the way they always had been.

In almost every little Mississippi town there were a few men who controlled the political and economic affairs of the community. This group usually included the local banker and a few of the top businessmen. A man or woman could not get elected to office or borrow money for any venture, however promising it might be, without their say-so. As the old saying goes, "If you didn't need money, you could borrow money; if you needed money, you couldn't borrow any." After I got to Jackson I saw the same thing happening on a larger scale.

When I graduated from law school, I needed some operating capital to rent an office and to live on while I was growing my practice. My father and I went to the see the president of the Bank of Oxford. He was a gray haired, older man who had been at the bank for many years. I needed $400, which was a lot of money in 1950. I thought that would give me enough to live on for four months. At the end of four months I believed I would have enough money coming in to pay my own way.

My father's business relationship with the banker was good, so I got the money but my father had to sign the note. Our visit lasted about fifteen minutes, and during our brief conversation the banker subjected me to a barrage of questions, almost like a cross examination. He wanted to know all about what I was going to do with the money, how I intended to spend the money, and most of all how and when I intended to pay it back.

I do not fault the banker for his caution in lending four hundred dollars to an unemployed and untested young attorney, but I relate this personal experience to say that if Mississippi had a more aggressive and creative banking system in the decades following the depression, the state's economic recovery could have been faster and much stronger.

Too many people had to depend on the loan sharks at the finance companies, which were charging thirty or forty percent interest, and by flipping the loans they could legally charge as much as sixty or seventy percent. Mississippi had been its own worst enemy, and the antiquated infrastructure of its business community stifled its development. During my administration I took on the loan sharks and secured legislation that facilitated the establishment of additional banking facilities. Twenty-seven new banks were chartered during my four years in office.

For many years there were several different levels of society in Mississippi based on such things as race, wealth, social standing, where you went to college, how much education you had, the neighborhood you lived in, and the kind of car you drove. The upper levels of the hierarchy controlled the state and opposed any change because the rules were designed for their benefit. The lower rungs of society were left to fend for themselves.

I believed that most of our social and economic problems stemmed from politics. The same group that controlled the economy also controlled the politics. If you did not have a relationship with Dr. Jones, banker Brown and businessman Adams, you could not get elected sheriff or supervisor. And if you were elected, you were likely to be controlled by the same crowd. Mississippi had been that way a long time.

After the Civil War L.Q.C. Lamar urged Mississippians to quit growing so much cotton, to start raising Jersey cattle, to attract industry into Mississippi, and to diversify the state's economy. I am sure my great-great-grandfather Ralph Lowe Waller must have known Lamar because his two sons served under him in the war. Whether he knew Lamar personally or not, Ralph Lowe Waller and his sons followed Lamar's advice. They diversified their farm and developed a small herd of Jersey cattle. But there were not enough Mississippians who could see the wave of the future and most of them continued doing things the old way.

The state's political and business leadership was determined to maintain the status quo. They were not willing to expand or diversify, and they kept industry out of the state. In small towns across the state whatever the first banker in town did, the second banker did, and the fifth generation banker did what the first generation banker did. Insurance agencies and retail businesses remained in the same families for generations. Mayors, aldermen,

city councils, and county supervisors were provincial and generally opposed new businesses and discouraged new subdivisions
because they feared an influx of new voters. Mississippi eventually became a closed society.

In 1964, the year I began my second term as district attorney,
Ole Miss history professor James Silver published a controversial
book entitled *Mississippi, The Closed Society.* In that book
Professor Silver accused the state's power structure of shutting out
ordinary citizens, maintaining racial segregation, and exercising
political and economic control of the state for its own self-inter-
est. I did not agree with everything he said, but in 1964 I had
been practicing law in Jackson for over a decade, and I knew that
much of what he said was true.

During one of my campaigns for governor I asked a man who
sold heavy road equipment to county supervisors how many honest supervisors had he known through the years. After a long
pause I asked him if he was going to answer my question. He said,
"I'm thinking." After another long pause he said, "I believe I have
met one." One honest supervisor out of the four hundred and ten
was obviously an exaggeration, but it was a testament to the
"good old boy" network that had controlled the state for so long.

Although I was born and raised in Mississippi, when I entered
politics it was like I was an outsider looking in, because small
farmers and entrepreneurs like my father and his neighbors in
Burgess had been left out, had been relegated to the fringes of
Mississippi society. When I ran for governor I was determined to
give ordinary citizens a voice and a chance to participate in their
government. That is why I was able to bring into my campaign
many people who had never been involved in politics before.

After five years into my law practice I saw an opportunity for
public service in the legal system, and I was in a hurry to get
involved. I wanted to make things better for my children than
they had been for my generation, and now I had Carroll to help
me. She was a partner in whatever good I may have accom-

plished. Carroll and the children were a popular attraction in all of my campaigns, especially after there were seven of us. The sight of our family having fun and campaigning together garnered me a lot of votes over the years. We have always done things as a family. We fished together, went to church together, and campaigned together.

I was in a hurry, but I had to earn the right to hold public office, so I started my political career by running for Hinds County prosecuting attorney in 1955. It was an office I was qualified to hold because I knew the law and how to litigate. I lost my first race by 226 votes out of more than 24,000 votes cast.

In the 1955 race I had the support of many of my new Jackson friends and clients. Charles Brady, one of my earliest supporters, was an accountant with a local automobile dealership and traveled with me throughout Hinds County. Brady was a native of the county and his father was a rural mail carrier. Between the two of them, they knew just about everybody in the county. Charles Brady was a tireless worker who made a substantial personal sacrifice to campaign for me. He is now deceased, and his memory is cherished by the Waller family.

Although I lost the race for county attorney, I was not the least discouraged and in a couple of years I let it be known that I would be a candidate in the 1959 Democratic primary for district attorney for the Seventh Circuit Court District that included Hinds, Madison, and Yazoo counties. Soon after I made my intentions public, Robert Nichols, the incumbent, told me that he would like to serve one more term and asked me not to run in 1959. If I would wait, he said, he would support me for the office in the 1963 election. I told him I was sorry, but I did not have time to wait.

Bob Nichols and his assistant district attorney Weaver Gore were jovial and friendly, and the 1959 campaign was never heated. In the 1950s political rallies were still popular, and at a big rally at Battlefield Park Bob Nichols was really getting into his speech, promising to shut down and arrest all the bootleggers in

Hinds County. From the back of the crowd a man shouted, "No, you won't." Nichols replied, "Yes, I will." After several exchanges of the promise and the rebuttal, Nichols paused and said, "I see the alcoholics are not anonymous tonight." As the years passed, both Bob Nichols and Weaver Gore remained my good friends.

I conducted a low budget, low-key campaign in 1959 with Carroll as my principal campaigner. Because of limited funds, we focused on personal contact. We began in our North Jackson neighborhood, knocking on doors, introducing ourselves, and asking the neighbors to talk to their friends and relatives about supporting my candidacy. Charles Brady was the closest thing we had to a full-time campaign worker. He traveled with me, usually at night and on weekends. My sister, Millie Burtschell, an official in a Jackson bank, was also a great help. My mother and father asked all their Oxford and Lafayette County friends to send postcards to their friends and relatives in the seventh district. Several Jackson attorneys, including Robert B. Hamilton, Wayne Nix, and Galloway Austin, also supported me.

Carroll spent as much time as she could on the campaign, working block-by-block in Jackson neighborhoods. She would park the car at one end of the block and walk to the other end, knocking on every door and ringing every door bell. I tried to make enough money to support my growing family, and at the same time run a campaign for public office.

I was not well known in Madison County and Yazoo County so I spent most of my time in those counties. I made most of the VFW picnics, the Saturday afternoon rallies, barbecues, and fish fries in all three counties during the summer of 1959. I handed out thousands of those cardboard fans that were so popular in funeral parlors before the days of air conditioning. In the days before television and sound bites, politics was a lot more personal and campaigning was a lot more fun. Whenever it was possible, Carroll and I would campaign together, and whenever we could we would take Bill, Jr., and Joy with us.

The Democratic primary election was a good old fashioned cliff hanger, at least for district attorney in the seventh district, and there was a huge turnout. We did not have voting machines and the counting took place at what the *Clarion-Ledger* called a "snail-like pace." With just two candidates for district attorney, Robert Nichols and myself, there would be no runoff. In the early returns I led in Hinds County by a margin of 13,632 to 13,622. In Yazoo and Madison the count was 2,849 to 1,850 and 1,342 to 1,296 in my favor. In the final tally the margin was larger, but still close. I remember that the balance in my bank account when the campaign started was $27,000, which was soon gone with about $10,000 in campaign loans and debts. Even so, that was a good investment, but it also shows that political candidates must have financial resources if they expect to win.

In the 1960s I served as prosecuting attorney in a district with a relatively low crime rate, at least by today's standards. The office of district attorney is a constitutional office and is charged with general law enforcement. Prosecutorial responsibility in the district was divided between my office and the three county prosecutors. The district attorney's office was responsible for the prosecution of felonies, and minor crimes were usually prosecuted by county attorneys. During my two terms in office, I had a good working relationship with the three county attorneys that included Paul Alexander in Hinds, Joe Fancher in Madison, and Griffin Norquist in Yazoo County. All of them were capable attorneys and willingly assisted me whenever I needed them.

Cases prosecuted by the district attorney usually involve murder, armed robbery, embezzlement, and other major crimes involving penitentiary sentences or the death penalty. I had two assistant district attorneys, Ed Peters and John H. Fox, III, my high school classmate. Peters would later be elected district attorney and would hold the office for more than thirty years.

The state's legal system was relatively inexpensive in the early 1960s. The three counties in the Seventh Judicial District did not provide financial support for the district attorney's office. Because I did not have an office in the courthouse, I worked out of my private law office. District attorneys could not be accused of seeking the office for financial gain. My salary was $3,600 a year plus an annual expense account of $3,000 from which I paid my travel expenses and my secretarial help. It probably cost me money to serve as district attorney.

The grand jury met three times a year in Hinds County and twice a year in Yazoo and Madison counties. I would be busy for three or four weeks after the grand jury met. Between court sessions there was not a lot to do as prosecutor, and I spent a considerable amount of time on my private law practice. The crime rate at the time was so low that my duties as district attorney were sporadic. But this was before the advent of the substance abuse problems we face today.

Stricter law enforcement I believe is the solution to the current drug problem. I do not favor long sentences for first-time offenders. I am not soft on crime, but I do not think that longer sentences are the answer. Mississippi's special drug courts have shown promising results in rehabilitating first-time offenders.

If we had a more vigilant and effective police force, and if drug dealers knew they were going to be caught and incarcerated, we would probably see a marked decline in drug-related crimes. We may not be able to stop the flow of drugs, but I believe that the traffic can be controlled. Among drug dealers in the city of Jackson today, a high probability exists that they will never be arrested and convicted.

We need a full-time strike force. You can not separate drugs from general crime because drug dealing leads to bank robbery and other serious crimes. The rising number of murders, auto thefts, burglaries, purse snatchings, and carjackings are usually connected to drugs. In my view, the solution is a highly trained, dedicated, and well-paid police force and particularly detectives who know how to make an arrest and collect evidence. These detectives should be paid two or three times more than they are making now and should be required to have the education and training necessary to do the job. From the courtroom looking out, police work is now more technical, and many of those trained for general patrol work, traffic control, and accident investigations simply can not efficiently work on cases involving drug-related crimes.

The public would be willing to support significant and expensive improvements in law enforcement to obtain superior police protection. We should recruit college graduates for the police program, give them legal training, and teach them the rules of evidence. I visualize these highly trained and educated police detectives working around the clock, seven days a week if necessary, as FBI agents do. Many police officers today have to take second jobs to support their families, and in some cases police officers have left a crime scene or interrupted an investigation because they had to get to their other job. Police officers today are meeting the day-to-day demands of the people, but the war on drugs and drug-related crimes requires much more.

We also need to unclog the court system. Most of the cases on the criminal court docket could be handled differently. The Hinds County Public Defender manages about two thousand cases a year, yet almost no cases are initiated on "information." Prosecutors can bypass a grand jury and charge someone on a document prepared by the district attorney known as an "information." The accused will waive his right to indictment, his lawyer can meet with the district attorney, and in ten days the case can be resolved or the accused can be incarcerated. This procedure would eliminate the long delay associated with grand jury sessions.

The court system needs streamlining at the arrest level, particularly in municipal courts, where most criminal charges are initiated. There needs to be one police detective in charge of a case from the beginning of the investigation to the sentencing of the guilty party. Some Mississippi courts are overwhelmed by the sheer number of cases and the time it takes to resolve them. In many instances justice is not being well-served. Unfortunately, most county supervisors, mayors, and legislators are not focused on improving our judicial system.

The scourge of drugs has changed everything and placed a

much greater burden on police officers and police departments. The criminal element is much more sophisticated today. Criminals know their rights and they know they can not be convicted without solid evidence. Mississippi's criminal justice system needs to be restructured and updated with one division handling drug related and violent crimes and another division addressing minor and non-violent crimes. The entire law enforcement process, from arrest to prosecution, needs to be restructured. There are too many insignificant steps in law enforcement that we have to take. A prosecutor in a murder case can not be effective if he or she has not been involved in the case from the time of the arrest.

Most Mississippians are not aware of the pressing need to upgrade and modernize our judicial system. So far, nobody has written a plan for a better judicial system, but I think many attorneys could do it. Many of the needed changes could be made without legislation. In some respects the Mississippi Supreme Court can augment changes by amending the procedural rules of courts. The state bar should have an interest in the reorganization of the judicial system. We should be creating committees within the bar to look at the system.

We have to alert the public that the cumbersome judicial system is not working in their best interest. The relentless increase in the crime rate requires some changes in the system. We have the same basic system we had in the 1920s, with the same law enforcement positions and procedures of eighty years ago. Law enforcement needs to be divided between routine beat duties of police officers and the more sophisticated criminal investigation responsibilities.

We had similar problems, but to a much lesser extent, during my two terms as district attorney. At times we had to delay presenting cases to the grand jury. We could improve the system if the grand juries met in continuous session. The state grand juries could meet, for example, at three o'clock in the afternoon, one day each week, and move these cases along. And defense lawyers could defend the cases against errors by the prosecution, all the way from the *Miranda* warning to defective wording in the indictment. Most of the appeals from criminal cases in the Mississippi Supreme Court today arise from defective language in the indictments or errors in the jury instructions. The Mississippi Supreme Court could influence many changes and improvements quicker than any other state agency or individual.

One of the things that lightened my schedule as district attorney was the large number of confessions we secured. We had as many as six or seven confessions for every ten cases we investigated. That was due to the quality of law enforcement and prosecution in those days. Criminal charges were based on solid evidence, and many people just decided it was not worth fighting the charges in court because they had no real chance of "beating the rap."

During my tenure as district attorney, Jackson had about as good a police department as we could have expected. M.B. Pierce, the chief of detectives, ran an effective detective bureau that included a team of well-trained and dedicated officers who were accountable to Police Chief W.D. Rayfield and Mayor Allen Thompson. As district attorney I reviewed the criminal files with Detective Pierce, identified the witnesses, gathered photographs, and was fully prepared for court. We held file management conferences on a regular basis before the grand jury met. In the early years we would have from forty to a hundred cases to present to the grand jury three times a year. By the time I left office in 1968 we were averaging about a hundred and sixty-five cases a month, but we were still closing them with about eighty-five percent guilty pleas.

As district attorney I had my share of high profile cases. Early in my term a prominent Jackson socialite stabbed her husband to death in their upscale home. She attacked him with a knife, inflicted fourteen stab wounds, and left him on the floor in a pool of blood. After he died, she moved the body from the floor to a bed and covered it with several blankets. She then wiped the blood from the floor as best she could and placed eight blood-stained towels in the washing machine. After I filed murder charges against her, a Hinds County grand jury indicted her. She pled not guilty by way of self-defense. The jury found her guilty, and the judge sentenced her to life in prison.

In another important case during my first term two men, one white and the other black, began arguing several hours into a fishing trip in rural Madison County after they had finished off a cooler of beer. The white man killed the black man. Although the case was tried primarily on circumstantial evidence, I convinced the jury that the defendant was guilty of second degree murder, and he was sent to the state penitentiary at Parchman for twenty years.

One of the most sensational cases I tried was the Kenneth Slyter case. Slyter was a white male accused of raping and murdering a fifteen year old girl he picked up at her home on the pretext of hiring her as a baby sitter. The girl's body was later found on the Natchez Trace, several miles north of Jackson in Madison County. Slyter backed his car over her several times and crushed her body. After we identified the tire marks on the girl's body and matched them to the tires on Slyter's automobile, a Madison County jury convicted him, and the judge sentenced him to death. On March 29, 1963, Slyter was one of the last men to be executed in Mississippi's gas chamber at Parchman. Mississippi later adopted the system of lethal injection.

I prosecuted several other capital crimes, and I had no reservations about asking for the death penalty because I believe it deters capital offences.

These three prosecutions do not demonstrate that there was no injustice in Mississippi's legal system, but they do undermine the national media's traditional view of Mississippi justice—the rich are never prosecuted, whites are not tried for violent crimes against blacks, and only blacks are executed in Mississippi. While I served as district attorney I was determined that justice and the rule of law would prevail in my judicial district, and the three county attorneys in my district had a similar commitment.

As district attorney I also made certain that indigents received a fair trial and were provided legal counsel regardless of race or economic status. When an indigent person needed legal assistance in court, I asked the judge to appoint a lawyer to defend him even though it was not required in felony cases until March 1963 when the United States Supreme Court issued the *Gideon* ruling.

During my eight year tenure as district attorney, we generally had high quality jurors who accepted their responsibilities of citizenship. People who asked to be excused from jury duty usually had a valid reason, and many times they offered to come back and serve at a later time. Unfortunately, that attitude has all but disappeared. Today, many people do not appear for jury duty. Many citizens do not want the responsibility for making life and death decisions, or they are simply unwilling to interrupt their lives for public service.

I had great respect for the judges who presided in the Seventh Judicial District. The judges were learned, legal scholars, and dedicated to the principle of justice for all. Perhaps they were a little stern, even severe. They were extremely conservative judges, but none of them ever impeded my pursuit of justice in their courts. Judge M.M. McGowan was active in several conservative causes in Mississippi. He had withdrawn from the Methodist Conference because he disagreed with the liberal direction in which the church was moving. He was a leader in the establishment of an independent Methodist congregation in Jackson.

Judge Leon Hendrick, the other circuit judge in my district, was as a high ranking lay leader in the conservative wing of the Presbyterian denomination. Judge Hendrick always took his charge to the grand jury seriously, and he gave the grand jury foreman clear and precise instructions. Judge McGowan handled the criminal docket in Yazoo County, and Judge Hendrick had the criminal docket in Hinds County. They split Madison County.

My campaign for reelection as district attorney in 1963 was certainly different from the 1959 race. I enjoyed a politician's fondest wish—I did not have an opponent. I was reelected district attorney for the Seventh Judicial District on August 4, 1963. About two weeks earlier Medgar Evers had been murdered at his home in northwest Jackson. Evers' murder changed the course of Mississippi history and had an effect on my life and political career that I could not have imagined at the time. I had met Medgar Evers on several occasions. Before June 12, 1963, I had never heard the name Byron De La Beckwith.

CHAPTER 8

The Beckwith Trials

*"Bill Waller made a stand forty-two years ago for
society, for Mississippi, and for what is right"*
—JUDGE BOBBY DELAUGHTER

W hen the United States Supreme Court issued the *Brown*
decision in 1954, I was twenty-eight years old and had
been practicing law for only four years. Like most Mississippians,
I did not realize the full import of that ruling. Even after the decision, Governor Hugh White and other public officials were still
determined to maintain racial segregation in the state's public
school system. As Mississippi's power structure had done so often
in the past, they refused to accept any changes in the status quo,
even those changes that were mandated by the United States
Supreme Court.

Resistance to the *Brown* decision became official state policy
under a 1956 statute that directed all public officials to "prohib-
it, by any lawful, peaceful, and constitutional means, the implementation of or compliance with the integration decisions of the

United States Supreme Court." To coordinate the state's policy of resistance the legislature established the State Sovereignty Commission and authorized the Commission "to prevent encroachment upon the rights of this and other states by the Federal Government." Sovereignty Commission members included the Governor, Lieutenant Governor, Attorney General, Speaker of the House, and prominent leaders of the Citizens' Council, which was established by a group of white men in Indianola two months after the *Brown* decision. The purpose of the Citizens' Council was to prevent the integration of the races in Mississippi, and the organization spread quickly throughout the state. Some of the state funds allocated to the Sovereignty Commission were secretly funneled to the Citizens' Council.

In 1959 when I was elected district attorney, Ross Barnett was elected governor on a campaign promise to keep Mississippi's public schools and colleges segregated. Paul B. Johnson, Jr., was elected lieutenant governor and issued a similar pledge. Few Republican candidates ran for office before the early 1960s, and most Democrats did not have any opposition in the general election.

When I was reelected district attorney in 1963, I did not have a Republican opponent, but the Republican Party did field a candidate for governor. Rubel Phillips was the first Republican to run for governor since Reconstruction and he received almost 140,000 votes. It took some courage for him to run as a Republican against Lieutenant Governor Paul Johnson in 1963 and to criticize both Johnson and Barnett for their handling of James Meredith's admission to The University of Mississippi. Phillips accused both of them of making a deal with President John Kennedy to admit Meredith, and he played several tape recordings of secret conversations between Governor Barnett and Attorney General Robert Kennedy.

Phillips ran again in 1967, the year I conducted my first statewide campaign. I had known Rubel at Ole Miss. He and his wife Margaret were great campaigners and were always cheerful and friendly. He is entitled to Mississippi Republican Party Membership Card Number One.

In the early 1960s as district attorney of the largest and only urban judicial district in the state, I was preoccupied with the criminal justice system and was not directly involved in the issues of civil disobedience and the civil rights demonstrations. Criminal charges stemming from the sit-ins and marches in Jackson were adjudicated in the municipal court, and civil petitions for injunctive relief were filed in the chancery court system. Misdemeanor charges filed against the demonstrators, such as trespassing or disturbing the peace, generally carried a $500 fine. The demonstrators were tried in Jackson's City Court rather than in a circuit court in which the district attorney's office had jurisdiction.

Beginning with an Easter boycott of downtown merchants in 1960, civil rights activities in Jackson and across the state accelerated into massive non-violent protests against Mississippi's system of legal segregation. In March 1961 the arrest of nine black Tougaloo College students for attempting to use the Jackson public library prompted demonstrations by Jackson State and Millsaps College students.

Later that summer, college students who called themselves "Freedom Riders" challenged the segregated interstate transportation facilities in the Trailways and Greyhound bus stations in Jackson. After observing the Freedom Riders and looking into their eyes, they never appeared to me to be the types who were violent or who would attempt to start a riot. They seemed calm and under control.

The direct action protests in Jackson, which eventually became known as the Jackson movement, attracted widespread attention and support from various civil rights organizations and enlisted an increasing number of young blacks into the civil rights movement. The older civil rights organizations like the National Association for the Advancement of Colored People, which had always used the legal framework to bring about racial changes, did not initially support the direct action protests in Jackson.

Unlike the leaders of the national organization, Medgar Evers, field secretary of the Mississippi NAACP, endorsed the demonstrations and soon became the most visible leader of the direct action protests in Mississippi. Before his appointment as the head of the state NAACP in 1954, Evers attempted to enroll at The University of Mississippi and break the color barrier in Mississippi. After his appointment as NAACP field secretary, Evers discontinued his effort to enroll at Ole Miss and concentrated on desegregating the public schools and other public accommodations and voter registration.

Although Evers did not pursue enrollment at Ole Miss, he encouraged his friend James Meredith to apply for admission to the university. After a two year legal battle, Meredith was admitted to Ole Miss on October 1, 1962. Meredith's admission caused a riot on the campus during which two people were killed. The Ole Miss riot prompted President Kennedy to reinforce the U.S. marshals at Oxford with several thousand federal troops. James Meredith was the first black student admitted to any white public school or college in Mississippi.

In the spring of 1963, with growing support from national organizations, and with an increasing number of Mississippi's black citizens joining the civil rights movement, Medgar Evers mailed a letter to political and business leaders announcing that the NAACP was determined to end all forms of legal segregation in Mississippi. He vowed to use picketing, marching, mass meetings, litigation, and "whatever legal means we deem necessary" to end racial segregation and discrimination.

Street demonstrations escalated, and Evers became much more visible as he took an active role in the Jackson movement. Jackson police arrested Evers and the NAACP's national executive secretary, Roy Wilkins, outside a Woolworth's store on Capitol Street as they observed a lunch counter sit-in. They were charged with "restraint of trade," and the national NAACP paid their bonds.

Mass marches and mass jailings became almost daily routines. As the size and the frequency of the demonstrations increased, Jackson Mayor Allen Thompson sought a restraining order to halt the marches. Judge J.C. Stennett, chancellor of the Fifth Judicial District, granted a sweeping injunction against Evers, the NAACP, Tougaloo College students, and other leaders of the Jackson movement. The injunction severely restricted the demonstrators' activities. As district attorney I was in almost daily contact with municipal officials while these marches and demonstrations were taking place.

At that time Jackson had a three-member city council, which worked closely with the police department to avoid any violence either by the protesters or those opposed to the protesters. We did not have two hundred people in the streets, half pushing for integration and half defending segregation. It was more like we had two hundred marching in the streets, and a few fanatics who might cause trouble.

Mayor Thompson, city officials, and most Jackson businessmen adamantly resisted any changes in race relations. They have been criticized for resisting the changes that were inevitable, and much of that criticism is justified, but the three-member city council probably saved Jackson from the extremists on both sides. Mayor Allen Thompson was the ceremonial leader of the council. The other two council members were R.S. "Sunny" Withers and Chalmers Alexander. They managed the city well. There were no factions on the city council then, and they controlled the police department. The officers of the department, in turn, respected the council. Police department officials and members of the council met on a regular basis, usually every day.

I did not know Medgar Evers personally, although I had met him at some of the meetings we had with the FBI and the Jackson Police Department. In those meetings Hinds County Attorney Paul Alexander and I talked about how to prevent riots and how to handle different situations that might arise during the marches and sit-ins. Although I did not always agree with him, I respected Evers and never thought of him as a troublemaker or a rabble rouser.

On May 20, 1963, Evers made a speech on a Jackson television station that brought considerable attention to him and to the racial changes that he was working to bring about. It was a calm and thoughtful explanation of what he was trying to accomplish and of the inevitability of change. He said that Mississippi, if left alone, could solve its racial problems. The speech was well received in both the white and black communities.

About three weeks later, shortly after midnight on Wednesday, June 12, 1963, Evers drove home from a meeting at the New Jerusalem Baptist Church. As he turned into the carport of his home in northwest Jackson his wife Myrlie, who was watching television with her children, heard the car, got up and turned on the carport light. Carrying a bundle of NAACP T-shirts, Evers got out of his car and walked toward the door of his home.

Byron De La Beckwith, lurking in a honeysuckle thicket a hundred and fifty feet away, propped his 30.06 Enfield high-powered rifle equipped with a telescopic sight against a sweet gum tree and fired one fatal shot. The single bullet struck Evers in the back and smashed through his chest. He fell forward and crawled on the concrete toward the back door of his home, leaving a trail of blood. The bullet shattered a window, slashed through an interior wall, ricocheted off the refrigerator, and came to rest on a counter top in the kitchen.

When she heard the shot, Mrs. Evers rushed out onto the carport and found her husband barely alive lying in a pool of blood. The rifle shot and Mrs. Evers' screams awakened her next door neighbor, Houston Wells, who ran outside and fired a pistol into the air to alert the other neighbors that something had happened to Evers. Jackson Police Department Detective Captain B.D. Harrell received a call that a shooting had occurred at 2332 Guynes Street and dispatched Detectives Fred Sanders and John Chamblee to the scene. They arrived at the Evers home about ten minutes after he had been shot.

Evers was placed on a mattress in a station wagon and rushed to University Hospital, escorted by a police squad car. Dr. Albert Britton, the Evers family's personal physician, also went to the hospital and was with Evers when he died shortly after 1:00 a.m. on Wednesday morning.

Upon learning that Evers had been murdered early Wednesday morning I, like most other Mississippians, was shocked and angered by the cold blooded murder of a fellow human being. Evers was not a black man or a civil rights activist to me. He was a man whose life had been taken by another man. As the prosecuting attorney of the jurisdiction in which the murder had taken place, I was determined to find the person who killed Medgar Evers, arraign that person before the bar of justice, and ask twelve good men to give him the death penalty.

One aspect of the Evers murder and the Beckwith prosecution that I think has not been adequately reported by either the state or the national media was the strong public support for a full and thorough investigation of the murder and the prosecution of the perpetrator. The circumstances of that murder—a man shot in the back at midnight, by a high-powered rifle with a telescopic sight, at his own home in front of his wife and children—genuinely shocked the people of Mississippi. The peace and dignity of Mississippi had been violated and most people wanted the assassin brought to justice.

I encountered almost no opposition or resistence to my investigation, and no one tried to persuade me not to prosecute Beckwith. In the weeks following the assassination a pall developed over the general public characterized by bewilderment and disappointment. The legal profession and the intellectual community were incensed by this cowardly act of violence. The response of the general public ranged from those who supported the prosecution of the assassin to the fullest extent of the law, to those who took a "wait and see" attitude, and a small minority who initially opposed the prosecution for whatever reason. Most of those in the last two categories eventually supported the prosecution because they came to see the Beckwith case as the trial of a man who murdered another man, and not as a discourse on race relations.

A small perverted element out on the fringe of society did not believe that it was a crime for a white man to kill a black man who was advocating racial integration, and they considered Beckwith a folk hero. This element opposed his prosecution, and when Beckwith took the stand he played to this small group. To my surprise this fringe element remained silent during the Beckwith trials.

I was determined to prosecute Byron De La Beckwith because I believed, based on the evidence that our investigation accumulated, that he murdered Medgar Evers. I wanted to demonstrate that a Mississippi prosecutor would try this case, however sensational and racially charged it might be, solely on the evidence. The district attorney's office moved with dispatch and with openness to show the world that there were those in Mississippi who would not tolerate racial assassinations or a man taking the law into his own hands.

The Ole Miss riot, the assassination of Medgar Evers, the murders of the civil rights workers in Philadelphia, the murder of Vernon Dahmer in Hattiesburg, and the death of the two students at Jackson State in 1970 made the people of Mississippi realize that violent resistance to change was a greater threat to society than the change they were resisting.

A few days after Evers' murder Jackson Mayor Allen Thompson appointed the city's first black policeman. Within the next few weeks several more black policemen were hired. Those appointments and several other steps Mayor Thompson took to meet some of the demands of the city's large black population relieved racial tension in the city to some extent.

During the investigation of the murder, John H. Fox, III, and I had the full support and cooperation of Jackson Police Chief W.D. Rayfield and his police officers, Hinds County Sheriff J.R. Gilfoy and his deputies, the Mississippi Highway Patrol, and the

FBI. These law enforcement agencies conducted an extraordinary investigation. Ten days after Evers' murder Beckwith was arrested, and two weeks later he was indicted.

Early on the morning of the murder Detective Fred Sanders found the lead bullet that struck Evers. Detective Sanders retraced its trajectory to a clump of trees and bushes on a vacant lot across the street from the Evers home, and adjacent to the parking lot of Joe's Drive-In restaurant, which faced U.S. Highway 49. In 1963 Highway 49 was called Delta Drive because it was the main highway from Jackson to the Mississippi Delta. That thoroughfare is now named Medgar Evers Boulevard.

Later that morning Jackson police detectives O.M. Luke and R.Q. Turner found the rifle, which had been carefully concealed in a honeysuckle thicket. Apparently, Beckwith intended to come back later and retrieve the rifle. Detective Sanders took the rifle to police headquarters where Detective Ralph Hargrove, the department's fingerprint expert, dusted it for prints. Detective Hargrove found several smudged prints on the rifle and one clear partial print on the scope that he believed had been made within the last twelve hours. After photographing the fingerprint lifted from the scope, Detective Hargrove sent the print to the FBI laboratory in Washington.

During my two terms as district attorney, I found that successful criminal investigations were usually a matter of just plain old hard work, and sometimes a lucky break. Everyone involved in the Evers murder investigation worked hard, but we also got a big break because of a picture in a newspaper. The Wednesday afternoon edition of the *Jackson Daily News* carried a front page picture of Detective Hargrove dusting the rifle found at the scene of the crime for finger prints. In Itta Bena, a small town about twelve miles from Greenwood, Thornton McIntyre, a twenty-five year old farmer and gun collector, read a description of the rifle pictured in the Jackson paper and called the Jackson police department.

Detectives Sanders and Chamblee went to Greenwood to

interview McIntyre. He told them that the rifle found at the murder scene might be the rifle he purchased several years earlier and
traded to Byron De La Beckwith in January 1960. They forward-
ed that information to the FBI, which began a search to determine if Beckwith's fingerprints matched the print on the scope.

As the information supplied by McIntyre was being investigated, I worked closely with Chief of Detectives M.B. Pierce and his
department to track down every possible lead. We found several
witnesses who would later testify that Beckwith had asked for
directions to Evers' home several days before the murder. We also
found witnesses who had seen a car similar to Beckwith's white
Valiant in Joe's Drive-In parking lot on the night of the murder.
The car was conspicuous because it had a long, two-way radio
antenna connected to the rear bumper.

While we pursued these leads, other agents were tracing the
distribution and ownership of the telescopic sight that had apparently been attached to the high powered rifle by an amateur
gunsmith. Eventually, the scope was traced to a sporting goods
store in Grenada. On June 21 FBI agents Walser Prospere and
Sam H. Allen questioned the owner of the store about the scope.
He told them that he had traded the scope to Beckwith for some
other firearms.

With each piece of new evidence I could see the case against
Beckwith tightening. We got the last bit of evidence we needed
for an arrest on Saturday afternoon, June 22. The FBI laboratory
matched the print on the scope with Beckwith's prints taken from
his military records. On the basis of that match, FBI agents
Walser Prospere and Thomas Hopkins arrested Beckwith at 10:30
p.m. on Saturday night in Greenwood at the office of his attorney, Hardy Lott.

Beckwith was an early member of the White Citizens' Council,
and just before he went on trial the Council organized a defense
fund that collected more than enough funds to pay his legal
expenses. Through his mother, Susan Southworth Yerger,
Beckwith's ancestry was steeped in southern traditions. Among

his most prized possessions were his guns and some memorabilia that he claimed once belonged to Jefferson Davis. When Beckwith was arrested, he was estranged from his first wife, Mary Louise Williams, who was in a Greenwood hospital.

The arrest was made late on Saturday night because Beckwith had been working at his job as a fertilizer salesman, and he wanted to go home, take a bath, and put on a nice suit of clothes with a white shirt and a bright tie before any pictures were taken. After his indictment Beckwith distributed his favorite picture of himself to reporters and asked them to use it in their coverage of the trial. Almost every reporter who covered the trial took notice of Beckwith's dapper attire, as well as his intense desire to be quoted in the media.

After they arrested him at Grenada, FBI agents Prospere and Hopkins brought Beckwith to Jackson Saturday night. The Sunday morning *Clarion-Ledger/Jackson Daily News* announced Beckwith's arrest of under the headline, "FBI Nabs Greenwood Man In Evers Murder." A front page article detailed his arrest but did not mention the fact that Beckwith was born in California. However, a later AP wire story indicated that his mother was a native Mississippian who was living in California when Beckwith was born, and moved back to the state when Beckwith was five years old. According to John Hammack and Charles Smith, who worked at the *Clarion-Ledger* in 1963, the wire service editor Harold Turnage mentioned to Purser Hewitt that Beckwith was born in California.

As executive editor of the *Clarion-Ledger* Purser Hewitt decided to make the fact that Beckwith was born in California the focus of a Monday morning article on Beckwith's arrest. Without informing AP reporter Dudley Lehew who wrote the Monday morning story, Hewitt added in the middle of the article the one-line sentence—"He was born in Colusa, Calif." Lehew's front page article appeared below the *Clarion-Ledger*'s most famous headline: "Californian Is Charged With Murder of Evers."

On Monday afternoon United States Commissioner John

Countiss, III, suspended the federal charges against Beckwith and transferred custody of Beckwith, who was then in the Hinds County jail, from federal to state authorities. After the Jackson police took custody, I formally charged Beckwith with Evers' murder.

At a contentious three-hour hearing the next day, I asked Municipal Court Judge James L. Spencer to hold Beckwith in confinement until the following Monday or Tuesday when I would seek a murder indictment against him from a Hinds County grand jury. Beckwith's defense team, Hardy Lott, Stanny Sanders, and Hugh Cunningham, argued that Beckwith should be set free. If not, they argued, he should be released on a reasonable bond. Judge Spencer accepted my claim that the evidence against Beckwith was so compelling that he should not grant bail, and he bound him over to the grand jury. On July 2 a Hinds County grand jury indicted Beckwith, and the following Wednesday he was arraigned before Circuit Judge Leon Hendrick in the Hinds County Courthouse.

In response to a motion I filed two weeks after the indictment, Judge Hendrick held a hearing on July 18 to consider Beckwith's mental condition. We asked the court to authorize a complete psychiatric examination of Beckwith by a board-certified psychiatrist. This was done for three reasons. First, I wanted to determine if Beckwith was mentally competent to stand trial. Second, if he were found competent that would eliminate an insanity plea, when he was brought to trial. And, finally, we expected to use the psychiatric diagnosis at the trial. I believed that Beckwith had some kind of mental disorder, or illusion of grandeur. He seemed proud of his arrest and enjoyed the attention he received, which led me to believe that Beckwith did not actually consider Evers' assassination a crime.

At the hearing I called four witnesses. Yerger Morehead, Beckwith's cousin and former guardian, and Dr. Roland Toms, a psychiatrist who had examined Beckwith during one of his stormy separations from his first wife, testified briefly about

Beckwith's mental state. Hugh Warren, a Delta planter who knew Beckwith well, described several conversations with Beckwith who told Warren that he always carried a pistol to church in case any black people tried to attend Sunday services. I called Jane Biggers, a reporter for *The Greenwood Commonwealth*, to testify about an article she had written about Beckwith, but Judge Hendrick ruled that her testimony would be hearsay and did not allow her to testify.

Following the testimony of my three witnesses, I introduced several court documents showing that Beckwith had physically threatened his first wife during their many estrangements. The only witness the defense called was Stanny Sanders, one of Beckwith's Greenwood attorneys. Sanders testified that Beckwith was sane and that he could prepare a rational defense. On the basis of the evidence presented at the hearing, Judge Hendrick ordered a psychiatric examination of Beckwith by a resident psychiatrist at the Mississippi State Hospital at Whitfield in Rankin County.

Beckwith was transferred from the Hinds County jail to the State Hospital on July 26. About a month later, Judge O.H. Barnett, the Rankin County circuit judge and a cousin of Ross Barnett, set aside Judge Hendrick's order and directed Rankin County Sheriff Jonathan H. Edwards to take custody of Beckwith and hold him in the Rankin County jail. I immediately appealed Judge Barnett's order. Three months later the Mississippi Supreme Court ruled that Beckwith could not be required to submit to a psychiatric examination, but did grant my request that Beckwith be returned to Hinds County to await his trial. Beckwith was transferred back to Hinds County on November 25, 1963, and two months later the first trial began.

The Beckwith trial was not just a high profile murder case, it was a national and international event. And Beckwith was not the only one on trial. I was on trial. John Fox, who was not only my assistant district attorney but also my law partner, was on trial. Beckwith's attorneys were on trial. The state of Mississippi

was on trial. Even the jurors were on trial. The major wire services and the *New York Times* published daily summaries of the
first trial in January 1964 and the second trial in April. Many
other newspapers and television networks also carried periodic
reports on the progress of both trials. John Herbers, who began
his career with the *Greenwood Morning Star*, covered the trial for
the *New York Times*. The international press, including the *Times*
of London, also attended the trials as did several freelance
reporters and photographers.

Both Jackson newspapers carried daily front page stories about
the proceedings and published many pictures of witnesses and
other participants in the trial. The editorial policies of the two
Jackson newspapers, which were owned by the Hederman family,
were extremely hostile to any political, social, or racial changes
in Mississippi. They were part of the old power structure that I
later called the "Capitol Street Gang."

Two days after Medgar Evers was murdered, a *Clarion-Ledger*
columnist insinuated "that desperately ruthless forces may have
used [Evers] as a sacrificial offering to rekindle the flames of
unrest here and spur the drive for 'victory' elsewhere." Though
willing to influence public opinion through its editorial pages,
the *Clarion-Ledger* and the *Jackson Daily News* provided open and
fair coverage of the trial.

Jerry DeLaughter covered both trials for the *Clarion-Ledger*. He
was a Mississippi College graduate and a distant cousin of
Assistant District Attorney Bobby DeLaughter, the chief prosecutor in Beckwith's third trial. Jerry DeLaughter's articles were
straightforward accounts of the trial proceedings and did not
reflect in any way the Hederman family's editorial policy. The coverage by the *Jackson Daily News*, most of which was written by
W.C. Shoemaker, was also straight news without any commentary.

Judge Hendrick did not allow cameras inside the courthouse,
but several sketches of the courtroom scene by editorial illustra-
tor and cartoonist Bob Howie appeared on the front page of the
Jackson Daily News.

John Fox and I prepared the case against Beckwith as thoroughly as we possibly could. It was based primarily on circumstantial evidence, but we still thought we had a good chance to get a conviction. As assistant district attorney, John performed outstanding work during the Beckwith prosecution, both in the pretrial proceedings and during both trials in 1964. He formed a bond with Chief of Detectives Pierce and Detectives Sanders and Chamblee and they worked tirelessly to formulate and construct the best prosecution possible. He sacrificed himself personally and financially by working day and night on the Beckwith case for months when he could have been making money in private practice. His small salary as an assistant prosecutor did not increase according to the hours he devoted to the case, and I was fortunate to have a colleague who shared my dedication.

John and I were more than colleagues, we were school mates and old friends. We grew up together in Lafayette County and we both graduated from University High School. His father, John H. Fox, II, was a legendary professor of law at The University of Mississippi. Professor Fox, whose long career at the law school included a two year term as acting dean from 1963-1964, was known as the "Great White Father" because of his domineering physical appearance topped with a shock of white hair and his omniscient, booming voice.

John is very bright and articulate, and helped me shape the strategy for the prosecution. I could not have had a better co-counsel. We had many discussions about how to maintain control of the trial and keep it focused on the fact that someone had murdered a man, and that the evidence showed that Beckwith shot and killed Evers. We could not allow the trial to become a debate about the civil rights movement or the history of race relations in Mississippi.

At the time of the Beckwith trials emotions regarding race relations were very intense, forcing all citizens to choose a side in the segregation controversy. A large majority of the white citizens believed in white supremacy and racial segregation, and had consequently developed a negative attitude toward blacks. Judge

Leon Hendrick suspected, and we agreed with him, that many of the veniremen would admit that they already had an opinion regarding the guilt or innocence of Beckwith, and that those opinions would be an honest, forthright statement of their convictions. Consequently, Judge Hendrick summoned a two hundred member venire for the trial.

As John and I were preparing the case against Beckwith we did not have the benefit of jury profiling experts or mock trials to ascertain how jurors might respond to the evidence we presented or to the arguments based on that evidence. Every good lawyer knows that many cases are decided when you pick the jury, and that is why John and I spent hours upon hours with Detectives M.B. Pierce, Fred Sanders, John Chamblee and other officials in the Jackson Police Department constructing a profile of a juror who would not be biased or prejudiced against the State and its case against Beckwith. Knowing that it would be impossible to take the issue of race completely out of the case and that a unanimous verdict was required, we designed a set of questions that would allow us to get into the minds of the prospective jurors. I wanted twelve good strong men who would be emotionally and mentally capable of deciding the case, not on the basis of race, but on the evidence we presented.

As difficult as it may be for some to understand now, in the early years of the twenty-first century, in 1963 there were white men in Mississippi who, like Byron De La Beckwith, did not actually believe that it was a crime for a white man to kill a "nigger" who was advocating racial integration and black voter registration. All of us in those profiling sessions agreed that we could not have such a man on the jury. We had to know if any of the veniremen believed that, so we decided to ask them: "Do you believe it is a crime for a white man to kill a 'nigger'?" And then we judged their response. The question, and the language, was repulsive to people in the courtroom and was offensive to John Fox and myself, but it was a question we had to ask because we had to know the answer.

That courtroom was a minefield, and John and I had to deal with the "us against them" mentality that was so deeply ingrained in the psychology of white Mississippians. We had to convince the jurors that John and I were one of "us" and not one of "them," and that we would try the case on evidence and not ideology. If we could do that, then we could take the next step, and argue on the evidence that Byron De La Beckwith had murdered Medgar Evers.

Because of the notoriety of both the victim and the accused, Judge Hendrick allowed an unusual procedure for questioning the veniremen. The two hundred man jury panel was sequestered in another part of the courthouse so that each prospective juror could be questioned individually on a number of subjects in addition to race. Each venireman's responses would be free of any influence by the answers of other veniremen. This allowed us to look at the juror's background, including education, occupation, age and other circumstances, so we were not forced to ask dozens of jurors the same questions at the same time in open court. Regardless of other factors, education and station in life had a lot to do with prejudices and opinions that could not be changed with evidence. Individual questioning of prospective jurors in capital murder cases is now standard procedure.

Judge Leon Hendrick was a distinguished Mississippi jurist and he presided over the trial with great dignity and decorum. He did not allow his courtroom to become a political forum.

Several books and articles have been written about the two trials in 1964 and the third trial in 1994. A complete account of all the testimony and the witnesses who appeared in the three trials can be found in Reed Massingill, *Portrait of a Racist*; Mary Ann Vollers, *Ghosts of Mississippi, The Murder of Medgar Evers, The Trials of Byron De La Beckwith, and the Haunting of the New South*; Adam Nossiter, *Of Long Memory*; Willie Morris, *The Ghosts of Medgar Evers*; Myrlie Evers, *For Us the Living*; R.W. Scott, *Glory in Conflict, A Saga of Byron De La Beckwith*; Bobby DeLaughter, *Never Too Late, A Prosecutor's Story of Justice in the Medgar Evers Case*; and Jeannine Herron, "Justice in Mississippi, Notes on the

Beckwith Trial," *Nation* (February 24, 1964, pp. 179-181). It is not my intention to provide a detailed account of the first two trials, but I do want to lay out the case against Beckwith that convinced me of his guilt.

In my opening statement, and in my closing argument, I told the jury that I would prove in ten ways that Beckwith was guilty. Beckwith had a motive, the ability, and the capacity to commit the crime. He planned the murder. The rifle found at the murder scene belonged to him, and he had recently acquired the scope that bore his fingerprint. A fingerprint expert testified that the print was no more than twelve hours old, and Beckwith had practiced firing the rifle and setting the scope at a Greenwood firing range shortly before the murder. He had a cut above his right eye that was recently made and was consistent with the kind of scar that would be made by a telescopic sight. He was identified as the man seeking the location of Evers' home four days before the murder. His car was seen near the Evers' home on the night of the murder. Beckwith offered no alibi for his whereabouts on the night of the murder until the last day of trial.

To prove our case, I called almost sixty witnesses and introduced more than fifty pieces of evidence. Walser Prospere testified to the circumstances leading up to Beckwith's arrest. Thornton McIntyre testified that he had traded the rifle that was found at the murder scene to Beckwith. Two prosecution witnesses identified Beckwith in a police lineup as the man who had asked directions to Evers' house four days before the murder. One of the most compelling items of evidence was the testimony of Dr. Forrest G. Bratley, Sr., a board-certified pathologist we employed to perform a physical examination of Beckwith. Dr. Bratley compared the crescent shaped contusion above Beckwith's right eye with the rifle scope found at the murder scene. Dr. Bratley testified that the contusion and the shape of the scope were a nearly perfect match. This was an important piece of circumstantial evidence.

Long before his arrest and even during his incarceration before the trial, Beckwith wrote dozens of letters and articles expressing his racial theories and his willingness to act upon those beliefs. During my cross examination I asked him several questions about those letters, specifically if he wrote the following sentence in a letter to the National Rifle Association on January 26, 1963: "Gentlemen: For the next fifteen years we here in Mississippi are going to have to do a lot of shooting to protect our wives, children and ourselves from bad niggers." He said that he had written that letter.

I then asked him about a letter to the editor that appeared in a Jackson newspaper on April 16, 1957. In that letter Beckwith wrote, "I believe in segregation like I believe in God. I shall oppose any person, place or thing that opposes segregation. I shall . . . bend every effort to rid the U.S. of the integrationists, whoever and wherever they may be." After I asked him if he wrote that letter he said, "I sure did write that." When I asked him if he still felt that way, he said, "Of course I feel that way."

My intent in presenting these and other similar statements that Beckwith had made over the years was to open a window into Beckwith's mind so the jury could decide for themselves if he was capable of killing the best known and most visible "integrationist" in Mississippi.

Beckwith's defense, which I described as "ridiculous" in my closing argument, was based on an alibi provided by three Greenwood law enforcement officers, two city policemen and an auxiliary patrolman. They testified that they had seen Beckwith in Greenwood just before and soon after the murder was committed. On the basis of their sworn testimony the defense argued that Beckwith could not have committed the crime because he was in Greenwood.

In 1964 the Mississippi rules of discovery in criminal cases did not require the defense or the prosecution to make any information available to the other side, and I did not know that these officers would testify in court until the last day of the trial. During my cross examination I asked the three officers why they had not notified the authorities about having seen Beckwith in Greenwood on the night of the murder. That information may have prevented the murder charges from being filed against Beckwith. They testified that they did not tell anyone about seeing him, because no one asked them if they had seen him. The fact that law enforcement officers did not reveal material facts regarding a case of this magnitude was unbelievable to me, and I highlighted the issue of perjury in my closing argument.

After the defense rested, John Fox presented what I thought was a compelling closing argument. After laying out much of our case he said to the twelve white, male, middle-aged Protestants on the jury, "As you enter upon your deliberations you take the conscience of Mississippi with you."

Although our case was based primarily on circumstantial evidence, I thought Beckwith's defense attorneys did little damage to our overall case in their closing arguments. Stanny Sanders pleaded with the jury not "to return a verdict of guilty . . . to satisfy the Attorney General of the United States and the liberal press."

The testimony of the three Greenwood policemen, which surprised everyone, was crucial to the defense. I tried to undermine their credibility by pointing out to the jury that they had waited six months, until the last day of the trial, to make that information available to the authorities. Their testimony must surely have provided "a reasonable doubt" to any juror who might have been looking for one. In my closing argument I told the jury, without specifically citing the three alibi witnesses, "Somebody is committing a palpable falsehood to you from the witness stand."

After the closing arguments and Judge Hendrick's instructions to the jury, the twelve tired men who had been sequestered for more than a week retired from the courtroom at 12:30 p.m. on Thursday afternoon, February 6, 1964. I think most people who had followed the case closely, including the local and national press, anticipated a quick decision, and most of them expected an acquittal.

Later that day as the jury was deliberating outside the courtroom, former governor Ross Barnett paid a brief visit to Beckwith.

After shaking hands, they talked for about five minutes and then Barnett left. Hugh Cunningham, one of Beckwith's attorneys, was a member of Ross Barnett's firm. Edwin Walker, the ex-general who had been so prominent in the Meredith riot on the Ole Miss campus, also paid a brief visit to Beckwith that afternoon.

When the jury had not reached a verdict by suppertime on Thursday, everyone began speculating about the outcome. We thought that a hung jury was the most likely outcome. At about 9:30 p.m. Judge Hendrick instructed Bailiff Ray Bonner to knock on the door of the jury room and ask if they had reached a verdict. A few minutes later, Bonner told Judge Hendrick that they had not. The judge then instructed the jurors to retire for the night and resume deliberations the next morning.

At 11:30 Friday morning Judge Hendrick brought the jury back into the courtroom and asked them if they had reached a verdict. When the weary foreman told Judge Hendrick that they had not reached a verdict and that it was not likely that they could reach agreement, the judge asked each juror if further deliberations might produce a verdict. They told him they had taken many ballots and that an agreement was not possible. Judge Hendrick thanked the jurors, instructed them not to discuss the case with anyone, and declared a mistrial.

Although one account had the jury dividing seven to five for acquittal, and another had the division six to six, we learned sometime later that the division on the panel was seven for a guilty verdict and five for acquittal.

After Judge Hendrick announced that he would set a date for a second trial, I filed a motion to deny bail to Beckwith, and Judge Hendrick bound him over until the next trial.

On April 6, 1964, we began jury selection for the second trial. We realized it would be difficult to get a jury that was not already influenced by the publicity of the first trial. But both sides agreed on a jury two days later and we began calling our witnesses.

The state's case was virtually the same as it was in the first trial except that one of the cab drivers who identified Beckwith as the man asking for Evers' address was no longer "positive" that the man was Beckwith. We felt sure that the change in his testimony was due to threats he had received between the first and second trials.

The defense put on a surprise witness who claimed that he owned a white Valiant similar to Beckwith's, and that his car was at the drive-in restaurant near Evers' home on the night of the murder. The three Greenwood policemen repeated their testimony providing Beckwith an alibi on the night Evers was killed. After Beckwith concluded his testimony, I cross-examined him for about three hours. I allowed him great latitude in answering my questions because I wanted the jury to understand that Beckwith was capable of killing a black man in cold blood.

On April 16 the ten-day trial ended, and the jury got the case. After deliberating for almost ten hours the jury foreman informed Judge Hendrick that they could not reach unanimous agreement. Judge Hendrick polled each juror and received a similar response. He declared a second mistrial and released Beckwith on a $10,000 bond. There were several accounts of the division among the jurors in the second trial, but according to the most reliable information I had, the jury was again hung by a vote of seven to five for conviction.

I believe the juries in both trials were good, honest, and fairminded men who wanted to do the right thing. The rule of law allows a jury to convict a person for a capital crime only by a unanimous verdict, and on evidence of guilt beyond any reasonable doubt. Jurors are historically reluctant to convict on circumstantial evidence. Unfortunately, most of our evidence was circumstantial, and defense witnesses placed Beckwith in Greenwood at the time of the murder. A juror inclined to sympathize with Beckwith could rely on that testimony, even if it was blatant perjury.

After the second trial Mrs. Evers came by my office and thanked me for my determination to bring Beckwith to justice. Our relationship during the second trial was more cordial than it had been during the first one. I think she may have had some doubts about my commitment during the first trial, and I can understand that. She was a grieving widow and mother who wanted to protect her children from the pain of a sensational trial. Mrs. Evers was an important witness. She could have helped the case, or she could have hurt it. She expected me to address her as "Mrs. Evers" and said she would not respond to my questions if I addressed her as "Myrlie." Forty-two years ago courtesy titles were not accorded to black women, and I believed my use of that title could undermine my relationship with the jury that I had so carefully cultivated. I phrased my questions to her in a manner that I did not have to address her by name. I was determined to keep the trial focused on murder rather than civil rights. Looking back, I may have been too blunt and brusque with Mrs. Evers.

During the first trial Homerita Welborn, a Hinds County court reporter, transcribed the testimony of witnesses, and I used that transcript during the second trial. When Mrs. Evers came by my office after the second hung jury, I gave her that copy of the transcript. Thirty years later when Hinds County District Attorney Ed Peters and Assistant District Attorney Bobby DeLaughter were gathering evidence for a third Beckwith trial, Mrs. Evers made that copy of the transcript available to DeLaughter. It was the only copy of the trial transcript that could be found.

In a hearing before Circuit Judge Breland Hilburn, a handwriting expert verified that the signature on the transcript was that of Homerita Welborn, who was deceased. John Fox and I testified at the hearing that we examined the transcript Mrs. Evers gave to DeLaughter and that it was the copy we gave Mrs. Evers in 1964. After that hearing, Judge Hilburn ruled that the transcript was authentic and could be admitted as evidence.

In his book about the third Beckwith trial, DeLaughter said that the transcript was one of the indispensable pieces of evidence in the prosecution and conviction of Beckwith in 1994. I met with DeLaughter several times during the months leading up to the 1994 trial. I liked him both as a man and as an attorney.

He approached the third trial from the same perspective that I approached the first two. DeLaughter knew that he could not put the civil rights movement or Mississippi on trial, if he wanted to get a conviction. He understood that the trial was about a murder and, as he put it, the "dastardly circumstances surrounding it."

Mississippi is not a big state, and there are not a lot of people here, so we often cross paths with each other, or with aunts and uncles or cousins. William Alexander Percy's nephew, Walker Percy, once said that everybody in Mississippi was either kin to each other or knew somebody who was.

I did not know Bobby DeLaughter personally until Jerry Mitchell, the *Clarion-Ledger* reporter who has won several prestigious prizes for his investigative reporting, started writing front-page articles about DeLaughter and the reopening of the Evers case. As it turned out, our paths had crossed many years earlier. When Bobby was in high school, his civics class visited the old Hinds County Courthouse to observe a trial. As it so happened, the trial in progress, in the same courtroom where Beckwith had been tried, was a murder case involving a prominent Jackson attorney, and I was the defense counsel. Bobby told Willie Morris, one of Mississippi's most beloved writers, that he was so captivated by the drama of the courtroom that he decided that day that he would be an attorney and someday a judge. DeLaughter skipped school for the next few days to observe the rest of the trial. Actually, his mother worked at the courthouse in the tax collector's office and allowed him to miss school. He came to the courthouse with her each morning and when she went to the tax collector's office, he went upstairs to the courtroom. Bobby DeLaughter is now a distinguished circuit judge for the Seventh Judicial District of Mississippi.

Over the last several years as I have thought about the first two Beckwith trials, I am convinced that the last thing Beckwith wanted or expected was a hung jury. I believe he would have preferred even a guilty verdict to no verdict at all. As I said in my closing argument at both trials, Beckwith did not kill Evers out of passion or revenge, but for a short-lived hold on destiny. In his peculiar world view—and in the minds of that small group who supported him—any verdict, whether it was guilty or not guilty, would have made him a man of destiny.

In several of his letters that I introduced into evidence, Beckwith spoke of his willingness to sacrifice himself for the cause. He said he would give himself up, if necessary. He would be a martyr for the cause. But what he really wanted and expected, I think, was to be acquitted. That would make him a big man, a hero to a fanatical few, and that was something that he had always wanted to be. A "not guilty" verdict would have given Beckwith and his speeches and writings worldwide infamy.

I think it never occurred to Beckwith that he would be found guilty. In the courtroom he did not have the demeanor of a man being tried for murder by a prosecuting attorney who was seeking the death penalty. It was like he was giving the performance of his life, and he was always dressed for the occasion, in French cuffs, gold jewelry, and a smile.

Several years later Beckwith described his performance in those first two trials this way, "Each morning I made a point of entering the court room dressed tastefully in the high style that was my custom . . . . Once inside, I made a point of nodding to those present, including spectators, guards, the jury, and the press, greeting them as cheerfully as though my only purpose in attending was to especially delight each and shower goodwill and fellowship on one and all."

As the prosecuting attorney, however, I was not among those whom Beckwith showered with goodwill and fellowship. "During the Jackson trial," he said, "it occurred to me to deliberately design an attack against Waller's pompous dignity . . . to shame and ridicule him and belittle him in the eyes of his supporters, the jury, the judge and the press." That was all right with me because I did not want his kind of goodwill and fellowship. For the most part, when he tried to pat me on the back, or poke cigars in my pocket, I just ignored him.

But the one thing we did not want was for Beckwith to be acquitted and then publish that book he had already started writing while he was in jail. He was going to call the book *My Ass, Your Goat, and the Republic*. He intended to brag about how he got away with killing Medgar Evers, like those two men who had been tried for killing Emmett Till. After their acquittal they were interviewed for an article in *Look* magazine and described how they had killed that teenager.

I did not want Beckwith to get away with killing a man and then go around bragging about it, which is exactly what he did. When he ran for lieutenant governor in 1967 his campaign slogan was, "Absolute White Supremacy under White Christian Rule." Ten years later, after one of my speeches during the 1987 governor's campaign, he came up to me and said, for the benefit of anyone who might be listening, "Mr. Waller tried to put me in the gas chamber twice. I told Mr. Waller back then I had a sinus condition and that smelly gas chamber would upset my sinuses." This encounter made the headlines of the July 26, 1987, Sunday issue of the *Clarion-Ledger/Jackson Daily News*. It was just that kind of bragging that would provide enough evidence for the third Beckwith trial, a murder conviction, and a life sentence.

During the thirty years between the end of the second trial in 1964 and the beginning of the third trial in 1994, there was continuing discussion about another trial. But a new trial could not be initiated without significant new evidence. An article by Jerry Mitchell in the October 1, 1989, issue of the *Clarion-Ledger* generated a great deal of controversy and support for reopening the Evers case. Mitchell reported that there was a possibility of jury tampering by the State Sovereignty Commission in the second Beckwith trial. That new information and the possibility that the jury pool could have been tainted prompted Mrs. Evers to issue a public statement asking for a thorough investigation.. After Mitchell's article and Mrs. Evers' statement, District Attorney Ed Peters ordered an investigation to determine if the Sovereignty Commission had contacted or attempted to influence any of the jurors in the second trial. By this time DeLaughter had taken a strong personal interest in the Evers case.

The jury tampering investigation found no evidence that the Sovereignty Commission had contacted any of the prospective jurors, but DeLaughter was determined to find some new evidence that would warrant reopening the thirty-year-old case. During the first two trials I thought if we ever found that one piece of evidence that would convict Beckwith it would probably come from Beckwith himself. That was why I allowed him to ramble on and on in his answers during my cross examinations. I believed that he would eventually convict himself, and that is what he did.

The evidence that Peters and DeLaughter needed for another indictment and a third prosecution was supplied by Beckwith himself, who could not seem to resist bragging about killing Evers. Amid all the publicity about reopening the Evers case, several people who had known Beckwith under a variety of circumstances informed the district attorney's office, and later testified in court, that Beckwith had not only bragged to them about killing Evers, but he expressed no remorse.

In January 1994, with this new evidence a Hinds County jury convicted Byron De La Beckwith for the murder of Medgar Evers, and Judge Breland Hilburn sentenced him to life in prison. In 2001 Beckwith died at University Hospital in Jackson.

A chapter in Mississippi history was finally closed.

CHAPTER 9

Mississippi Standing Still

*"We need new leaders who will move with speed and daring,
and govern with honesty, dignity and statesmanship."*

1967 CAMPAIGN SPEECH

A fter the commotion of the Beckwith trials subsided, I settled
back down into the routine of a Mississippi district attorney
and continued to build my law practice. My firm had grown to
five partners and we had an expanding group of clients. Although
there were no specific plans to run for another office when my
second term expired in 1968, some of my new-found friends
encouraged me to do so.

The prosecution of Byron De La Beckwith made Mississippians
proud of their state for the first time in many years, and they
wanted to get Mississippi moving again. They wanted leaders
who would talk about the future, about their hopes and aspira-
tions, and not about holding on to the past and resisting change.

Many of them said to me, "Why don't you run for governor?
Mississippi needs new leaders who are not afraid to take on the

John Fox, my co-counsel, and Judge Leon Hendrick, who presided
over the 1964 Beckwith trials

With Joe Fancher, my campaign chairman, announcing my
candidacy in 1967

A 1967 campaign brochure

Campaigning at the Neshoba County Fair   PHOTOGRAPH COURTESY MDAH

Governor's Staff 1972-1976, Hinds, Madison, Rankin District

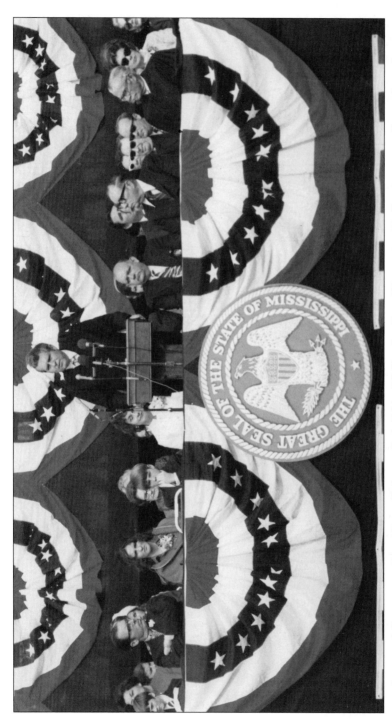

Inaugural Ceremony: Front Row, (left to right), Eddie Waller, Lt. Gov. Winter, Joy Waller, Emma Waller, Bob Waller, Carroll Waller, Governor Waller, Mississippi College President Lewis Noble, Governor Williams, Chief Justice Tom Brady

Carroll and I opening the Inaugural Ball

My first State of the State Address, with Senate President Pro Tempore Bob Perry (left) and Speaker of the House John Junkin (right). Seated below, left to right, Jesse White, Secretary of the Senate, James A. "Jeep" Peden, Reading Clerk, and Herman Glazier, Executive Assistant to the Governor.

PHOTOGRAPH COURTESY MDAH

The College Board, seated (left to right): Ira Morgan; Miriam Q. Simmons; Thomas N. Turner, Sr. Milton Brister; M. Paul Haynes. Standing (Left to right): Sylvia Thornton, Board Secretary; Travis E. Parker; Bobby L. Chain; Dr. Verner S. Holmes; Boswell Stevens; Ross L. Franks; Dr. R. C. Cook; W. M. Shoemaker; Dr. Robert W. Harrison; Dr. E. E. Thrash, Executive Secretary. After the death of Ira Morgan, I appointed Mike Sturdivant (not pictured) to fill his term.

Seated to my left at one of the four Governor's Conferences on Education
are The University of Mississippi Chancellor Porter L. Fortune, Jr.,
Lt. Gov. Winter, Superintendent of Education Garvin H. Johnston,
and Senator Herman DeCell

Announcing the passage of the $1000 teacher pay raise: (left to right),
W. S. Griffin, Governor Waller, Rep. George Rogers, C. J. Duckworth,
Sen. Jack Tucker

William L. Waller Technical Center at Northeast Mississippi Community College

Signing the $600,000 highway bill: (left to right), Sen. Ebb Horton; Sen. Thomas N. Books; Sen. Perrin Purvis; Lt. Gov. Winter; Rep. Thomas Hickman; Rep. Henry Jones

I was the first Mississippi governor to attend a Choctaw Indian Fair. Sitting directly behind me is Chief Phillip Martin   PHOTOGRAPH COURTESY MDAH

Signing SB1857 creating the Wildlife Heritage Committee that arranged for the purchase the Pascagoula River bottomland. Charter members were (seated) Sen. Ray H. Montgomery; (standing left to right) Bruce H. Brady; William Y. Quisenberry, III; Avery Wood; Rep. James H. Neal; Rep. Charles M. Deaton; William H. Allen; Rep. Tommy A. Gollott; Sen. William C. Rhodes

Visiting with Dr. Billy Graham on one of his trips to Jackson

Elvis making a donation to the victims of a tornado in McComb

The Republican Governors Conference at the 1973 Ole Miss-Tennessee Game in Jackson: (left to right), Christopher Bond of Missouri, Ronald Reagan of California, Winfield Dunn of Tennessee, and Jack Williams of Arizona

Welcoming Texas Senator Lloyd Bentson (on the far right) to Mississippi, with Jackson Mayor Russell Davis (to my right) and Fayette Mayor Charles Evers (to my left)   PHOTOGRAPH COURTESY MDAH

My Farewell Address   PHOTOGRAPH COURTESY MDAH

old political machine." Most of the people who talked to me about running for governor had never participated in politics before, but they realized that they and their children had a stake in Mississippi's future.

It was obvious to me and to the people who encouraged me to run that Mississippi was standing still, and that the old guard could not get the state moving again, and certainly not get it moving in the right direction. Our leadership had developed the notion that any significant change was not good and should be resisted. This state of mind was a result of all those years when our leaders tried to avoid desegregation, and what they called "federal encroachment on states' rights."

Working class Mississippians who paid most of the taxes, women and blacks, and young Mississippians like those in the Junior Chamber of Commerce, or Jaycees as they were called, had long been excluded from the political process, but they were becoming more politically astute. I believed it would be their votes that would elect a new class of leaders. My 1967 campaign for governor was directed primarily to them.

When I announced my candidacy on November 15, 1966, at the old Heidelberg Hotel in Jackson, Lieutenant Governor Carroll Gartin and Jimmy Swan were already in the race. Swan was an arch segregationist and a radio personality from Hattiesburg. He had announced he was running in April 1966.

Lieutenant Governor Carroll Gartin had also announced his intention to run for governor. Gartin had lost the governor's race to Ross Barnett in 1959, but then defeated Evelyn Gandy for lieutenant governor in 1963. He was generally considered the front runner in 1967, and his popularity had narrowed the field of prospective candidates. But his sudden and unexpected death on December 19, 1966, changed the political landscape and over the next few weeks the names of several possible candidates surfaced.

During the early speculation Jackson Mayor Allen Thompson and Mississippi Supreme Court Justice Tom Brady, who wrote a scathing criticism of the *Brown* decision entitled *Black Monday*, were considered likely candidates but they did not enter the race. There was some talk, especially among Ole Miss alumni, that Chancellor John D. Williams might run for governor. It was also rumored that Robert "Blowtorch" Mason, a welder from Magee who ran for governor in 1959 and 1963, would conduct a third campaign, but Mason decided at the last minute not to enter the 1967 race.

There was also some discussion about a potential candidate who never actually intended to run. Many of Governor Paul Johnson's supporters urged Mrs. Johnson to run as a surrogate candidate for her husband as Mrs. George Wallace had recently done with success in Alabama. As the various candidates lined up for the coming campaign, and the speculation about her candidacy increased, Mrs. Johnson held a press conference at the Governor's Mansion on February 9, 1967. After thanking her potential supporters for their interest in her candidacy, she said, "I am realistic enough, however, to know that the enthusiasm for my candidacy constitutes a tribute to my husband's administration as governor during the crucial three years just passed." She then said that she would not be a candidate and that she looked forward to returning to private life and their home in Hattiesburg. Just before the filing deadline, however, Governor Johnson announced that he would run for lieutenant governor.

William Winter announced his candidacy in the spring of 1967 and conducted a vigorous campaign. William Winter and I basically appealed to the same constituency, but he got a lot more of their votes in 1967 than I did.

After the Democratic Party stripped him of his congressional seniority, Congressman John Bell Williams announced that he would run for governor. Williams had campaigned for Republican Barry Goldwater in the 1964 presidential election against President Lyndon B. Johnson. Goldwater carried Mississippi with 87% of the popular vote.

Williams had represented Mississippi's third congressional district since 1946 and was a ranking member of the Democratic caucus. Williams would probably have remained in Congress if his seniority had been restored. Hodding Carter, III, who had recently taken over the Greenville *Delta Democrat-Times* from his father, and the Mississippi Young Democrats helped persuade the congressional Democrats to reject Williams' appeal for the restoration of his congressional ranking.

Williams conducted an unusual, stealth campaign, and I rarely saw him at the political rallies where the other major candidates appeared. He was not a crowd pleaser, but he was a wounded World War II veteran and that made him popular with the voters. He also appealed to the state's pronounced opposition to President Johnson and the national Democratic Party, which Williams said had insulted Mississippi by taking away his seniority, and that it was a slap in the face of every Mississippian.

The other major Democratic candidate in the race was former governor Ross Barnett, who was making his fourth campaign for governor. Barnett lost in 1951 and 1955, and was elected in 1959. After sitting out a term because the 1890 constitution prohibited governors from succeeding themselves, Barnett ran again in 1967.

I never dreamed nearly twenty years earlier, when my father took me into Ross Barnett's office and asked his old Mississippi College classmate to help "my boy" get started in the practice of law, that I would someday be running for governor of the state of Mississippi, and that Barnett would be one of my opponents. Barnett was sixty-nine, and the oldest candidate in the race. I was the youngest at forty-one. After the death of Carroll Gartin, Barnett was generally considered the front runner. Tom Ethridge, a *Clarion-Ledger* columnist, even speculated that Barnett might win the race in the first primary.

The last candidate to formally file for the 1967 governor's race was Rubel Phillips, a former Democratic public service commissioner who switched to the Republican Party in the early 1960s. Phillips was making his second run for governor after losing to Paul Johnson in 1963. Phillips would meet the winner of the Democratic primary in the general election in November.

Two minor candidates, Vernon E. Brown and C. L. McKinley, filed for the office but neither of them conducted an active campaign. A.B. Albritton, a *Clarion-Ledger* staff writer, reported that McKinley was seen only once after his announcement. McKinley worked in Pennsylvania as a pipe-fitter during much of the campaign and listed a trailer park in south Mississippi as his home address. McKinley sent several tape-recorded messages to political rallies around the state and asked the rally organizers to play the tapes for the audiences. Brown, the Stone County Tax Assessor, made several appearances during the first primary, including the Neshoba County Fair, but he did not conduct an extensive campaign.

In addition to the eight candidates for governor and a large field for other statewide offices, there were six candidates for lieutenant governor. Governor Paul Johnson narrowly missed making the second primary, in which Charles Sullivan defeated Roy Black. Also running for lieutenant governor was Byron De La Beckwith, who announced his candidacy soon after I announced that I was running for governor. Beckwith was selling subscriptions to a Jackson weekly newspaper when he filed for office. Although he did not actually campaign for the office, and the only major speech he made was at the Neshoba County Fair, Beckwith still received 34,675 votes.

Early in the 1967 campaign, I realized that to run for governor you had to have a lot of stamina and a lot money. And I soon learned that there was a direct correlation between the public's perception that you could win and the financial contributions they would make to your campaign. It was not my purpose to get in the 1967 race as a "warm up" for a later campaign. I entered the race to win, and I campaigned on that basis.

I announced my candidacy early because I knew it would be an uphill battle to get myself known around the state, and I had a lot of ideas that I wanted to put before the people of Mississippi. Someone said I was better known outside Mississippi than inside the state, and I am sure that both helped and hurt my campaign.

My state campaign manager was Joe Fancher, a classmate at the Ole Miss law school who had also worked with me on several criminal cases when he was Madison County Attorney. Joe and I were novices in the rough and tumble game of Mississippi politics, and we both learned a lot as the campaign progressed.

In its June 25, 1967, Sunday edition, the *Clarion-Ledger/Jackson Daily News* carried a picture of me milking a cow and announced that I had won second place among the candidates who entered a milking contest sponsored by the Biloxi Merchants Association. At long last my boyhood experience on my father's Lafayette County farm had paid off. That second place finish no doubt endeared me to the voters who had not yet mechanized their dairy operations and won me an undetermined number of votes. Troy Watkins of Natchez, a candidate for lieutenant governor, beat me by less than half a bucket.

Although I advanced a wide range of issues throughout the 1967 election, my platform was largely established by the time the campaign was in full swing. The central theme of my campaign was expressed in a statement I made on August 5 at Booneville: "Yesterday's politics won't solve tomorrow's problems."

Most of Mississippi's public policies and its political structure had been established in the horse and buggy days, and I wanted to help move our state into the progressive modern era. I was running as an independent Mississippi Democrat with no affiliation with any machine, group, or organization. And I offered the voters alternatives to the old ways of the past. We needed to jump start Mississippi again, like Governor Hugh White had done with the Balance Agriculture With Industry program that created thousands of new jobs during the depression in the 1930s. As I said over and over during the campaign, to get Mississippi moving again we needed to replace the tired old machine politicians with new leaders who would "move with speed and daring" and who would govern with "honesty, dignity, and statesmanship."

At the top of my agenda was the improvement of the state's public school system, and the first step in that process was the reinstatement of compulsory education. I made a solemn pledge to the people of Mississippi that we would provide our children an adequate education by qualified teachers who would no longer be the lowest paid in the nation. I also pledged to take politics out of education by supporting an appointed superintendent of education at the state and the local level. Elected school officials often spent too much time getting reelected and not enough time educating our children.

During the heat of the 1967 campaign, a legislative study underscored the pressing need for major improvements in the state's school system. The Booze, Allen and Hamilton Study of Public Education in Mississippi, which was authorized by the legislature in 1966, reported that Mississippi school children scored at or near the bottom in almost all educational categories.

Although the two previous governors boasted of the number of industrial jobs that were created during their administrations, most of them were minimum wage jobs. While I did not disparage those jobs, I thought we were not doing enough to attract heavy industry into the state. We should have been doing more to bring the kind of industry into Mississippi that would complement centers of expertise that already existed, such as the aeronautical engineering program at Mississippi State University.

I pledged to work with major industrialists in America and abroad to secure for our state a larger share of the heavy industry that was going to Alabama, Georgia, Louisiana, and other southern states. As part of a broad economic development program, I recommended the construction of agricultural packaging and processing plants. By manufacturing and marketing more finished products we could keep a larger portion of our agricultural dollars in the state.

In 1967 there were thousands of small farmers and businessmen in Mississippi who could have benefitted from an infusion of new capital. My platform included the establishment of a low interest, small loan program for beginning entrepreneurs on the same principle that we granted tax exemptions and long term, low interest loans to the industries we were trying to lure to Mississippi.

I also recommended that the family car, like the family home, be exempt from ad valorem taxes. If we could give a billion dollar corporation a tax exemption to build a shipyard in Pascagoula, we could surely give the overburdened middle class taxpayer an exemption on the family car that had become as much a necessity as the family dwelling.

Another group of hard working middle class citizens who were being penalized because of outdated public policy were Mississippi truckers. The varying weight limits on the state's primary and secondary highways were creating unnecessary hardships for the trucking industry and were a negative factor in economic development generally. The weight limits on state highways varied by as many as twenty thousand pounds from the "cross-country loads," and some truckers had to transfer their cargo to smaller trucks when they made deliveries to small towns in Mississippi. In a speech on July 27 to the Highway 82 Club, I discussed this situation and said that if I were elected governor I would recommend legislation to alleviate that problem.

At a rally in New Albany sponsored by the Jaycees, I noted that most of the candidates in the race were speaking in glittering generalities and did not get specific on the issues. My opponents talked about their belief in our way of life, good government, low taxes, and love of country. Those were the same old tired political phrases that I had heard since my boyhood days on the farm, and I thought the people of Mississippi deserved better.

One of the subjects that I thought required a straightforward discussion was the issue of law and order, an issue that was important to me because of my background as a prosecuting attorney. The 1960s was a time of such rapid and sweeping changes that we just could not keep up with it all, and sometimes the changes got out of hand. In Mississippi the real threat to law and order did not come from the Vietnam war protest, the increasing use of mind altering drugs, or the sexual revolution, but from the far ends of the racial divide. At a Rotary Club luncheon in Laurel on April 25 I addressed the issue of law and order and racial violence.

In that speech I said that every Mississippian had the right to sleep safely in his own home and to know that his children were protected by custom and law. I asked the Rotarians if they wanted Mississippi to be ruled by cross burners or by the rule of law. And as a fifth generation Mississippian I said that the "hooded cowards" of the Ku Klux Klan did not represent our southern heritage.

I also said that when Stokley Carmichael or the black separatists in the Republic of New Africa movement shouted "Black Power" and called on black men to commit acts of violence, they did not speak for black Mississippians. Like their white neighbors and friends, black citizens wanted to live in peace and dignity. I tried to convince those Rotarians and everyone else who read or heard about that speech that the lawless elements in our state existed because of our collective silence. Like most other white men in Mississippi I had not raised my voice against the Klan or its sympathizers, but now that I was asking the people to elect me their governor I would no longer remain silent.

There were some courageous sheriffs and mayors and a few newspaper editors like Hodding Carter of the Greenville *Delta Democrat-Times*, Ira Harkey of the *Pascagoula Chronicle*, Oliver Emmerich of the *McComb Enterprise-Journal*, George McLean of the *Tupelo Daily Journal*, Hazel Brannon Smith of the *Lexington Advertiser*, and P.D. East of the *Petal Paper* who spoke out against racial violence. I commended them, and I also praised Governor Paul Johnson for his commitment to law and order and encouraged those Rotarians not to be intimidated or afraid, to report crimes to the police, and to testify against people who committed acts of violence. I was pleased by the response to the speech, and all across the state people were telling me that they were ready to accept the changes that they knew were inevitable.

In many other campaign speeches across the state I said that law and order was not only necessary for the safety of our own people, but it was necessary if we were serious about attracting new industry and tourists to the state. I believed that tourism was one of our state's most promising opportunities for economic development. But we had not developed the great potential of the Gulf Coast as a convention site or as a vacation destination. I recommended a convention center for the coast and an active program to attract tourists to Mississippi. At that time we had no tourist attraction like Six Flags or Disney World, and we did not have facilities on the coast that could accommodate a national convention.

At almost every campaign stop in 1967 I talked about the antiquated character of state government, which was still operating under a constitution that was drafted in the nineteenth century, and I recommended a broad range of reforms. At my June 25 kickoff rally in Oxford, I said, "My program for Mississippi is down-to-earth, specific, positive, and we could achieve these goals if we moved with speed and daring."

Among the reforms that I recommended in that Oxford speech were:

- modernizing the judicial system
- upgrading qualifications for justices of the peace
- gubernatorial succession
- professionalizing law enforcement
- expanding the training of highway patrolmen and local police
- separating the duties of the county tax collector and the county sheriff
- allowing the sheriff to succeed himself
- placing more county officials on a salary basis rather than a fee system
- an appointed statewide highway management system
- ninety-day, annual legislative sessions
- reducing the residency requirement for voting from two years to six months

I also recommended a public relations agency to improve

Mississippi's image and to correct the often inaccurate and misleading statements appearing in the national media. As I have thought about our state's national image over the years, I believe that we deserve some of the criticism we have received. But the national media has made us a convenient scapegoat and rarely gives us credit when we deserve it.

In addition to these recommendations, most of which have been enacted over the last three or four decades, there were two other major issues that I raised in almost every campaign appearance. First, I was appalled to learn that sixty state agencies maintained two hundred and thirty-three separate bank accounts, and that Mississippi's idle funds were deposited in non-interest bearing accounts. The state was losing millions of dollars every year while bankers were making millions off the taxpayers of Mississippi. I could find no evidence that any interest had ever been paid on public funds that were deposited in state banks. Naturally, bank officials and their shareholders opposed any change in the state banking laws.

I raised the banking issue repeatedly throughout the campaign because one of my major reasons for running for governor was to bring sound business practices to state government. And I assured the people that if I was elected governor the state's idle funds would be deposited in interest-bearing accounts.

The other major issue I raised repeatedly was the heavy cost of the "brain drain." At rallies in Meadville, Columbia, Bay St. Louis, Raleigh, Cleveland, Corinth, and at other stops around the state, I said that if we expect our bright young men and women to stay in Mississippi we must attract more of the blue chip, high-paying industry that was going to other southern states. We educate our young men and women and they go out of state to find better paying jobs. This was a vicious cycle, but it could be stopped with creative and positive leadership from the governor and the legislature. The out-migration of talent left some of the smaller towns and cities without enough qualified people to staff new industries or businesses.

Industrial development and the creation of better paying jobs would also reduce the state's dependence on federal welfare programs, which today includes about 39% of the state's population. I said many times during the 1967 campaign that elderly people and those who were unable to work should continue to receive federal assistance. I also said that the welfare system perpetuates a welfare culture, generation after generation, and that the real solution to rising welfare costs is jobs. The way to end poverty is to put people to work. I believe that a strong work ethic has made this country what it is, and that able-bodied men ought to work if there is a job available to them.

As the first Democratic primary was winding down, none of the other candidates were addressing these important issues, except William Winter, but he was having to spend much of his time defending himself from Ross Barnett, Jimmy Swan, and John Bell Williams. They accused him of voting for John Kennedy in 1960 and Lyndon Johnson in 1964, and of being too "liberal" for Mississippi. Williams labeled Winter "Kennedy's Candidate." Ross Barnett called Winter "Little Boy Blue." He called John Bell Williams "Johnny Come Lately" Bell Williams, and a "middle of the roader," and said that sometimes it was hard to figure out just which side of the road he was on. Winter labeled Barnett "an arranger" for working out a secret deal with Attorney General Robert Kennedy to admit James Meredith to Ole Miss, and called Williams "a quitter" for abandoning his congressional seat in Washington and coming back home to Mississippi.

The press and his supporters labeled Jimmy Swan a "segregationist." Although there were already more than 6,000 black students enrolled in the white public school system, Swan still promised to keep the schools segregated and proudly claimed to be a modern day Theodore Bilbo. The *Clarion-Ledger* called C.L. McKinley a "phantom" candidate because he made so few public appearances during the campaign.

No one called me anything, so I got to label myself. Early in the campaign I described myself as an active conservative.

Actually, the *Clarion-Ledger* staff writer Kenneth Fairley labeled me a "dark horse."

Because the candidates were more specific about the labels they placed on each other than they were about the important issues facing the state, I suggested that all of the candidates for governor begin meeting at courthouses across the state for some good old fashioned political debates. I thought it was important for the voters to see us all together and compare our ideas and hear our solutions for the state's problems. After none of the candidates agreed to that proposal, I then suggested that we meet in a series of televised debates. Most of the ten television stations in Mississippi agreed, at my request, to make free time available for a live, unrehearsed debate between the candidates running for governor. William Winter and Vernon Brown agreed to public debates, but Jimmy Swan, John Bell Williams, and Ross Barnett would not consent to live, unrehearsed televised debates. Neither would they agree to meet in a series of public forums organized by the Mississippi Jaycees.

I spoke at several rallies that were sponsored by the Jaycees. These energetic, independent thinking young men realized that Mississippi was standing still, and I enlisted thousands of them into my campaign. James Rankin, the 1967 state president of the Mississippi Jaycees, became one of my strongest supporters and held a leadership role in my second campaign. During the 1971 campaign the Jaycees were among my strongest and most influential supporters.

I also made a direct effort to attract women to my campaign. Two weeks before I formally announced my candidacy, I spoke to the Pre-Law Club at Millsaps College. During a discussion with the students, they asked me if I thought women should be allowed to serve on juries. The fact that women could vote, hold public office, own their own businesses, and practice law, but could not serve on juries was just one more glaring illustration of Mississippi's outdated political system.

In a speech to the Jackson chapter of the American

Association of Business Women, I assured them that I would support their right to serve on juries and that I would appoint women to the Agricultural and Industrial Board, the College Board, and other important state agencies. I also appealed to Governor Paul Johnson to release the report of the Commission on the Status of Women, which the legislature had authorized in 1962 and was submitted to the governor on June 2, 1967.

Women voters responded to my campaign because I promised to enlarge the role of women in state government, and some of my most active supporters in the 1967 campaign were women. For many of them it was their first time to participate in the political process. Among those women volunteers were my sister Millie Burtschell, my sister-in-law Patsy Waller, Joanne Pittman, Martha Carr, Betty Jeter, Betty Cryder, Ginny Hamilton, Betty Lake, Carol Robinson, Dorothy Allen, Frances Roebuck, Sandy Fischer, Barbara Fortenberry, Anne Gardner, Francis Gatewood, Norma Price, Marjorie Murley, Elise Wise, Faye Dixon, Victoria Webb, and Bonita Metcalf.

I also received a lot of support from women because Carroll was so active and visible in my campaign. In Mount Olive on July 25, Carroll drew a crowd of over three hundred women to a morning coffee hosted by my cousin, Faye Gatewood Dickson and her daughter, Sue Tyrone. In 1967 politics in Mississippi was still a personal and a family affair.

Although my appeal to black voters was indirect, I did get some support from the increasing number of black voters, largely because of my prosecution of Beckwith. Charles Evers worked quietly behind the scenes for me and made a financial contribution to my campaign. Several months after the campaign, in the winter of 1967, he was in my office and we talked about Mississippi politics. During the conversation I said, "You know, Charlie, someday it might be just you and me running against each other." Evers smiled at the thought, but neither of us could have imagined what would happen just four years later.

The polls and predictions during the 1967 campaign were a hit and miss proposition and changed dramatically as the first primary came to a close. Four months after *Clarion-Ledger* columnist Tom Ethridge wrote that "the biggest question seems to be the size of the Barnett majority," a statewide poll of eight hundred voters showed William Winter leading the race with 45%, followed by John Bell Williams at 31%, and Barnett a distant third with 8%. Republican Rubel Phillips had 7%, and I was in fifth place with 4%. Jimmy Swan had less than 1% and 4% were listed for others or undecided.

An informal sampling of members of the Mississippi Legislature by the *Clarion-Ledger* in early July indicated that William Winter had peaked and was in a downward trend. Almost all the legislators agreed that Ross Barnett's campaign was "gaining new support and strength daily" and that he was now leading the race. Most legislators predicted a Barnett versus Williams race in the runoff election, but some thought that Jimmy Swan might surprise everyone, and that he could even make it into the second primary.

About a week later a poll released by Joe Abram, an independent pollster from Biloxi, seemed to validate the predictions and opinions of the legislators. Abram's poll had Barnett leading the race at 31%. Winter was close behind at 29%, Williams had 24%, Swan was at 9%, and I trailed with 6%.

At this stage in the campaign I was not too discouraged because I had a sense that, despite the polls, a lot of people had not really made up their minds. Some polls estimated that the undecided or silent vote was between thirty and forty percent, and I believed that many of those undecided voters would break for me.

In the late stages of the campaign, when it became increasingly evident that Winter and Williams were surging into the lead, Barnett claimed that he was still in the lead and attacked both of the front runners. Barnett ridiculed Williams as "an absentee congressman" and criticized him for collecting his $30,000 annual salary even though he was not performing his congressional duties. Williams shot back at Barnett, accusing him of making a "secret deal" with the Kennedys to let James Meredith in Ole Miss.

Just before the end of the first primary, Meredith endorsed Ross Barnett and announced that he would campaign for him in fourteen cities. Barnett accused William Winter and James Meredith of forming the "most diabolical alliance . . . in the political history of Mississippi" and repudiated Meredith's endorsement.

Jimmy Swan's increasing appeal to the old line segregationists precipitated Barnett's decline in the closing days of the campaign and apparently cost him a place in the runoff. During the last few days of the first primary, Swan made a direct racial appeal and reiterated his earlier promise to keep the schools segregated. James Saggus, an AP reporter, quoted Swan as saying, "To grant equality to the Negro is to make savagery equal to civilization." Swan's stern rhetoric and the perception that Barnett's strength was declining caused a large number of Barnett's former supporters to switch to Swan.

On August 6, two days before the first primary vote, the Greenville *Delta Democrat-Times* formally endorsed me for governor of the state of Mississippi. Hodding Carter, III, wrote in an editorial that "Mississippi badly needs the best leadership it can find. Bill Waller would provide it." That so-called "liberal" newspaper endorsed this "self proclaimed conservative" with a caveat: "We have not always agreed with every stand he has taken, but have been impressed from the start to the finish by his willingness to take stands free of the overblown generalizations which have marked the other candidates."

I authorized Joe Fancher to issue the following statement: "I appreciate [Mr. Carter's] frank statement that he does not always agree with me. Likewise, I don't always agree with the writer since I am a conservative. I am glad the *Delta Democrat-Times* understands and appreciates my conservative program for Mississippi and my hard-nosed, business-like approach to state government."

I did appreciate the *Delta Democrat-Times'* endorsement and I thanked Hodding Carter for it. As I recall his was the only newspaper that endorsed me.

When the votes were finally cast on election day I did not win, but I did make history and there is a Claude Sutherland photograph on the front page of the *Clarion-Ledger* to prove it. I was the first Mississippi politician to campaign by helicopter. On Monday morning Carroll and I boarded a helicopter for a full day of appearances that took us from Pascagoula to Biloxi, Gulfport, Hattiesburg, Laurel, Meridian, Jackson, Vicksburg, and Greenwood. The picture in the *Clarion-Ledger* was taken when Carroll and I made an afternoon stop in Jackson. The paper called the helicopter jaunt "one of the most spectacular moves of the closing hours" of the campaign. Someone said that even though I did not win, I achieved one of my campaign promises. I had moved Mississippi politics from the horse and buggy era into the age of the helicopter.

The turnout in the first Democratic primary was the largest in Mississippi history, and it took a long time to count the ballots because only ten counties used voting machines. Perhaps for the first time in Mississippi history, a computer tabulated the results of a state election. President Robert Mayo of Hinds County Junior College in Raymond made his institution's computer available to Hinds County officials. Beth Day and Ross Martin programed the Model 1620 computer to count the ballots used by the county's new voting machines.

Although only 650,000 were expected to vote in the first primary, more than 684,000 votes were cast for the seven gubernatorial candidates. That was an increase of more than two hundred thousand from the 475,000 votes cast in the 1963 election. This increase was a sign that more people were getting involved in state politics, and that spelled trouble for the old guard.

Another major reason for the increase in voter turnout was the large number of black voters who had registered in the mid-1960s. According to the *Clarion-Ledger*'s estimate at the time of the first Democratic primary, black registration had increased from 30,000 in 1963 to 180,000 in 1967.

A substantial black voter turnout resulted in the election of 22 of the 108 black candidates running in the 1967 election. Among those twenty-two elected officials was Robert Clark of Ebenezer in Holmes County. The first black man elected to the state legislature since the early 1900s, Representative Clark enjoyed a distinguished thirty-six year tenure in the Mississippi legislature, rising to the rank of speaker *pro tempore*. During my administration I enjoyed an excellent working relationship with Representative Clark.

When all the results were in, William Winter led the ticket with 222,001 votes and John Bell Williams received 197,778. The final tally validated what several observers had predicted. Many of Barnett's supporters moved to Swan. In the final count Swan came in third with 124,361 votes, and Barnett was fourth with 76,053 votes. I was fifth with 60,090. Vernon Brown received 2,051 votes, and C. L. McKinley got 1,671. John Bell Williams eventually defeated William Winter in the second Democratic primary, and later defeated Republican Rubel Phillips in the November general election.

Based on the most reliable figures available, *Jackson Daily News* staff writer Charles Gordon estimated that there were 750,000 registered voters at the time of the first primary. The 684,000 votes cast in the first primary was not only the highest vote total in the state's history, but the turnout represented an astounding 91% of the registered voters.

Soon after the first primary, supporters of William Winter and John Bell Williams sought my endorsement and the support of those who had voted for me. I remained neutral during the runoff but encouraged my supporters to stay active in Mississippi politics.

The 1967 election was a turning point in Mississippi's political history. It was the last election in which major candidates campaigned against progress and for the status quo and made direct appeals based on race. I think voters decided during that election that holding onto the past was another lost cause, and that significant changes were necessary to improve the quality of life for everyone.

The 1967 campaign was also the beginning of the end of those old fashioned campaigns dominated by big political rallies where hundreds of people gathered for a barbecue or a fish fry and a day-long round of speeches by candidates from governor to constable.

During the long campaign my law partners John Fox and Robert Pritchard, in addition to supporting my campaign, maintained the law firm and continued to serve our clients. After the campaign the firm expanded and eventually included Tom Coward, W.W. Pierce, Bill Gowan, Barry Powell, Sam Wilkins, James H. Neeld, and Don Lacey. Our diverse practice included commercial, family, personal injury, and some criminal law.

In January 1968 the firm acquired an old building across the street from City Hall near the state and federal courthouses. Working closely with the carpenters and builders, we redesigned and renovated the old building into a comfortable and convenient law office. After almost forty years it is still the office of Waller and Waller and a pleasant place to work.

Because of my eight years as district attorney of the largest judicial district in the state, many people involved in the criminal justice system, or members of their families, often sought my counsel. Some of them were often in financial straights and I sometimes offered my services either pro bono or for a minimal fee.

One such case involved Wesley Wilson, who owned the Jackson Brace Company and was a personal friend of many years. The Wilson family asked me to represent his younger brother, Charles Clifford Wilson, one of the Klansmen charged in the murder of Hattiesburg civil rights leader Vernon Dahmer.

In July 1968 Clifford Wilson was tried on state murder and arson charges. When the Hattiesburg jury could not reach a verdict, Judge Stanton Hall declared a mistrial. In January 1969 Wilson was retried and a jury convicted him on both counts.

When the jury could not agree on a penalty, Judge Hall sentenced Wilson to life in prison.

While his murder conviction was on appeal to the Mississippi Supreme Court, Wilson was tried in federal court at Meridian on charges of conspiracy to deny Dahmer his civil rights. It was at this time that the Wilson family asked me to work with his two attorneys, Harold Melvin and Leonard Melvin of Laurel.

On May 10, 1969, when a federal jury in Meridian could not reach a verdict in Wilson's trial on the federal conspiracy charges, U.S. District Court Judge Dan M. Russell, Jr., declared a mistrial. Wilson was then returned to Parchman to serve his life sentence.

In his book, *Attack on Terror: The FBI Against the Ku Klux Klan in Mississippi,* Don Whitehead wrote that Wilson's arrest was "shocking" to the Laurel community because he was such a model citizen. A sharecropper's son, Wilson was the thirty-six year old father of four children and the owner of the Laurel Brace and Limb Company. He was the 1965 president of the Laurel chapter of the Mississippi Jaycees, and was named "Man of the Year" in Laurel just before his arrest in 1968. Wilson was cited for his work with the Boy Scouts and with crippled and retarded children.

In all three of Wilson's trials numerous character witnesses, including bankers, physicians, public officials, and his colleagues in the Jaycees, testified on his behalf. All of them were bewildered that such a good man had committed such a heinous crime.

When I took office in January 1972 Wilson was on emergency leave from Parchman. Governor John Bell Williams had granted him a leave, which I later extended, because one of his children was undergoing surgery and his wife was ill.

Early in my administration I established a work release program for inmates at Parchman. Among the first group released under this program were eight black and seven white inmates. One of the fifteen inmates was Clifford Wilson. After his release Wilson worked in a mental retardation center in Ellisville. Wilson's release was extremely controversial and prompted a demonstration at the Capitol by a small group of blacks and a counter demonstration by a few whites. The coverage of the demonstration by one of the local television stations was so inflammatory that I filed a complaint with the Federal Communications Commission.

In 1975, after numerous meetings and consultations with prison officials and members of Wilson's family, I commuted his sentence to time served. This was a form of parole that I extended to approximately three hundred inmates during my administration with virtually no recidivism. I carefully considered each reprieve before granting it, and I believed it was the right thing to do.

One of my firm's most interesting and successful clients in the late 1960s was Fred Adams, Jr., an ingenious young entrepreneur. He was the prototype of the young businessmen that I believed Mississippi needed if we were going to make any real economic progress. Fred Adams was our client primarily because he and Bob Pritchard were classmates at Mississippi State and were close friends.

Adams was a pioneer in the poultry industry and established a restaurant chain, "Chicken Chef," which unsuccessfully challenged the large established restaurant chains such as Kentucky Fried Chicken. Even though that enterprise failed, his Jackson-based company Cal-Maine Foods, Inc., is now the largest shell egg producer and marketer in the nation. Cal-Maine Foods owns more than twenty-five million chickens and sells more than six hundred million dozen eggs a year, which is about thirteen percent of the national market. Among Cal-Maine's most popular products is Egg-Land's Best, a low-cholesterol egg. Pritchard and two other members of my firm, W.W. Pierce and Jim Neeld, withdrew from the firm when they became general counsel for Adams Enterprises.

Unfortunately, there were many other young businessmen who were not successful because they lacked the financial resources that Fred Adams enjoyed early in his career. The lack of venture capital continues to be a problem for our home-owned business infrastructure.

Although I had a successful law practice and my family was growing up and enjoying life, I still felt that there was some unfinished business. I wanted to be governor of Mississippi because I thought its citizens deserved better leadership than it had been getting from the "good old boys." After the 1967 campaign I knew that I would run again, it was just a matter of when. Politics is largely a matter of timing, a lesson that I would learn the hard way in the 1978 Senate race.

I had decided that I would not run for governor in 1971 if William Winter was going to run. We talked several times, and he told me that he was going to run for lieutenant governor and encouraged me to make another run for governor. After those conversations, I began making plans for another campaign.

As with all political races financing is the threshold problem. Having little or no personal wealth and with a young family, I had to do some planning and soul searching between 1967 and 1971. I stayed in contact with my key supporters and fund-raisers like Al Biggs, Charles Brady and Dr. Marshall Fortenberry of Jackson, D.A. Biglane of Natchez, Bobby Chain and Wiley Fairchild of Hattiesburg, Woodrow Stephens of Wiggins, Nolen Clark of Waynesboro, George Dale of Moss Point, and many others. Most of them assured me that I would have a much better chance in 1971, but that I would definitely be the underdog to Lieutenant Governor Charles Sullivan.

Carroll and my entire family encouraged me to make another campaign. My law partners were also encouraging, particularly Bob Pritchard. Bob enjoyed politics, had a wide circle of friends, and was an effective fund-raiser.

I had to know that the financial resources would be available before I could make another commitment to run. In all of my campaigns we raised money by collecting ten dollars here and fifty dollars there, which made it even more imperative that we have the kind of commitment necessary to raise several hundred thousand dollars through small contributions. After my key supporters assured me that I would have that kind of backing, I decided to run again.

CHAPTER 10

Campaign of 1971

*"In one of the major political upsets of the century,
Bill Waller beat Charles Sullivan in the second primary."*
—EARLE JOHNSTON

In the spring of 1971 as the likely candidates for governor were lining up, Charles Gordon of the *Jackson Daily News* wrote that I just might be the "man on horseback" that many voters were hoping to see in the contest. Even though I finished fifth in 1967, I was convinced by the way people had responded to my campaign that they were ready to elect someone who offered an alternative to the old status quo machine politics. They were tired of politicians, bankers, and big shots in Jackson deciding who would run for governor and who would win. As I had in my first race for governor, in the 1971 campaign I ran against the old guard and the Jackson political machine, which I called the "Capitol Street Gang."

Under the existing political system, you had to stand in line and wait your turn to be governor. Charles Sullivan's 1971 campaign slogan was a candid expression of that tradition—"It's Charlie's Time." Sullivan ran for governor in 1959 and 1963, for lieutenant governor in 1967, and was running for governor again in 1971. This time the "Capitol Street Gang" was backing Sullivan, and most of the state's daily newspapers endorsed him.

The "Capitol Street Gang" included the powerful Hederman family, who owned both daily newspapers in Jackson and one of the two Jackson television stations. One of the four Hederman brothers was a member of the Board of Trustees of Institutions of Higher Learning. Another was a member of the Board of Directors of the Research and Development Center. A third brother was President of the Pearl River Valley Water Supply District, which controlled the Barnett Reservoir and was responsible for naming it the "Ross Barnett Reservoir." The fourth brother was a member of the Mississippi Memorial Stadium Commission that would not allow integrated professional football teams to play in Mississippi's largest football arena. The editor of a Hederman-owned Jackson newspaper was also on the Agricultural and Industrial Board.

A.B. Albritton, the Jackson correspondent for the Memphis *Commercial Appeal,* noted that during the 1971 campaign the Hederman press "attacked . . . Waller for all he was worth . . . and has not been hesitant to take a few pot shots at the governor since he assumed office either."

Another powerful element of the "Capitol Street Gang" was the small ruling elite that dominated the Mississippi Legislature. When Speaker of the House Walter Sillers died in 1966 he had been in the legislature for half a century. He had been speaker for a quarter of a century. His successors, John Junkin and Buddie Newman, served for almost another quarter of a century. The chairmen of the legislative appropriations and finance committees controlled the purse strings of state government and were ranking members of that ruling elite. The courthouse and city hall "gangs" in towns and cities across the state were also vital members of the old guard.

The source of the old machine's power was its control of the state's economic resources and its use of racial politics. The people in power played on the fear of integration and practiced "status quo politics." They said that any significant political or social change might upset the status quo and disturb the state's racial traditions, so to be on the safe side, things must be kept the way they are and always have been.

Because no one offered a better alternative to this way of thinking, the people neglected their own economic interests and did not challenge the political machines. I had seen this way of thinking in my boyhood and wondered why so many good people accepted "status quo politics." John Fox said that I started running for governor when I was in high School. If that is true, it was because of my desire to offer the people an alternative to the do-nothing, hold-onto-what-you-have machine and to give ordinary citizens an opportunity to participate in their government.

The 1971 campaign was a lot more fun than 1967. In many ways running for governor was more enjoyable than being governor. Willie Morris once asked former governor J.P. Coleman, who was then a judge on the U.S. Fifth Circuit Court of Appeals, if he ever thought about running for governor again. Judge Coleman said he enjoyed his campaigns for governor, and that he would like to run again, but he was afraid that he might get elected.

I ran as an underdog and outsider in 1971, as I had in my first race, and few of the state's newspapers and almost none of the state's "political observers" considered me a viable candidate. Bill Minor, the Mississippi correspondent for the New Orleans *Times-Picayune* and one of the keenest of those observers, and my friend of many years, wrote that I was not considered a major candidate at the start of the campaign and was certainly not considered Sullivan's strongest rival. Most observers believed that Jimmy Swan would be Sullivan's major challenger.

By the time all the candidates filed or announced that they planned to run for governor the number of prospective candidates reached an all time high of eleven. In 1971 the Mississippi

Democratic Party was divided into two factions, the Loyalists and the Regulars, and each faction nominated a candidate for governor.

The Mississippi Loyalist Democratic Party nominated Charles Evers, and he prepared to run as a candidate in the August 3 Democratic primary. The Loyalists were a biracial faction of the Mississippi Democratic Party that had been recognized as the official state party at the 1968 Democratic National Convention. The Loyalists planned to run a large number of candidates for various offices, including Robert Clark for lieutenant governor. However, Clark declined the nomination and was reelected to the state House of Representatives.

The Regular Democratic Party of Mississippi, the traditional all-white faction, did not have standing with the national Democratic Party, but was recognized under state law as the official Democratic Party of Mississippi. After Secretary of State Heber Ladner ruled that the Loyalist Democratic Party did not have legal standing under state law and was not entitled to use the term "Democratic Party," Evers announced that he would run as an independent in the November general election.

Rubel Phillips, who ran for governor as a Republican in 1963 and 1967, announced that he would not be a candidate in 1971. The leadership of the Mississippi Republican Party did not want to split the white vote and allow Evers to be elected by a plurality of votes.

Three candidates announced that they would run for governor but did not file with the secretary of state. Robert Derwood Ladner, a Long Beach businessman and a third cousin of Theodore Bilbo, announced his candidacy for the Democratic primary in early June. He said he did not agree with Bilbo's racial beliefs and would ask Charles Evers to be his running mate as lieutenant governor. He also promised to appoint blacks to high level positions if elected. Soon after his announcement Ladner dropped out of the race, apparently for health reasons.

The other two prospective candidates were Independent C.L.

McKinley of Pascagoula and Republican Harold B. Gregory, a Holly Springs farmer. McKinley, who ran for governor as a Democrat in 1967, promised a campaign like no one had ever seen before. In one respect McKinley's campaign was different. During the height of the campaign, McKinley was arrested on a firearms violation. However, he was given a suspended sentence after explaining to the judge that he was the target of an assassination plot that might be connected with the assassinations of President Kennedy and Dr. Martin Luther King, Jr.

McKinley also vowed to put Claude Ramsey in jail if he were elected. Although he was a pipe fitter and worked at Ingalls Shipyards in Pascagoula, McKinley was anti-union. He accused Ramsey, the head of the AFL-CIO in Mississippi, of trying to keep him from getting a job in the Pascagoula shipyards.

Harold Gregory spoke at the Neshoba County Fair on July 29, but I never ran into him anywhere else on the campaign trail. He did not qualify as a Republican candidate, and his name did not appear on the ballot in the November general election.

In addition to Evers, McKinley, Gregory, and Ladner, seven Democratic candidates announced for the August 3 Democratic primary. Roy Adams, a former highway commissioner for the northern district, was supposedly recruited by Senator James Eastland's forces to run against Charles Sullivan. State Senator Edwin Pittman of Hattiesburg, and Jackson attorney Andrew Sullivan also announced. Jimmy Swan, who claimed to have Senator Eastland's support, and Circuit Judge Marshall Perry of Grenada, an old line segregationist, also entered the race. Swan and Perry were the last two candidates for governor who campaigned on a segregationist platform. Lieutenant Governor Charles Sullivan and I brought the total number of candidates up to eleven.

Although I started the race far behind the front runners, I believed my 1967 campaign had helped change the way people were thinking and convinced many of them that some changes had to be made in the way the state was being governed. The integration of the public school system in the spring of 1970 brought fundamental and sweeping changes to Mississippi. Whites and blacks had to accept those changes and learn to live in peace and harmony. Most of my strongest supporters in 1971 were rank and file Mississippians, and I encouraged them to consider the changes facing Mississippi not as problems but as opportunities.

I will mention many names in this chapter, but these are the men and women and young people who believed in what we were trying to do together, and gave so freely of their time and their money to make my campaign a success. The least I can do in return for their support is to share these pages with them.

The ten dollar and twenty dollar contributions from the "little guys" were the start-up funds needed to build a successful campaign. I would rather have ten supporters who make a ten dollar contribution than the one supporter who makes a hundred dollar contribution. If a small modest income supporter makes a contribution, he considers it an investment in his future and he will bring along his friends and relatives. Had it not been for these supporters I would not be writing these memoirs. And whatever good I might have done, they made it possible.

As we began organizing a team that would campaign in more than three hundred towns and cities across the state, we held an old time family reunion involving three or four generations of the Waller family and scores of unpaid volunteers. Carroll was the most effective campaigner, and many good friends like Martha Carr traveled with Carroll on a regular basis. Virginia Hamilton, Tuggie Lake, Carolyn Stephenson, and Paula Cazenaul were also regular campaigners. As the campaign progressed we found that Carroll and the children attracted a great deal of attention and created a positive image for my campaign.

Bill, Jr., was a student at Mississippi State University and campaigned at night and on weekends, making campaign speeches wherever he was needed. Our daughter Joy, who was seventeen at the start of the campaign, also traveled with Carroll to many rallies. Her remarkably effective "my Daddy" speeches had a special appeal to the new eighteen year old voters.

The Twenty-Sixth Amendment giving eighteen year olds the right to vote was ratified just before the first Democratic primary. Many of those new and energetic voters were attracted to my campaign because of Joy and Bill, Jr., and because I talked about the future and not the past.

I will always be grateful to the support I received from the Waller family, including my aunts, uncles, and even distant cousins. My father and stepmother, Percy and Emma Waller, worked tirelessly as did my brother Don and his wife Patsy and their entire family. My sister Millie Burtschell often went to rallies with Carroll and the children at a considerable personal sacrifice, since she was a senior vice-president at Deposit Guaranty Bank with many responsibilities. I can not overstate the importance of my family connections, because they constituted the core of the campaign.

My cousins Ralph and William Edward Metcalf, who were boys when I visited them in Cleveland during the Great Depression, were men now and they and their wives Dolly and Bonita helped me get elected governor of Mississippi.

Among my most active and strongest supporters in Lawrence County, which I carried by an almost two to one majority over Charles Sullivan, were Carroll's aunt Anita and her husband Ernest Clinton.

Dr. John Waller of Monticello also supported me from the beginning to the end of that long campaign. Although we were not related, he jokingly claimed to be my cousin during the campaign. The day after I was elected a nurse asked him if the new governor was his cousin, and he boasted, "He's my brother."

High school friends in Jackson and Oxford, Carroll's classmates and alumni at Mississippi College, fellow church members, legal and professional associates, and many others with some connection to me or to my family and friends joined my campaign. Mississippi College is a small school, but its alumni have a strong presence in local government and business in central Mississippi, and its alumni were loyal to Carroll.

Of the thousands of congratulations I received from my supporters after the election, one that was special to me was from Dr.
J.E. Tramel, Jr., the superintendent of schools in Brookhaven. In
our youth Dr. Tramel and I went to school together at Black Jack
in rural Panola County. In a letter responding to his best wishes I
said, "With your continued support, we will build a greater
Mississippi" and assured him that "Black Jack shall rise again!"

My desire to serve all of the people of Mississippi was deeply
rooted in the sense of pride I had in my state that goes back
through my family for five generations.

In my second race we had a much larger campaign staff, and
considerably more money, and strong local organizations in most
of Mississippi's eighty-two counties. I did not have a large campaign staff in 1967, and almost all of them were unpaid volunteers, but I stayed in touch with them. When I announced my
candidacy in the spring of 1971, I already had a large volunteer
army of supporters.

As I have mentioned before, one of those who was with me
from 1955 to 1971 and thereafter was Charles Brady of Jackson,
who eventually became the general agent of an insurance company with agents in several counties. He introduced me to his company's agents around the state, and many of them joined my campaign. Brady later served as Chairman of the State Tax
Commission for several years.

Jackie Gardner, another insurance executive with statewide
connections, logged thousands of miles in his personal airplane
flying me to meetings with his agents and enlisting their support
for my campaign. He and his wife Anne were from Leflore
County and worked tirelessly to build support for me in Byron De
La Beckwith's hometown of Greenwood.

My local campaign committees worked hard, but they also
liked to have fun. My Sunflower County committee, which
included Dick Barrett and Joe Buchanan, always served water-
melons on those hot summer days when I came to town to make
a speech. They advertised a special and unique brand of water-

melons that were available only at my rallies, which they called "Waller melons."

Avery Wood of Greenwood, a cousin of Anne Gardner, joined us in 1967 and remained one of my most loyal supporters. During the 1971 campaign a Jackson automobile dealer provided Avery a mobile home to travel around the state and make speeches on my behalf. Sometimes my brother Don traveled with Avery, and they would take turns speaking at rallies. Don was fond of telling about a rally they attended in Rienzi, a small town in Alcorn County in the northeast corner of Mississippi. Being from the flatlands of the Mississippi Delta, Avery did not know much about Mississippi's northeast hills, and he kept asking Don how to pronounce the name of the town. Don explained that it was pronounced "Rye-enzy," and Avery practiced it over and over as they drove north toward Rienzi. When Avery got up to speak, the first words out of his mouth were, "We are glad to be here in 'Renzy' to tell you why you should vote for Bill Waller." I lost Alcorn County in the first primary, and I have often wondered how many votes old Avery might have cost me. But I appointed him chairman of the Mississippi Game and Fish Commission anyway.

Don was also fond of telling about people getting me confused with Alabama's famous governor, George Wallace, who was then at the height of his popularity. When Don would introduce himself and say he was speaking on behalf of Bill Waller who was running for governor, people would often say, "Oh, yeah, I know about that Wallace fellow, and I'm going to vote for him." There is no telling how many votes I may have gotten from people who thought they were voting for George Wallace, or maybe his cousin.

Among my many other volunteers were A.B. Biggs, Gene McKey, and Dr. Marshall Fortenberry of Jackson; David Bennett of Ashland; George A. Schloegel of Gulfport; Robert G. "Bunkey" Huggins of Greenwood; my cousin Howard Davidson, an automobile dealer in Booneville; J.E. Moore of Jumpertown; and James Noble and his wife Patricia of Brookhaven. James was a classmate at the Ole Miss law school. Also instrumental to my

successful campaign were George Dale of Moss Point; Joe
Fancher of Canton; Murry Cain of Winona; Bernice Hale of
Pontotoc, my second grade teacher; Zack Stewart, later northern
district highway commissioner; Audie Randle of New Albany;
Dr. and Mrs. Fayette Williams of Corinth; Hubert Hodges and
John Risher, an electronics entrepreneur from Philadelphia;
Woodrow Stephens of Wiggins; E.U. Parker, a blind insurance
agent from Laurel; Chet Dillard, a former district attorney from
Laurel; Alvin Coleman, a merchant from Ackerman; Dr. Horace
May and his son Bill, now a prominent attorney from Newton;
D.A. Biglane and his son James from Natchez; Columbus attor-
ney Dudley Carter; Jessie Adcock, a real estate developer from
Biloxi; Sam Provenza, a Pepsi-Cola distributor in Greenville; and
Bob Ashley, a newspaper editor in Hazlehurst.

In the summer of 1970, while I was organizing my campaign
staff, a young advertising executive and political consultant from
Memphis was attracting attention in political circles for his work
on Dale Bumpers' campaign for governor in Arkansas. Bumpers,
an almost unknown small town lawyer, was elected governor of
Arkansas in his first statewide race, and Deloss Walker received
much of the credit for his successful campaign.

Charles McKellar, a former associate in the Godwin
Advertising Agency in Jackson who worked with me in the 1967
and 1971 campaigns, suggested that I contact Walker to see if he
would be interested in working on my campaign. I was initially
reluctant about hiring an out-of-state company to conduct my
campaign. My initial misgivings were validated when a
Hederman newspaper published an editorial cartoon depicting an
oversized milk cow grazing in Mississippi, with her hind legs in
Memphis, where she was giving her milk in Tennessee.

Despite my hesitancy I contacted Walker. We had a long and
friendly interview, and I realized that he was interviewing me
while I was interviewing him. At that stage in his career, Walker
only worked for contenders and did not contract with incum-
bents. I met with him several times, and we liked each other

immediately. I think he was drawn to my campaign because I was fighting the establishment and because I would give middle class and working people an opportunity to participate in their government. The Mississippi Jaycees were among my strongest supporters in 1971 and most of them knew Walker personally. He had been the national Jaycees president, and the Mississippi Jaycees urged me to bring him into the campaign.

After several meetings I asked Walker to join my campaign, and he agreed to do so. He worked well with Hermit Jones of Canton, my campaign manager. Walker was a political genius and was one of the reasons I was elected. He had a quick response policy and would not let any attack by my opponents go unanswered. I actually welcomed attacks from other candidates because that meant I was moving up in the race.

After Walker agreed to work on my campaign he made several additions to the staff, including James Rankin, a former president of the Mississippi Jaycees, who had worked with me in 1967, and J. C. "Sonny" McDonald of Kosciusko, another former president of the Mississippi Jaycees. McDonald was my statewide coordinator and he added Jackson attorney Gene Wilkinson and Ralph Sowell, a Jackson printer, to the campaign staff.

Mrs. Marvin H. Jeter, Jr., was the statewide ladies' chairman and Louise Scott Hardy, an honor graduate of Murrah High School in Jackson and a student at Agnes Scott College, was the state coordinator for youth activities. Louise's father was Dr. James Hardy, the renowned medical professor at The University of Mississippi Medical Center who performed one of the first human heart transplants. Professor Hardy encouraged Louise to take the position on my campaign staff and attended several of our rallies in Jackson. Another physician who strongly supported me was Dr. Marvin Jeter, Jr., the husband of our ladies' chairman. Dr. Jeter was a native of West Point and a highly regarded internist.

In most political campaigns money is scarce and is usually thirty to sixty days behind the need. When you need money, you sometimes do not have the credibility to raise it, particularly if you are an outsider or a newcomer to politics. It is difficult to raise money if you are not considered a viable candidate, but you need money to become a viable candidate. Walker's solution to the problem was to begin raising money early in the campaign and hold it in reserve. Then as the campaign got underway we would have the funds to get our message out.

Deloss Walker had extensive radio and television experience and understood the importance of the media in reaching those voters who did not ordinarily attend political rallies. We used a radio talk show to increase my name recognition. The radio programs also identified me as a major candidate, and convinced people that I had something important to say about the real issues facing the state. Walker had his own studio and video production system, and a camera team followed me around the state. We would use the footage from my campaign speeches to create spontaneity and originality in my television ads.

The extensive use of television was another of Walker's innovations. In the early 1970s people were not turning out for political rallies. We would go to a rally in a small town and find less than a hundred people there, and most of them would be family and friends of local candidates. There were few undecided voters at political rallies in the summer of 1971, so we had to find another way to reach them, and television was the most effective way.

We also created an eight page tabloid newspaper that focused on my family. We used family photographs, including a picture of my father plowing a field on his tractor, and several pictures of my children.

In my 1971 campaign appearances I raised the issues of consumer protection laws, elimination of the state sales tax on prescription drugs for elderly citizens, double homestead exemptions for the elderly, and protection of Mississippi's environment.

I also cited the need to update the statutes that governed Mississippi's municipalities and the need for more autonomy for towns and cites, which were virtually the wards of the state legislature. I favored giving a larger share of gasoline taxes to municipalities since a greater proportion of automobile travel was on city streets rather than on state highways.

In Biloxi, on August 17, I pledged to strengthen Mississippi's pollution control laws and to establish a long range program for protecting the environment. In that televised discussion I said, "To bring industry to Mississippi at the cost of destroying our clean environment would be a poor bargain. A generous God has blessed Mississippi with clean air, pure water, fertile soil, and abundant natural resources. I promise that as your governor I will always work to see that clean air, pure water, and other resources will be here for our children and the generations of Mississippians yet unborn." My commitment to protect the environment was formed during those carefree summer days when we played on the sandy beach of Maybelle's Lake and went fishing in Clear Creek.

During the last two weeks of the first primary I sensed a major shift in the electorate. As late as July 22 over fifty percent of the voters were still undecided, and I felt they were breaking toward me. Carroll, Don and Millie all said they could sense that, and my campaign staff had the same feeling. Deloss Walker knew that the electorate was fluid, and in the last week of the first primary we directed our television ads and our radio spots toward those who were trying to make up their minds.

My campaign against power politics and the "Capitol Street Gang" struck a cord with Mississippi voters, and by the end of the first primary the other candidates joined the chorus. Ed Pittman claimed that Mississippi was a "closed society" and placed the blame squarely on the politics of the old guard. Jimmy Swan criticized the "fat cats" and "special interest groups in Jackson." Judge Perry called for "an election not an auction." Even Charles Sullivan accused me of being in cahoots with the old machine and claimed that he was a man of the people.

According to one observer my campaign "caught fire" in the last week or so before the first primary election. I felt good about my chances because other candidates were criticizing me. One candidate even called Charles Sullivan and me "the gold dust twins of liberalism." Deloss Walker assured me that to be linked with the acknowledged frontrunner, especially in a negative way, was a good sign.

Toward the end of the first primary I began getting calls from some of Senator Eastland's key supporters who told me that they were beginning to support my campaign because the tide was turning in my favor. In the last month of the first primary I talked several times with D.A. Biglane of Natchez, one of Eastland's advisers and one of my strong supporters in 1967. He assured me that there was a groundswell of support for my candidacy.

The results of the first primary were just about what I expected. Charles Sullivan led the ticket with 288,219 votes, and I got 227,424. Swan was a distant third with 128,946. Immediately after the first primary, Sullivan's campaign boasted that his 60,000 vote lead would be virtually impossible for me to overcome, and that no candidate in history had lost the second primary after leading by such a large margin.

As the Sullivan camp increased the use and visibility of his popular slogan, "It's Charlie's Time," I countered with my slogan, "It's Time for a Change."

During the second primary there was an interesting twist on my campaign against the political machine. In several campaign speeches Charles Sullivan challenged me to provide the names of the machine politicians and accused me of going to the leaders of the old guard and asking for their support. Sullivan based that charge on the fact that Senator Eastland was supporting me in the second primary. In the first primary, Eastland supporters had been divided between Roy Adams, Ed Pittman, Jimmy Swan, and me.

Although the senator never publicly endorsed me, many of his long time supporters were working on my behalf, and some of his major donors were contributing to my campaign. But some of the senator's inner circle, including his son-in-law Champ Terney, an attorney in Indianola, were supporting Charles Sullivan.

I met with Senator Eastland several times during the second primary. He was an unusual man, quiet and unassuming. During those meetings I would bring him up to date on the campaign. He had a phenomenal memory and would ask about individuals by name in small towns across Mississippi. He would give me the names of people I should see throughout the state. He had friends and supporters in almost every community, and he knew how many votes he could deliver in every county. In these private meetings the senator never asked me for anything, and I never offered him anything for his support.

Senator Eastland supported me because he thought I had a good chance of beating Charles Sullivan. The long-standing animosity between Senator Eastland and Charles Sullivan originated in the 1960 presidential election when Sullivan backed Mississippi's unpledged presidential electors. Sullivan publicly criticized Eastland, and they had an ugly exchange at a Delta fish fry over the senator's support for John F. Kennedy and the national Democratic Party. Sullivan accused the state's senior senator of being disloyal to Mississippi and to the people who elected him.

The ill will between Sullivan and Eastland intensified during the 1963 gubernatorial election when Sullivan, after being eliminated in the first primary, publicly endorsed J.P. Coleman over Paul B. Johnson, Jr., who was fondly known as "Little Paul" by his friends and supporters. Senator Eastland had a long-standing political and personal friendship with "Little Paul," whose father, Governor Paul B. Johnson, Sr., had appointed Eastland to the Senate in 1941 after Senator Pat Harrison died.

In response to questions about Senator Eastland's support I said, "It is true that I have fallen heir to support which in earlier elections went to others. But my appeal from March to date has been for all the votes of all the people of the state."

During the second primary the *Grenada Sentinel*, which had supported Judge Marshall Perry in the first primary, endorsed Charles Sullivan. That gave Sullivan fifteen of the twenty daily newspapers. He also had the endorsement of several weeklies.

In contrast, only two dailies, the *Daily Corinthian* and the *Natchez Democrat*, endorsed my candidacy. The weekly *Copiah*

County Courier, which was edited by my good friend Bob Ashley, and the *Neshoba Democrat*, a weekly newspaper published in Philadelphia, also endorsed me.

I was especially pleased that the *Neshoba Democrat* endorsed me because its fine young editor, Stanley Dearman, was my kins-man. Since his days as editor of The University of Mississippi stu-dent newspaper, *The Daily Mississippian*, Stanley had been fight-ing the state's machine politicians and "status quo politics." He and his newspaper deserve a great deal of credit for supporting racial harmony in Philadelphia and for finally bringing some clo-sure to the 1964 murder of the three young civil rights workers.

In the closing days of the second primary there was an army of volunteers working day and night for me, and I was working hard to keep up with them. After observing my work ethic in the early stages of the campaign, Deloss Walker introduced the campaign slogan, "Waller Works." In the last few days of the campaign I knew that we would win, and I think everyone else, the paid staff and the volunteers, were confident that we would win. But that did not mean we let up. We worked until the polls closed on election night.

My staff reserved a large ballroom in the Heidelberg Hotel, and we invited everyone who wanted to share that special night with us. As the results started coming in, it was clear that I had not only overcome a sixty thousand vote deficit, but that my margin of victory would be more than sixty thousand.

There is no scene so jubilant and happy as a ballroom full of workers and supporters who gradually realize that they have just won a long, hard political campaign. And I might add, because I have been in both kinds, there is almost nothing as sad and somber as a loser's ballroom.

The staff and I rested for only a few days before getting back to work because there was still two more months to go before the general election on November 2. Even though Charles Evers was a charismatic leader and had a special appeal, no one really believed that he had a chance of winning the election.

Nevertheless, I was determined to control the election by continuing to discuss the real issues and not allow myself or the campaign to be distracted or caught up in the white versus black character of the election. During the general election two totally unexpected issues surfaced and attracted a great deal of attention from the voters and the press.

The first issue was the condition and future of Mississippi's antebellum Governor's Mansion, which occupied a prominent place on Capitol Street in downtown Jackson. After Governor John Bell Williams added an expensive driveway and built a security fence around the Governor's Mansion, an inspection of the building revealed significant structural damage. The cost of repairing the one hundred-and-thirty-year-old building was estimated at $1.2 million.

Soon after that report was issued Governor and Mrs. Williams decided for safety reasons to vacate the Governor's Mansion. Many people criticized Governor Williams for adding an expensive driveway and a $175,000 security fence around a building that was not safe to occupy. Governor Williams also raised the question of building a new executive residence in a residential section of Jackson and converting the downtown mansion into a historical museum.

In a speech at Prentiss on October 12 Carroll briefly outlined the history of the Governor's Mansion and asked women across the state to help her save the "historic home of our heritage." I supported Carroll's effort to save the building, and I pledged to move my family into the Governor's Mansion if I were elected.

The other issue that surfaced during the general election was the validity of a thirty-six year old statute and its potential effect on my candidacy. The Corrupt Practices Act of 1935 limited a gubernatorial candidate's campaign expenditures to twenty-five thousand dollars for each primary, or a total of fifty thousand dollars for both. The law required all candidates to file an itemized statement of expenditures with the secretary of state within thirty days after the primary elections. If a candidate won the second primary but exceeded the allowed expenditures, he would be disqualified.

On April 9, 1970, well before the 1971 gubernatorial election, the Mississippi Legislature repealed this antiquated law. But the statute was not approved by the U.S. Department of Justice as required by the 1965 Voting Rights Act until September 16, 1971, more than a month after I had won the second Democratic primary. Charles Evers announced that he would file a lawsuit challenging my nomination under the 1935 statute, which he contended was still in force because its repeal had not been approved at the time of the Democratic primaries.

A possible legal challenge to my nomination created near panic among some of my supporters and speculation about what would happen if a protracted court battle resulted in my disqualification. Would Governor Williams remain in office until it was all sorted out? Would William Winter, the incoming lieutenant governor, become the governor if I was disqualified? Or would Evers be declared the winner by default?

Some Democratic nominees for state and local offices were so concerned about disqualification under the 1935 statute that their wives filed as independent candidates for the same offices. On election day, voters were greeted with the spectacle of some Democratic candidates being challenged by their wives.

I was not as worried about my disqualification under the 1935 law as I was about the mounting support for Carroll as an independent candidate. Because Carroll was so popular with the voters across the state, I was not really sure whether they wanted Carroll as an alternative candidate, or just a stand-in for me.

On the day before the September 23 filing deadline for independent candidates, Mississippi Supreme Court Justice Tom Brady filed as an independent candidate for governor. After the U.S. Justice Department ruled that the 1935 Corrupt Practices Act was not valid and that Democratic candidates were no longer in legal jeopardy, Justice Brady urged voters around the state not to vote for him but to vote for Bill Waller.

Justice Brady had earlier explained to me that he qualified in part because he was concerned about my safety, and he feared there might be an attempt to assassinate me. I was not concerned about that possibility. The Highway Patrol provided security for me and my family after I won the Democratic nomination

My last major campaign speech during the general election was on October 30 at an alumni meeting of Sigma Phi Epsilon fraternity. I talked about the "brain drain" and asked them to help me change Mississippi so its young men and women would stay in the state. To encourage greater participation in public affairs by young people, I also recommended that we allow college students to vote by absentee ballot.

The final results of the general election did not surprise me, although my margin of victory was greater than expected, and I got more black votes than had been predicted.

On the night of the election, when the outcome had been decided, Charles Evers caught up with Carroll and me at a television station where I had made a brief statement about the election and my plans for the future. He shook hands with Carroll and me, congratulated us, and wished me well. We congratulated him on his campaign and wished him well.

The 1971 general election was historically significant by almost everyone's account, and there are many assessments of that election. The local, state, national, and even international media felt obliged to scrutinize and analyze the election. In his book, *Amazing Grace: With Charles Evers in Mississippi*, Jason Berry chronicles the 1971 general election from inside the Evers campaign.

Hodding Carter, III, of the *Delta Democrat-Times* provided one of best assessments of the campaign just before the general election. "While it is true," he wrote, "that Waller has become closely allied with powerful forces of the Old Guard during the general election, he is not one of them, and it is they who have rushed to him rather than he to them. His rhetoric . . . has been in refreshing contrast to the campaign oratory of every serious candidate for governor of this century."

Although Carter was a member of the Loyalist faction, he did not endorse Charles Evers. In an editorial published the day before the election he wrote, "Two native sons who happen to like each other personally have clashed in an historic campaign in which race has been ever present but racism has been muted if not entirely laid to rest. They have kept the campaign cleaner and on a higher plane than any we can recall. They have asked for the votes of all their fellow Mississippians and they have meant it. The state can be well served by either, although one is white and the other is black."

In my losing campaign of 1967, Mr. Carter endorsed my candidacy. At that time I admitted that we disagreed on some issues, but I thanked him for his endorsement. In 1971 we may still have disagreed about some things, but I wholeheartedly agreed with the last sentence in his editorial.

"It's a good time to be a Mississippian."

CHAPTER 11

The Transition

*"I am determined to move Mississippi out of the
horse and buggy era into the modern age."*

1971 CAMPAIGN SPEECH

Several days after my election I received a telephone call from
Governor Jimmy Carter of Georgia inviting me to the
Southern Governors Conference, which he was hosting in
Atlanta. I immediately accepted his invitation and looked for-
ward to getting away for a few days and meeting my fellow south-
ern governors. My election was part of a broader political devel-
opment in the early 1970s when several governors who were not
identified with the old political machines were elected in the
Deep South. Among that "new breed" of southern governors
were Dale Bumpers of Arkansas, Winfield Dunn of Tennessee,
John West of South Carolina, Ruben Askew of Florida, and
Jimmy Carter of Georgia.

After the governors conference I made a quick trip to

Washington to meet with Mississippi's congressional delegation and President Richard Nixon. The President assured me that he would support my progressive program for economic development in Mississippi.

The 1971 legislature had provided funds and office space in the Executive Building across the street from the Capitol for an orderly transition from Governor Williams' administration to mine. The day after my election, I started putting my team together and began selling the new image of Mississippi as a beautiful place with friendly people, fresh air, clean water, and good hunting and fishing.

During the transition I met with the budget commission and members of the legislature at four regional meetings sponsored by the Mississippi Economic Council. At those meetings, which included the chairmen of the legislative finance and appropriations committees, I realized that the governor's authority over the state budget was even more limited than I had previously thought. And I learned that unless I assumed a deferential attitude, as many of my predecessors had, my relationship with the legislature would be adversarial.

Hovering over my transition was the specter of national politics and Mississippi's role in the Democratic Party convention at Miami. At the governor's conference in Atlanta and at a press conference the day I opened my transition office, I got several questions about the division between the Loyalists and the Regulars and about the prospective presidential bid by Governor George Wallace. I said that I would not endorse Governor Wallace, because I preferred a candidate who had a chance to win the election.

I wanted to reestablish Mississippi's rightful place in national politics, and I encouraged all Mississippi Democrats to participate in the party caucuses to select delegates to the Miami convention. I said, "We intend to have no fallouts, walkouts or throwouts. We expect to have a delegation representative of all the people." I fully expected the Loyalists and Regulars to merge peacefully and voluntarily. I appointed a five-member delegation, including two blacks, to represent the Regulars at a meeting with a similar group from the Loyalists.

But the two factions failed to reach a compromise. I thought the Loyalists were asking for too much and were willing to give too little. The Regulars asked Judge Dan M. Russell, Jr., to decide which faction had the legal and constitutional right to the name "Democratic Party of the State of Mississippi," and to enjoin the Loyalists from representing Mississippi at the Democratic Convention. I also met with the Democratic credentials committee in Washington and asked that the Regulars be seated at the Miami convention.

Judge Russell ruled in favor of the Regulars regarding the right to call themselves the "Democratic Party of the State of Mississippi." On appeal, however, the Fifth Circuit Court reversed Judge Russell's decision, and the credentials committee refused to seat the Regulars at the party convention. I was offered a seat at the convention as an honorary delegate but declined the offer.

After Cliff Finch was elected governor in 1975 the two groups finally reached a compromise. Aaron Henry, former leader of the Loyalists, and Tom Riddell of the Regulars, were named co-chairmen of the unified Mississippi Democratic Party. Loyalist Pat Derian and Jan Little, a member of the Regular faction, were named co-vice chairmen.

The forty-five days between my election and the inauguration were hectic, and I anticipated the inauguration with great excitement. On Monday, January 17, 1972, I attended the swearing in of Lieutenant Governor William Winter. During my administration Governor Winter and I shared the common goal of making Mississippi a better place for all of its citizens. Governor Winter has enjoyed a long and distinguished career, and his contributions to Mississippi are unsurpassed by any modern statesman.

The day of my inauguration began with a prayer service in the sanctuary of the First Baptist Church. The Reverend Herman Milner, my kinsman and pastor of the Van Winkle Baptist Church, delivered the invocation. My pastor Dr. Larry Rohrman

and my former pastor Dr. W. Douglas Hudgins spoke briefly. The
youth choir, which included our daughter Joy, sang "I Am
Thankful To Be An American."

In my inaugural address I pledged to modernize state government, strengthen the free enterprise system, and improve the
quality of education. I promised that during my four years in
office I would not stand idly by and observe the God-given talents of one Mississippian wasted, because every adult illiterate,
every school dropout, and every untrained child is an indictment
of us all. [See Appendix A]

The four living governors, J.P. Coleman, Ross Barnett, Paul
Johnson, and John Bell Williams joined me at the reviewing
stand in front of the Governor's Mansion for the inaugural
parade. Ray Cannada of Edwards was the general chairman of the
parade, which included more than two hundred units and took
more than two hours to pass the reviewing stand.

The inaugural reception was held in the Old Capitol because
the Governor's Mansion was closed. It was the first inaugural
reception held in the Old Capitol since its restoration under
Governor Coleman in the 1950s.

Later that night I spoke briefly about a new day of promise to
the two thousand young men and women at the youth ball in the
Heidelberg Hotel. I thanked them for their support and invited
them to join me in shaping Mississippi's future.

After a long and busy day Carroll and I opened the inaugural
ball at the Mississippi Coliseum to the "Magnolia Waltz," which
had been composed especially for this event by Mrs. Gladys
Stogner. Mr. and Mrs. Gene Wilkinson and Dr. and Mrs.
Marshall Fortenberry served as general chairmen of the inaugural
ball, and Mr. and Mrs. W.A. Miller, Jr., were the general chairmen of decorations for all of the inaugural day ceremonies.

Even before my inauguration the press began to speculate
about who would stay and who would go in state government.
Because of constitutional limitations on the office, the governor's
most significant influence was in the power of appointment. And

it was not the high and mighty offices but the local jobs, like game wardens, that generated the most intense interest.

Early in my administration I appointed a Charles Sullivan supporter to a job at the weigh station in his home county because he needed the job, and I thought he deserved it. I was assailed by my own supporters in that county. You would have thought I had appointed a socialist to the position. But when I appointed Charles Sullivan to a high position in the Mississippi National Guard there was little or no opposition. I wanted to be fair and to appoint competent, deserving individuals.

When I took office in 1972 there were about a hundred and fifty state agencies, boards and commissions and approximately 37,000 state employees. That was one state employee for every sixty citizens in the state. With that ratio we should have had the most effective state government in the Union. But we did not, and I was determined to reorganize the executive branch.

Shortly after I appointed Dr. Robert Robinson as Director of the Department of Welfare he told me that there were several employees who never came to work, and that some came in late, left early, and often took Fridays off. I also learned that the clerical staff at state colleges and universities closed their offices when classes were not in session.

I considered my election a mandate for me and all other state employees to update, modernize, and professionalize state government. Because that was one of the primary themes of my campaign, I directed all state employees to be at work on time and to work a full eight-hour day, including Fridays. I also directed the state colleges and universities to keep their offices open during spring break, Christmas holidays, and between semesters even though classes were not in session. My directives, understandably, were not popular with state employees, but I had promised to bring sound business practices to state government. I intended to translate the slogan "Waller Works" into official state policy.

My earliest staff appointments included Allen Haliburton, state Senator Ollie Mohammed of Belzoni, and J.C. "Sonny"

McDonald as my first chief of staff. Charles McKellar served as my press spokesmen throughout my term. Wayne Edwards also served as one of my press secretaries. His skill in working with both the state and national press was exceptional. Wayne is one of those rare political advisers who could have enjoyed a success-ful national career as a consultant had he chosen that field. He is now a member of a public relations firm in Nashville.

I asked Herman Glazier to continue as the liaison between the governor's office and the legislature, and I appointed James Chastain, A.I.A, Director of the State Building Commission, Harold "Hap" Owen as Director of the A&I Board, and Dr. Alton B. Cobb as Director of the Department of Health. Dr. Cobb served in that position for almost two decades and is an exemplar of the public servant.

For the military department I appointed E.A. "Beby" Turnage of Monticello as Adjutant General of the Mississippi National Guard, with the rank of major general. A decorated World War II veteran with a distinguished career in the Mississippi Army National Guard, Major General Turnage was chancellor of the Thirteenth Chancery Court District at the time of his appoint-ment. Following his term as adjutant general, Turnage was appointed Dean of the Mississippi College School of Law. The readiness center in Monticello is named in his honor.

I appointed E.H. "Mickey" Walker, Jr., of Starkville assistant adjutant general for the Mississippi Army National Guard. Lieutenant General Walker, also a decorated World War II veter-an, was serving as Executive Director of the Mississippi National Guard Association at the time of his appointment. Following Lieutenant General Walker's service in my administration, he was appointed Deputy Director of the Army National Guard for the National Guard Bureau in Washington. In 1982 President Reagan appointed him Chief of the National Guard Bureau and promoted him to the rank of lieutenant general. The Armed Forces Museum at Camp Shelby was recently named in honor of Lieutenant General Walker. I appointed Charles Sullivan, my run-off opponent in the 1971 Democratic primary, as Assistant Adjutant General for the Mississippi Air National Guard. The Air National Guard base at Thompson Field in Jackson is named in honor of Brigadier General Sullivan.

In 1975 I had the privilege of administering the oath for Bill, Jr., to become a second lieutenant in the Mississippi Army National Guard. He was a Distinguished Military Graduate of the ROTC program at Mississippi State University. His first assignment was platoon leader in the National Guard Unit in my hometown of Oxford, then known as Detachment 1, Troop B, 1st Squadron, 108 Armored Cavalry. He completed his military career in January 2004 having attained the rank of brigadier general.

Two members of my staff that I was especially close to were Ron Little and Harold Cross, the pilots who flew the state-owned airplanes. It is just my nature to be in a hurry and to give orders, but on one occasion I instructed Harold Cross about something while in flight, and he reminded me that when we were on the ground I was governor, but when we were in the air he was in charge. Harold had been an Air Force pilot during the Vietnam War and joined the Mississippi Air National Guard about the time he came to work for me. Governor Haley Barbour appointed Harold Adjutant General of the Mississippi Air National Guard in January 2004.

I used the state planes so much that the Jackson press began keeping track of the cost of every flight and duly reported the figures after each trip. I made no apologies for using the state-owned airplanes because I had promised the voters that I would move Mississippi forward with all resources available, including time-saving aircraft.

When J.C. McDonald resigned as my chief of staff to accept an appointment to the Probation and Parole Board, I appointed George Dale in his place. Dale continued in that position for the remainder of my term and was a valued member of my administration. In 1975 Dale was elected Insurance Commissioner, and reelected for seven consecutive terms. Commissioner Dale is now the dean of state insurance commissioners and is presently working overtime to meet the insurance needs of the victims of Hurricane Katrina.

In 1967 George Dale was assistant principal of Moss Point High School when I asked him to be my campaign manager for Jackson County. Although we lost that first election, Dale was one of the main reasons that I carried Jackson County in 1971. It was the only county I carried on the Mississippi Gulf Coast.

Early in my administration Dale's primary duty was to interview the horde of office seekers and try to match them with appropriate positions in state government. My brother Don was so swamped by office seekers that he could hardly get his crops planted. Political patronage is a fact of life in politics, but George and I were committed to the appointment of the best people available.

On the day Governor Hugh White left office in 1956 he told his successor J.P. Coleman, "Beware of Parchman." Unfortunately, John Bell Williams did not pass that wisdom on to me, and two of my most controversial appointments involved Mississippi's ancient, antiquated penal system. My first appointment as superintendent of Parchman was a distant relative of Carroll's, but if you only read the Jackson newspapers you would have thought he was my brother-in-law. He resigned after being accused of purchasing penitentiary supplies from another relative.

Following that fiasco I was determined to find a professional with no ties whatsoever to the state of Mississippi. After an extensive search I hired Jack Reed, a penologist from California. It took the Senate two months of wrangling to confirm him. The new superintendent was the first professionally trained administrator of Parchman and held that position throughout the remainder of my term, but he was also occasionally embroiled in controversy.

Because the public welfare system involved so many people either directly or indirectly, I was determined to appoint the best person I could find to head the Department of Welfare.

Representative Clarence Pierce of Carroll County strongly recommended Dr. Robert Robinson, a professor of business and economics at the University of Louisiana at Monroe. Robinson was a native of Choctaw County and had a Ph.D. in economics from Mississippi State University. Although he took a cut in salary, Robinson accepted the appointment.

Dr. Robinson found the office in shambles and the records in disarray. He immediately initiated a new records system to comply with federal regulations. Many of the department's three thousand employees had been hired at the behest of powerful legislators without regard for qualifications. The department's director of public relations rarely came to work and did little to inform the public of the department's function. He was a former legislator and a close friend of the chairman of one of the legislative finance committees.

After Dr. Robinson discussed the situation with me I directed him to dismiss the public relations director and replace him as soon as possible. After the dismissal of that individual several lawmakers and other public officials badgered Dr. Robinson, but he did not reinstate him. When Hap Owen resigned for health reasons, I appointed Dr. Robinson Director of the A&I Board. During the last three decades Dr. Robinson has served several governors in a variety of positions and is currently Executive Director of the Division of Medicaid for the Haley Barbour administration.

I appointed Lee Spainhour Sutton Director of the Department of Human Resources. Mrs. Sutton was a Certified Public Accountant and managed the agency that dispensed the largest portion of the state's federal funds. She personally directed the management of all funds for the Office of Economic Opportunity and for the Head Start Programs throughout the state. Many of the programs were reorganized and equity funding was a primary objective during her tenure as director of Human Resources. Mrs. Sutton was the first woman to head a major state agency.

Because education was such a high priority for me, I wanted an educational expert on my staff. In one of my many discussions with my brother Don about getting good people in my administration, he told me about a young Ole Miss professor who was renting our grandfather's old home place in Burgess. That was the house where as a boy I went in the late afternoons to enjoy a Coca-Cola and spend time with my grandfather Morgan Waller.

Soon after our discussion Don introduced me to Dr. Milton Baxter, a professor in the School of Education at The University of Mississippi. Dr. Baxter was a thirty-three year old native of Petal, and a graduate of Mississippi College. He also had a Ph.D. from the University of Alabama.

Dr. Baxter joined my administration, and in addition to being my educational advisor, he was also the Executive Director of the Education and Training Program. Dr. Baxter served throughout my four year term and two years into the term of Governor Cliff Finch.

During the 1971 campaign I promised the voters that I would appoint qualified people to public office, and that race would not be a consideration in my appointments. The first blacks I appointed to office were members of my personal staff. James Rundles helped me identify and recruit blacks for a variety of appointments. Also on my staff were Ed Cole, Charles Evers' 1971 campaign manager and later chairman of the unified Mississippi Democratic Party, and Tom Espy, whom I later appointed to the Minority Business Development office. Geraldine Yates worked with Dr. Baxter in the manpower training program. I also appointed Dr. John Cameron of Jackson to the manpower program.

By midway through my term I had appointed blacks to almost one-fourth of all state agencies and I had appointed the first black man to a statewide law enforcement agency. The Mississippi Highway Patrol was integrated during my administration, and the Department of Public Safety actively recruited black patrolmen.

Among the blacks I appointed to various agencies and commissions were Gwen Loper, the first black woman appointed to a state board. I appointed her to the Board of Mental Health. I named Dr. Albert Lott, a Brookhaven physician and a member of the local school board, to the Select Committee on Higher Education, and Cleve McDowell, the first black student admitted to the Ole Miss law school, to the State Penitentiary Board. I appointed Marvin Morgan, a *cum laude* graduate of Alcorn State, to the Board of Public Welfare; Dr. A.L. Johnson, president of Prentiss Institute, to the Probation and Parole Board; and Dr. Robert Harrison to the Board of Trustees of Institutions of Higher Learning. Nathan Hodges, the owner of the Hodges Funeral Home in Oxford, was appointed as the first black to serve on the State Board of Embalming.

Other blacks I appointed to various public offices included Dr. Walter Washington, president of Alcorn State University; Dr. John Peoples, president of Jackson State University; Dr. Estes Smith, a professor at Jackson State; Cornelius Turner, a Jackson businessman; Helman Johnson, of Marion County; and Gloria Ross, of Jackson.

Almost as important as my appointment of blacks to significant positions in state government was the decision of the First Baptist Church of Jackson, on the tenth anniversary of the death of Medgar Evers, to open its doors to blacks and to accept them into the fellowship of the state's largest Southern Baptist congregation. Also, on the tenth anniversary of Evers' death I proclaimed a statewide day of remembrance in his honor.

During my administration there were several judicial vacancies that I filled by appointment. When Associate Justice Tom Brady died in 1973, I appointed Judge Vernon Broom of the fifteenth circuit court to fill that vacancy. I named Robert J. "Rip" Prichard, III, a Picayune attorney, to Judge Broom's position. Judge Prichard is currently the longest-serving circuit judge in the state. In addition to his judicial duties, he presently co-chairs the Uniform Criminal Rules Study Committee.

Three circuit court appointments went to Ruble Griffin of Bay St. Louis, who replaced Judge Harry Walker in the second district; Francis S. Bowling of Jackson replaced Judge M. M. McGowan who resigned his judgeship in the seventh district; and Clarence Morgan of Kosciusko in the fifth circuit court district, upon the death of Judge Marshall Perry. I also filled three vacancies in the chancery court system. Those appointments went to Melvin Bishop and Betty B. Tucker of Jackson, and J.W. Walker of Mendenhall. Judge Tucker was the second woman to serve as a chancery judge. Lenore Prather was the first woman chancellor. Judge Prather later served as chief justice of the Mississippi Supreme Court.

I appointed Glen Davidson to fill the vacancy of district attorney in the First Judicial District. He later served as U.S. attorney for the Northern District of Mississippi, and in October 1985 President Reagan appointed him United States District Judge for the Northern District of Mississippi. Judge Davidson is now the Chief Judge for the Northern District of Mississippi.

In the early 1970s no state agency, board, bureau, or commission was beyond the reach of politics, not even law enforcement. When I appointed W.O. "Chet" Dillard commissioner of the Public Safety Commission, which included the Highway Safety Patrol, the Law Enforcement Training Academy, and the state crime laboratory, he was shocked by the condition of the facilities. The ceiling in the Highway Patrol building on Woodrow Wilson Drive was literally falling down, and the only laboratory equipment available to Dr. Arthur Hume, the director of the crime lab, were a couple of old microscopes. In spite of the increasing number of drug-related crimes, Dr. Hume did not have the modern equipment necessary for specimen analysis. Dr. Hume, a renowned forensic toxicologist, worked for many years to improve the efficiency and credibility of the state crime laboratory.

We were able to build a new headquarters for the Highway Patrol and to modernize the crime laboratory. Under the direction of Tom Shelton, former sheriff of Hinds County and director of the Training Academy, we also upgraded the academy to FBI standards. Commissioner Dillard, Tom Shelton, and Dr. Arthur

Hume deserve high praise for their dedication and improvement of law enforcement in Mississippi.

On the night of Dillard's appointment, and before he actually assumed the office and moved into the building, Highway Patrolman Reese Shook arrested and jailed a prominent member of the legislature for DUI. When the news got out, the local press converged on the jail and demanded to know what had happened. Unknown to me and to Commissioner Dillard, Interim Commissioner Wood Stringer called Patrolman Shook into his office and directed him to tear up the ticket.

Commissioner Stringer was a personal friend of C.B. "Buddie" Newman, the chairman of the House Ways and Means Committee. They lived in the same apartment building, and Newman was related to the state representative who was arrested.

The wire services picked up the details of the arrest and the destruction of the ticket, and the news soon spread around the country. To make matters worse Commissioner Stringer ordered the transfer of Patrolman Shook from Jackson to the Batesville patrol office. The transfer gave rise to a joke that quickly made the rounds in Jackson, "What's the quickest way to get from Jackson to Batesville? Arrest a member of the legislature."

After Patrolman Shook refused to be transferred, the story intensified and Commissioner Dillard and I were bombarded with calls and letters demanding an explanation of the entire matter. In his 1992 memoirs entitled *Clear Burning*, Commissioner Dillard wrote that the swirling controversy over Patrolman Shook's arrest and the incarceration of a member of the Mississippi legislature was his "baptism in the fire of high powered politics."

Charles McKellar, my press secretary, tried valiantly but without much success to explain that Mississippi's antiquated constitution protected members of the legislature from arrest under certain conditions, and that the interim commissioner had ruled that the state representative Patrolman Shook incarcerated was immune from arrest. Few people accepted that explanation, and the story lingered for some time and then eventually faded away.

I was surprised by the intensity of the first major controversy of my administration, but not deterred. I had waited too long and worked too hard to get where I was to be intimidated by a public clamor over whether a member of the legislature could be arrested for driving under the influence of intoxicants.

CHAPTER 12

Straight Ahead

"It's a good time to be a Mississippian."

—HODDING CARTER, III

Since the Civil War, the history of Mississippi had been like a winding country road leading to nowhere in particular. A poll tax and literacy requirement had disfranchised half of the state's population and made the other half apathetic toward politics and government. For nearly a century, the people of Mississippi were encouraged by their leaders to think slow and small, to resist change and to hold onto the past regardless of their economic or social standing. The political and economic leadership resisted any movement to expand the economy and modernize state government. They generally opposed new business and capital entering the local economy that they did not control. I was determined to change that mind set and to rejuvenate both the private sector and state government.

When I took office in January 1972, the antiquated structure of state government was the product of an outdated constitution and a handful of legislators who had controlled both houses for more than fifty years. The system had splintered the executive branch of state government into sixteen elected offices. When the legislature enacted a highway construction program the three elected highway commissioners, rather than the governor, implemented the program. When the legislature passed educational legislation the elected state superintendent of education, rather than the governor, implemented the legislation. The distribution of executive authority among sixteen elected and autonomous officials diminished the power of the governor, and made Mississippi's chief executive the weakest in the nation. Because the governor could not succeed himself, he was virtually a lame duck from the beginning of his administration.

The sixteen elected officers in the executive branch included the governor, lieutenant governor, attorney general, secretary of state, commissioner of insurance, state auditor of public accounts, superintendent of education, state treasurer, commissioner of agriculture, land commissioner, three public service commissioners, and three state highway commissioners.

Thanks to John Ed Ainsworth, who served as land commissioner, that office was abolished and its functions were transferred to the secretary of state in 1980. William Winter, who was the elected state tax collector, also persuaded the legislature to abolish that position in 1964. I recommended an appointed highway commission, an appointed state superintendent of education, and a lay board of education. But no significant changes were made in any of the executive offices or in the governor's authority over the executive branch during my administration.

The executive branch also included approximately one hundred and fifty boards and commissions. Members of the legislature served on the most important boards and commissions, and for all practical purposes the lieutenant governor, as the presiding officer in the Senate, was a member of the legislative branch. In the 1930s Mississippi paid the Brookings Institution thousands of dollars to study the structure of state government. On the basis of its comprehensive study, the Brookings Institution recommended major revisions at the state and local level. None of the major recommendations were adopted, however, and Mississippi maintained the old cumbersome system that had been devised in the nineteenth century.

I may have asked the people to think too fast and too big, and I may have asked too much of the legislature during the first session of my administration. I thought our legislature was too large for the population of the state, and I recommended that the number of legislators be reduced from 52 to 30 in the Senate and from 122 to 82 in the House. Obviously, this recommendation did not endear me to the members of the legislature.

My effort to reorganize state government was not aimed just at the legislature. I also recommended that the number of state boards and commissions be reduced to approximately fifty, and I called for an open meetings law that would enable citizens to find out what was happening in their government.

In my first address to a joint session of the legislature on January 25, 1972, I presented a comprehensive agenda that included the following recommendations:
- a $600 million highway program
- construction of a network of four-lane highways throughout the state
- governmental reorganization
- creation of a Small Business Administration
- restructuring the A&I Board and the R&D Center
- reorganization of the state park system
- creation of a state tourism agency
- establishment of a Department of Administration
- expansion of the Department of Revenue to consolidate other agencies
- an absentee voter law
- transfer of Bureau of Drug Enforcement to the Department of Public Safety

- make National Guard eligible for Veterans Farm and Home Board loans
- increase the amount of veterans' loans from $16,000 to $20,000
- abolition of the State Sovereignty Commission
- creation of a state agency for public relations
- establishment of more degree granting branches of colleges and universities
- equalization of property assessments.

In conclusion I issued a standing invitation to members of the legislature "to visit me on any subject at anytime of the day or night" and predicted that the 1972 session would be "the most productive session of the legislature in the history of our state." [See Appendix B]

Soon after my address to the joint assembly, and before I was even comfortably situated in my Capitol office, a legislative delegation did indeed pay me a visit. The delegation, as best I recall, included the speaker of the house, the chairman of the House Appropriations Committee, the chairman of the House Ways and Means Committee, the chairman of the Senate Finance Committee, and the chairman of the Senate Appropriations Committee. The visit was a display of solidarity among the leaders of both houses and an early warning of things to come.

Sitting across the table from me was the old guard that I had campaigned against. They had supported Lieutenant Governor Charles Sullivan and had fully expected him to win. To the legislative leadership I was an interloper in the governor's office. The speaker of the house and the legislative leadership informed me that we would get along just fine if I followed the governor's traditional role, which was to make speeches, attend ceremonies, and cut ribbons. I explained to them that I would not be a ceremonial governor, and abruptly ended the meeting. Maybe I should have been more diplomatic about it, but I was elected because I promised to bring change and progress to Mississippi.

From the beginning of my administration my relationship with the legislature was antagonistic because I asserted the authority of the governor, and I might have been too combative. After a speech by a member of the House of Representatives that I thought seriously misrepresented my position on a particular matter, I walked onto the floor of the House and accosted him.

By the 1970s the Capitol building was not large enough to accommodate the governor's administrative offices and the increasing number of legislative committee staff members. To create additional space for legislative functions and to the relieve the overcrowding, the legislature moved the governor's support staff to the Walter Sillers Building across the street from the Capitol. As a courtesy to the governor, and to provide a more convenient location during legislative sessions, I was given a "ceremonial office" located between the House and Senate chambers. Throughout the remainder of my term some legislators, both privately and publicly, referred to me not as "the Governor" but as "the Occupant" of the office in the middle of the Capitol.

At the first opportunity I demonstrated my intention to exercise to the fullest extent possible what little power the governor had. During the first session of my administration the legislature passed a law removing the Department of Audit from the elected office of State Auditor Hamp King to an individual who would be appointed by the legislature. This bill clearly violated the separation of powers doctrine, and I vetoed it. That was the first of thirty-two bills that I vetoed, which was more than any of my predecessors. Another bill I vetoed was the 1973 appropriation for the Sovereignty Commission that in effect abolished the agency. The commission served no useful purpose, and I thought those funds should be allocated to a public relations department to promote tourism.

During the second year of my administration Bill Minor wrote in the New Orleans *Times Picayune*, "The legislature had finally come to the realization that it no longer had a governor with a rubber stamp." In the final analysis, however, the legislature wielded the power, and for the first time in more than forty years the legislature overrode a governor's veto.

One of the mistakes I made with the legislature was not to organize my supporters and to form some sort of alliance with the progressive members of both houses. But I had campaigned against political cliques, rings, and gangs and I did not want to replace one clique with another one. My often stormy relationship with the legislature resulted primarily from my reluctance to form alliances, my determination to increase the governor's authority in formulating the state budget, and my relentless support for a succession amendment.

I kept this issue constantly before the public and the legislature, and I even recommended a constitutional amendment that would preclude me from seeking a second term. Although virtually everyone agreed that the governor of Mississippi was the weakest chief executive in the nation, I could not persuade the legislature to allow the people to vote on the issue. Ironically, the Senate repeatedly approved the succession amendment, but the House defeated it each time it was presented. I was convinced that the voters would approve a succession amendment if they were given the opportunity.

When it became increasingly evident that a succession amendment would not pass the House of Representatives, especially one that would allow me to succeed myself, there was some speculation that Carroll would run as a surrogate for me. But Carroll and I did not even consider the possibility of her running for governor in 1975.

Eventually, the legislature did propose a constitutional amendment, and the voters ratified it by a substantial majority in 1986. Governor Ray Mabus, who was elected in 1987, ran for reelection in 1991 but was defeated by Kirk Fordice, the first Republican elected since Reconstruction. Governor Fordice, who had never held public office before running for governor, was also the first governor to serve two consecutive terms. He was reelected in 1995.

Under the 1890 constitution members of the legislature were not term-limited, and legislators from small safe districts could build up years of seniority and eventually become chairmen of the powerful appropriations and finance committees. Over the years this small group of "good old boys" gradually expanded its reach into the executive branch and eventually assumed the power to both formulate and enact the state budget. During my administration the Budget Commission included the governor and lieutenant governor, the president *pro tempore* of the Senate, the speaker of the house, the chairmen of the Senate Finance and Appropriations Committees, the chairmen of the House Appropriations and the Ways and Means Committees, and other members of the House and Senate appointed not by the governor, but by the lieutenant governor and the speaker of the house.

The oldest tradition in American democracy is that those who hold the purse strings hold the power to govern. The legislature's control over the state budget allowed it to aggrandize its power and to curtail the power of the governor.

I did everything I could to expand the governor's role in formulating the budget, but it took a lawsuit, a state Supreme Court decision in 1983, and the Administrative Reorganization Act of 1984 to finally give the governor any real authority over the state budget.

Even though I did not have the level of cooperation from the legislative leadership that I would have preferred, I had a good working relationship with many of the rank and file members of both houses. And with their help I was able to get much of my legislative agenda enacted into law. [See Appendix D]

I would be remiss if I did not mention a number of legislative statesmen in both houses who were not part of the old guard and were willing to support my legislative program as outlined in my first address to the joint assembly. I remember fondly all those conferences we held, and the fact that they were always willing to help me move some legislation forward, even though some of it was controversial.

The positive thinking leadership in the Mississippi Senate

included William B. Alexander of Cleveland, Daniel Boyce of Rankin County, Herman DeCell of Yazoo County, Dale Ford of Taylorsville, Bob Hardy of West Point, William Hickman, Jr., of Brookhaven, Ebb Horton of Louisville, J.C. "Con" Maloney, Jr., of Jackson, James Molpus of Clarksdale, Charles Pickering of Laurel, William Powell of Liberty, Fred Rogers of Meridian, Charles "Son" Rhodes of Pascagoula, Martin T. Smith of Poplarville, Theodore Smith of Corinth, Donald Strider of Charleston, Emerson Stringer, Jr., of Columbia, Jack Tucker of Tunica, and Sam Wright of Clinton.

The members in the Mississippi House of Representatives included Gerald Blessy of Biloxi, Ben Camack, Jr., of Hazlehurst, Charles Capps of Cleveland, Milton Case of Canton, Robert Clark of Ebenezer, Mike Cooke of Tupelo, Raymond Comans of Decatur, Devan Dallas of Pontotoc, Billy Gibson of Bruce, Hervey Hicks of Yazoo City, Robert "Bunky" Huggins of Greenwood, Leo Hughes of Madison, Carroll Kennedy of Brandon, Max Kilpatrick of Philadelphia, Richard Livingston of Pulaski, Hainon Miller of Greenville, Joe Moss of Raymond, Jerry O'Keefe, Jr., of Biloxi, George Rogers, Jr., of Vicksburg, and Martha White of Baldwin.

These legislators did not agree with me on every issue, but as a rule we worked together to pass the bills that we thought were in the best interest of Mississippi. It took courage for them to support legislation that the leadership opposed, and these men and women deserve much of the credit for many of the laws we passed in the early 1970s. One of our finest legacies was the elimination of the exorbitant interest rates that loan sharks had been charging working class Mississippians for many years.

However sweeping my agenda might have seemed, I really had only four basic goals and objectives. I wanted to improve the quality of education, to modernize state government, to bring sound business practices to government operation, and to strengthen the free enterprise system to give every person a decent chance for a better life.

In my effort to attract blue chip business and high-wage industry to Mississippi, I spent a lot of time with national and international corporate executives promoting the state. I thought Mississippi was on the brink of significant economic advancement, and we needed to develop the full potential of the Tennessee Tombigbee Waterway and the port of Gulfport. To get Mississippi products into the international marketplace, I conducted several trade missions to Europe, the Middle East, Asia, and South America. Paul Fugate, who played a major role in my economic development program and worked with Dr. Robinson at the A&I Board, accompanied me on several of those missions.

The development of Mississippi's economic potential required a modern highway system. When I started school in 1932, Governor Theodore Bilbo wanted to move Ole Miss to Jackson because the university was inaccessible to large parts of the state except by rail. After the legislature refused to relocate the university, he asked them to build good roads to Oxford. In his request for a comprehensive state system of paved roads Governor Bilbo said, "Not kings, nor Congresses, nor courts, nor constables, nor ships, nor soldiers, but roads rule the world. Good roads are the only royal lines in a democracy . . . the only legislature that never changes, the only court that never sleeps . . . the high priest of prosperity."

However eloquent Bilbo's rationale for a state system of good roads might have been, the old guard was slow to act. When I was elected governor almost forty years later there was still not a four-lane highway leading to the state university from any direction—north, south, east, or west.

During my administration we completed a $300 million dollar highway construction program that had begun in 1969. We also initiated another $600 million dollar program, which was the largest public works appropriation in the history of Mississippi. The bill included funds to four-lane the stretch of Highway 6 from Oxford to Interstate 55 at Batesville. There was at last a four-lane highway leading to The University of Mississippi.

I not only wanted to expand the state highway system, I wanted to make the roads safer. In 1972 Mississippi had the highest rate of traffic fatalities in the United States. I discussed this with Public Safety Commissioner Chet Dillard and we made safety a priority for the Mississippi Highway Patrol. During the next four years traffic fatalities declined from 951 in 1971 to 607 in 1975. Mississippi led the nation in the reduction of highway deaths in 1975, and received a $500,000 grant from the National Safety Board to continue our safety program.

Unlike some of my predecessors who were reluctant to accept federal grants because of the anti-discrimination guidelines that accompanied them, I not only accepted federal funds I actively pursued them. We needed the money and could put it to good use for all our citizens. The distribution of funds, both federal and state, is a delicate matter because there is always some individual or agency that will claim they are not getting their fair share. The reallocation of funds, after they have been initially distributed, is even more delicate and almost always prompts complaints. There were two instances during my administration when the reallocation of federal funds generated an intense controversy.

The first case involved a seven-county consortium in north Mississippi that was receiving federal manpower training grants when I took office. After I established a statewide manpower training program the grants that were going directly to those counties were discontinued. Those seven counties became part of the state program and began receiving funds through my office. One powerful member of the legislature accused me of taking money from the consortium and spreading it over the state. I could not convince him that those counties were still receiving their fair share of the grant money, and he remained unfriendly to me and my agenda for the rest of my term.

The second case in which I reallocated federal funds produced even more controversy. In 1972 Mississippi was receiving $7,000,000 in federal funds from the Office of Economic Opportunity "to provide quality health care services to the

poor." Approximately $5.5 million, or almost 80% of those
funds, were allocated to a hospital in Mound Bayou, a small rural
community in the Delta. When I learned that the hospital
employed only 12 physicians and dentists among its 468 employees, and that $4 million was going to salaries and only $300,000
to medical supplies, I directed Mrs. Lee Spainhour Sutton, the
state director of the OEO, to reduce the annual appropriation to
the Mound Bayou project and distribute the remaining funds
proportionately and equitably to other OEO projects around the
state. It was clear to me that too much money was going to
salaries and fringe benefits and not enough to medical services.
The reallocation of those funds prompted an angry response
from some black leaders, but I was committed to bringing sound
business practices to state government and believed that this
reallocation was justified.

Throughout my adult life, I have compared Mississippi to our
neighboring states that have capitalized on their natural resources
to attract tourists from all over the country, and I have wondered
why we did not make a greater effort to attract tourists. During
my administration improving and promoting our tourist attractions was a high priority. One of the significant achievements of
my administration was the construction of the Gulf Coast
Coliseum, which has brought hundreds of conventions and thousands of tourists to the Mississippi Gulf Coast.

Both my supporters and my opponents joked about my plan to
create a major tourist attraction on the Barnett Reservoir, which
they called "Waller World." It is not a laughing matter that
Mississippi has lost millions of dollars of revenue by not developing our natural resources and promoting tourism.

I wanted to attract industry to Mississippi, but not at the
expense of the environment and our natural resources. I promised
"to protect our clean air, pure water, and natural resources for our
children, and for the generations of Mississippians yet unborn." A
rare opportunity to fulfill that promise occurred when the
Pascagoula Hardwood Company announced its intention to sell

a 32,000 acre tract of pristine hardwood bottomland along the Pascagoula River.

The purchase and preservation of this vast wilderness was an extraordinary achievement by a remarkable group of individuals, and is a rare example of cooperation among conservationists, corporate executives, stockholders, and public officials. The project was conceived during long conversations among Graham Wisner, an heir of the Pascagoula Hardwood Company, David Morine, of the Nature Conservancy, Avery Wood, Director of the Mississippi Game and Fish Commission, and Bill Allen, a member of the board of directors of the Game and Fish Commission and chairman of the Mississippi Wildlife Heritage Committee. I endorsed the project from its conception and supported the necessary legislation to purchase the land.

A small group of men and women who were dedicated to the preservation of this wilderness area skillfully guided several bills through the legislative process. On March 11, 1974, I signed Senate Bill 1857 creating the Mississippi Wildlife Heritage Committee, which would oversee the project to its completion. On April 3, 1975, I signed House Bill 914, authorizing fifteen million dollars in general obligation bonds to purchase the Pascagoula River swamp land from the Pascagoula Hardwood Company. I asked the legislators and other supporters of the project who had worked so diligently to secure the passage of these bills to join me at the signing ceremonies in my office.

The Pascagoula purchase was the largest tract of land dedicated to wildlife management ever acquired by any state using only state funds, and it is the largest bottomland overflow swamp in the lower forty-eight states that has protected status. Donald G. Schueler recounts the fascinating story of the Pascagoula project in his book, *Preserving the Pascagoula*, which the University Press of Mississippi first published in 1980 and reissued in 2002.

During my administration there were two projects to which I committed a great deal of time and energy. One was the preservation of the Pascagoula wilderness area. The other was the establishment of the dental school, the college of veterinary medicine, and the school of architecture. Both projects required extremely delicate negotiations among sometime conflicting and rival interests within the legislature, in the private sector, and among college alumni organizations. The preservation of the Pascagoula bottomland and the establishment of the three professional schools are premier examples of what government can accomplish when rival interests work together for the broader interest of society.

In addition to preserving the Pascagoula River bottomland, I supported and signed legislation that provided tax incentives to encourage the reforestation of thousands of acres of idle land. Dick Molpus, who later served as secretary of state, was the president of the Mississippi Forestry Association and he and his father, Richard Molpus of Philadelphia, helped me persuade the legislature to pass this bill. The law not only helped revive an important Mississippi industry, it also protected large stretches of land that had been damaged by years of erosion following the great lumber boom of the 1920s.

While I was concentrating on how to persuade the legislature to pass my progressive agenda, the Reverend Sun Myung Moon and Elvis Presley came to town. When Sun Myung Moon visited Jackson one of his local followers asked my office to name the Reverend Moon an "Honorary Colonel" in a formal ceremony during a meeting with his supporters. Since Senator James Eastland had already honored Moon in a similar fashion, someone in my office prepared and signed my name to a document naming Moon an honorary member of the governor's staff. George Dale presented the document to the Reverend Moon on my behalf at a meeting in which the Reverend Moon preached a sermon in what he thought was Chinese.

I was not aware of any of this until the next day when the Hederman press revealed to the world that I had named the Reverend Moon an "Honorary Colonel." The *Baptist Record*, the official newspaper of the Mississippi Baptist Convention, castigated me and said that my action insulted "all Christians of good will." I had to fend off questions for weeks about the event, which I had nothing to do with and did not even know about until it hit the front page. The Sun Myung Moon incident was nothing, however, compared to the uproar created when Elvis came to town.

After he became a world celebrity Elvis Presley, who genuinely loved his home state, rarely performed in Mississippi because the state imposed a ten percent entertainment tax. When Elvis agreed to donate part of the proceeds of a special concert in the Mississippi Coliseum to the victims of a recent tornado in McComb, the state waived the tax. As a courtesy to me, in part because I supported the waiver of the entertainment tax, the promoters of the concert sent me forty complimentary tickets.

Tickets to the Elvis event were in great demand, and the concert immediately sold out. Many people stood in line for hours only to be told that there no more tickets available. When the *Clarion-Ledger* revealed on page one that I had been given forty free tickets, presumably to distribute among my wealthy friends, the telephones in my office began ringing and did not quit until minutes before the concert began. The brunt of those calls and complaints was borne by Chief of Staff George Dale. When the tickets first went on sale, Dale's wife, Yvette, stood in line for four hours to purchase their tickets. By the night of the concert, Dale was so exasperated by all of the hullabaloo that he and his wife gave their tickets away and stayed home.

In spite of the controversies that distracted me and my staff, we tried to remain focused on the important issues and the reasons the voters elected me. One of those reasons was my promise to improve the quality of education.

CHAPTER 13

Education—The Highest Priority

"The establishment of the dental school, the college of veterinary medicine, and the school of architecture are among the most important educational achievements in Mississippi during the twentieth century."

—BOBBY CHAIN

In the early 1970s Mississippi was near the bottom in per capita income and other economic indicators primarily because of the low skill level of its adult population. After the *Brown* Decision in 1954 the legislature repealed the compulsory attendance law, and the school drop-out rate increased dramatically. Consequently, Mississippi had a large adult population without the necessary academic or vocational training for jobs in the private sector. Many of them were eventually added to the welfare rolls. Federal grants were available for vocational training under the manpower training program, but Mississippi's political leaders did not pursue those grants.

The acceptance of federal grants could create significant problems for Mississippi politicians and college presidents. Before the

Veterans Administration would authorize a hospital in Jackson, Governor J.P. Coleman had to sign an agreement that the hospital would open its facilities to blacks and would not discriminate in its hiring practices. The old guard bitterly denounced Governor Coleman for agreeing to those regulations, and he recalled several years later that nothing in his long career had surprised him as much as the angry response to the integration of the VA Hospital. He said he signed the compliance agreement because Mississippi desperately needed the medical facility, and it was the right thing to do.

Dr. Richard A. McLemore, who was president of Mississippi College from 1957 to 1968, had a similar experience. To qualify for the federal student loan program, Mississippi College officials agreed to administer the funds without regard to race. Several members of the Mississippi College board of trustees, which included a member of the Hederman family, publicly denounced President McLemore for signing the compliance agreement. The lingering controversy eventually led to McLemore's resignation in 1968. After his tenure at Mississippi College, Dr. McLemore served as Director of the Mississippi Department of Archives and History.

It was reprehensible to me that the state's political leadership would refuse to accept funds that could help educate and train its citizens, and deny them any real chance to make a good living for their families.

Mississippi's public school system ranked near the bottom in almost all categories of measurement. Except for Arkansas, we had the lowest paid teachers in the country. The low salaries made it difficult for the public school system to attract quality teachers, and many of them were not certified in the courses they taught. The student-teacher ratio was too high and the expenditure per pupil was much too low. The top ten or fifteen percent of our students could compete with students anywhere in the country, but it was the other eighty-five percent of the children who were being short-changed by the system.

Because of my knowledge of the problem and my own early

education in Burgess and Black Jack, the improvement of our educational system was the highest priority of my administration. I believed the entire system, from kindergarten to the universities, needed an overhaul. I wanted to bring substantive and significant changes to the system.

The public school system was a large and complex mechanism that had evolved over time, and it had serious problems that would not admit to quick and simple solutions. Sometimes I might have been too much of a "hands on" governor, but I did not have time to work through the bureaucracy in the state Department of Education. I was sometimes criticized for going around the Department of Education, but it seemed to me that they were they ones who had allowed the system to deteriorate and had done little to correct it. They had not convinced the legislature that significant reform was necessary and that the entire system was seriously underfunded.

My plan for educational reform included a four-point strategy. First, I appointed a director of education and training in the governor's office. Second, I asked a group of private citizens and professional educators to study the existing system of education to find out what was working and what was not, and what was needed to make the system better. Third, I held annual Governor's Conferences on Education to get the people thinking and talking about education. Finally, I submitted a set of recommendations to the legislature and pushed as hard as I could for their enactment.

I was not an expert in the field of education and wanted the best advice I could get, so I appointed Dr. Milton Baxter as Director of the Office of Education and Manpower Training. One of Dr. Baxter's first appointments in his office was Harold Bishop, the son of Mayor Edward S. Bishop of Corinth. Mayor Bishop was the state's first black mayor of a predominantly white city. After working with Dr. Baxter for several months, Harold enrolled at the University of Alabama. When he graduated he was named a special assistant to the president of the university.

Soon after his appointment Dr. Baxter met with the superintendent of education to assure him that we wanted to cooperate with the Department of Education. Since I had campaigned for an appointed superintendent and a lay board of education, and was the first governor to have my own Office of Education, the state superintendent was somewhat suspicious of my intentions. I did not intend to intrude upon the superintendent's responsibilities, but I did not want to have to get his permission or approval for my educational agenda.

In addition to helping me shape my educational reform program, Dr. Baxter also directed the Mississippi Manpower Training Program, which was funded by the U.S. Department of Labor and had 350 employees. Because most of the people who received vocational training under this program were high school dropouts, I encouraged Dr. Baxter to include some academic instruction along with technical training.

At the time I was elected governor, the Manpower Training Program had an annual budget of $120,000,000, but the program was available in only fourteen counties. Through Dr. Baxter's tireless efforts he secured additional funds and expanded the program. By the end of my term, manpower training funds were distributed statewide and there were training programs in all eighty-two counties.

President Harold T. White of Northeast Mississippi Community College also worked closely with me on manpower training. He was one of the leaders in the seven-county consortium in northeast Mississippi that received Department of Labor funds for technical and vocational training before Dr. Baxter established the statewide program. An enlightened and innovative educator, President White provided day care services to young mothers enrolled in college classes at the Booneville campus. Northeast Mississippi Community College was also one of the first academic institutions in Mississippi to offer a program in restaurant management. Two of that program's most illustrious alumni are President White's two sons, Hal and Mal, who are the proprietors of a famous eatery in Jackson.

In the 1960s racial violence largely overshadowed the rising scourge of illegal drugs. As prosecuting attorney of a judicial district with an urban population, I was aware of the impending crisis of drug abuse, and to combat that problem I established a Council on Drugs in my Office of Education and Training. The director of the council worked closely with other health agencies and with law enforcement officials. With the support of Senator Theodore Smith of Corinth, the Council on Drugs eventually became the Department of Mental Health.

After many long conversations with Dr. Baxter, I decided to appoint two committees to study public education. Because the dual, segregated public school system was integrated in the spring of 1970, I wanted a comprehensive study of the new unified system before we made any significant recommendations. We were dealing with new circumstances, and we needed new solutions. One of the committees, the Public Education Study Committee, focused on the broader issues of the school system and the education establishment. The other committee, the Quality Education Committee, concentrated on the day-to-day operation of the local schools.

Because the college boom had peaked and enrollment had leveled off by 1970, I appointed a Select Committee on Higher Education to study the duplication of degree programs and the possibility of consolidating or closing some of the eight institutions of higher learning. The numerically-driven funding formula had encouraged institutions to offer popular degree programs to attract more students and to increase their share of the state appropriation for higher education. That strategy led to duplication and a waste of the state's limited resources. I also wanted the Select Committee to consider reducing the twelve-year term for members of the Board of Trustees of Institutions of Higher Learning. While these various studies were underway, I visited as many public schools as I could, most of the junior colleges, and all of the senior colleges and universities.

Among my many visits to colleges around the state I remember two in particular. One of them was a visit to Mississippi Valley State College. Eugene McLemore, the student body president, invited me to address the alumni and students during the 1974 homecoming festivities. Mississippi Valley was established at Itta Bena in 1950, and I was the first governor to attend a football game at the college that was made famous by Willie Totten and Jerry Rice. Willie Totten returned to his alma mater and is now the head football coach.

After graduating from Mississippi Valley, McLemore earned a law degree from Ole Miss and practiced law in Jackson. He has also held several governmental positions in Hinds County and is currently the pastor of the Lynch Street AME Church in Jackson. We have remained friends through the years. Eugene is the brother of Dr. Leslie McLemore, a professor of political science at Jackson State University and a member of the Jackson City Council.

The other visit that I remember so well was to Northeast Mississippi Community College. President Harold White invited me to deliver the commencement address on the twenty-fifth anniversary of the college's first commencement ceremony. I spoke on the "Southern Century" and the bright future of the South, and challenged those graduates to stay in Mississippi and help shape that future.

In the 1970s the state's junior college system was one of the best college buys in the country and one of Mississippi's most valuable assets. Because of my relationship with President White, a longtime friend and supporter, I forged a strong working relationship with the junior college presidents. President Terrell Tisdale of Jones Junior College became an active consultant and advisor as did Frank Branch of Holmes, Clyde Muse of Hinds, Billy Thames of Copiah-Lincoln, J.T. Hall of Delta Junior College, Horace Holmes of Southwest, William Scaggs of

Meridian Community College, and Marvin White of Pearl River. Dr. J.J. Hayden of Perkinston Junior College was a leader in the expansion of the junior college curriculum and the establishment of branch campuses. The community college system was especially helpful in coordinating and implementing my manpower training program.

Unfortunately, my relationship with the institutions of higher learning was not as cordial. The presidents of the colleges and universities were angry because I vetoed a library catch-up funding bill. I vetoed the bill to force the reallocation of building funds to the general operating budget that included library expenditures. I thought a reallocation was necessary because the postwar enrollment boom had run its course, and I did not think the institutions should keep adding expensive new buildings. A few months after I vetoed the library bill the State Building Commission issued a moratorium on all preplanning for future construction.

The Board of Trustees of Institutions of Higher Learning maintained an informal "pecking order" among the colleges and universities that was for all practical purposes official state policy. At the top were The University of Mississippi, Mississippi State University, and the University of Southern Mississippi. Mississippi State was accorded university status in 1958, and the University of Southern Mississippi was elevated to university status in 1962. The other five institutions of higher learning, Mississippi State College for Women, Delta State College, Jackson State College, Alcorn State College, and Mississippi Valley State College were in a separate category from the three universities. This educational hierarchy existed because alumni of the three universities had dominated the College Board since the early 1960s, and alumni of these three schools also held high ranking positions in both houses of the legislature.

As a matter of fairness and equity I thought the five colleges should also have representation on the Board of Trustees, and I considered this carefully in making my appointments to the

College Board. Appointments to the Board of Trustees of Institutions of Higher Learning are among the most important decisions a governor makes during his four-year term. Until I took office I did not realize how prestigious this position was. It is probably the most sought after appointment in state government. The members of the Board of Trustees of Institutions of Higher Learning have virtually complete control over higher education, including budgetary operations, capital improvements, the curriculum, and the selection of college administrators.

Mindful of the power vested in the College Board, I was careful in selecting my five regular appointments. Because of the death of a board member, I also made a sixth appointment. I appointed four trustees to a twelve-year term, and the LaBauve Trustee to a four-year term. This special trustee was established to oversee the funds that Felix LaBauve of Hernando bequeathed to The University of Mississippi in 1879. The legislation creating the position provided that the trustee serve a four-year term and be a resident of DeSoto County. I appointed Ross Franks of Hernando as the LaBauve Trustee. After this position was abolished in 1987, the governor appoints four members, and all Board members now serve nine-year terms.

Some of my most ardent supporters who sought appointment to the College Board were well advanced in age, and I was reluctant to appoint them to a twelve-year term on a board with such demanding responsibilities. The previous group of trustees appointed by the outgoing governor were all past their sixtieth birthdays, and three of the appointees were Ole Miss graduates to one Mississippi State graduate, giving Ole Miss seven of the thirteen members. Most of the recent governors had attended The University of Mississippi, and they tended to appoint Ole Miss alumni to the Board. Ole Miss graduates in the legislature also influenced the governor's appointments.

Even though I am a loyal Ole Miss law school graduate and love the university, I thought the College Board should represent all eight institutions of higher learning. Since the student body of three of the state senior colleges were predominantly black, I appointed Dr. Robert Harrison, a dentist from Yazoo City. Dr. Harrison was the first black to serve on the College Board. Many prominent Yazoo County citizens including John Holmes, a renowned trial attorney, recommended Dr. Harrison as a person of superior intellect and competence. He was an outstanding member of the Board of Trustees and commanded the respect of his fellow trustees and administrators at all of the senior colleges.

While I was considering my appointments to the Board of Trustees, I learned that there had been only six women members of the College Board in the twentieth century. And after learning that no graduate of Mississippi State College for Women had ever served on the Board, I appointed Miriam Simmons. A gifted high school principal from Columbia, Mrs Simmons was dedicated to the education of our young people, and was the first MSCW graduate to serve on the Board of Trustees of Institutions of Higher Learning.

My third twelve-year appointment went to Travis "Red" Parker, a long-time resident of Drew, and a graduate of Delta State College. He was a successful Delta planter and businessman and possessed a first rate mind. Parker was the first graduate of Delta State College appointed to the College Board, and he made a significant contribution to higher education during his tenure on the Board.

The fourth twelve-year appointment was Bobby Chain of Hattiesburg and a graduate of the University of Southern Mississippi. Chain was a building contractor and had served on numerous boards, including the board of directors of the Deposit Guaranty National Bank, which was then Mississippi's largest bank. Chain became the de facto chairman of the "Waller appointees" and was a progressive leader throughout his twelve years of service, devoting much more of his time than was required.

After the death of Ira "Shine" Morgan of Oxford, I appointed Mike Sturdivant to fill his unexpired term of four years. A Delta

planter and businessman from Glendora, Sturdivant was a graduate of Mississippi State University and devoted a great deal of his
time to the work of the College Board. All six of my appointees
were diligent and committed to the improvement of higher education for all of the citizens of Mississippi.

During my administration the U.S. Department of Justice
imposed additional desegregation requirements on the state's colleges. Dr. Robert Harrison and Bobby Chain, along with
Executive Secretary E.E. Thrash, made more than one hundred
trips to Washington to negotiate a final plan with the
Department of Justice. Senator James O. Eastland was immense-
ly helpful in these negotiations, as he was in many other projects
initiated during my administration.

Establishing parity among the eight senior colleges became one
of my educational objectives because under the existing system a
degree from one college was not accorded the same value as a
degree from another institution. This was brought to my attention by Representative Charlie Capps of Cleveland who informed
me that a woman who recently graduated from Delta State with
a 4.0 grade point average, and had impeccable recommendations,
was denied admission to the medical school on three occasions. I
was dumbfounded by the fact that she was denied admission and
that many out-of-state applicants were admitted. An official at
the medical school implied that applicants from other senior colleges, including private schools such as Millsaps and Mississippi
College, were ranked above Delta State. Eventually, we were able
to get this Delta State graduate admitted to the medical school.

I thought that a practical remedy for this kind of discrimination among the state's institutions of higher learning would be to
discontinue the numerically-driven funding formula, allocate certain degree programs to particular institutions, equalize the funding formula for all institutions, and elevate the five colleges to
university status. It was not my intention to weaken or compromise the educational standing of the three large universities but

rather to enhance and upgrade the academic programs at the other five colleges.

Elevating the five colleges to university status was controversial, but it was actually not my first choice. My preference was to consolidate the eight institutions into four universities. Not even my own appointees to the College Board, however, were willing to take such drastic action, and there was virtually no public support for closing any of the institutions.

An issue of some interest to the Mississippi legal community surfaced during my administration and generated much discussion and maneuvering. After Governor Bilbo failed to relocate The University of Mississippi to Jackson, there was an effort to move the medical school and the law school to the state capital. Eventually, the medical school was moved to Jackson in 1955. In the early 1970s the effort to move the law school to Jackson was renewed. I strongly opposed the relocation of the law school. After the Mississippi College School of Law was established in 1975, and a new law building was constructed in Oxford, the effort to move the law school to Jackson was abandoned.

One of the most important educational legacies of my administration was the establishment of three new professional schools. As I said in an earlier chapter, the establishment of a dental school, a college of veterinary medicine, and a school of architecture was extremely important to me because for decades we had been sending our bright young men and women out of state for training in these professions. Many of them did not return to Mississippi, and that "brain drain" had been costly to the state. Before the creation of these schools, our taxpayers had subsidized institutions in Tennessee and Alabama that trained most of the dentists, veterinarians and architects in Mississippi. If our young men and women did not have to go out of state for their professional training, we would not have to worry about them coming back to Mississippi.

With the full support of my appointees on the College Board

and my allies in the legislature, and after months of hard work and lobbying by Ole Miss alumni such as Dr. Marshall Fortenberry and Mississippi State graduates like Dr. Hugh Ward, we persuaded the legislature to authorize a dental school at the medical center. After the creation of the dental school, Ole Miss and Mississippi State graduates then lobbied for the establishment of a college of veterinary medicine and a school of architecture at Mississippi State. In a rare display of cooperation between Ole Miss and Mississippi State alumni, the advocates of these new programs joined forces and secured legislative approval for the three professional schools.

In working with the various groups that were supporting the new professional schools, I was astounded to learn from Dr. Fortenberry and Dr. Ward that there were some dentists and veterinarians who opposed the new schools. In contrast, the Mississippi Chapter of the American Institute of Architects fully supported the establishment of the school of architecture, which is today one of the premier programs in the country.

In addition to establishing the new schools, we also persuaded the medical school to increase the entering class from fewer than 100 students to approximately 150. Other improvements in higher education included the expansion of the health care-related professions, including physical therapy and a B.S. degree program in nursing at Delta State University.

The early 1970s was a time of extraordinary expansion of college opportunities for our young people. I cannot overemphasize the commitment of my College Board appointees to those expanding opportunities and the leadership that Bobby Chain provided during his twelve year tenure. Dr. Shelby Thames, who is now president of the University of Southern Mississippi, began the polymer science program at USM during the term of my College Board appointments. That program eventually achieved worldwide prominence. The University of Southern Mississippi was also authorized to grant engineering technology degrees, and the Gulf Coast Research Laboratory received significant new funding and greatly expanded its research facilities.

Delta State University established a Department of Commercial Aviation that now offers both undergraduate and graduate degrees. Many of the department's graduates are employed as corporate or airline pilots. My cousin Charles Metcalf is currently an instructor in the aviation program.

With the full support of my College Board appointees many necessary capital improvements were made on all eight campuses, including a new football stadium at USM. At The University of Mississippi a new law school, a student union, an athletic dormitory, and a physical education building were constructed in spite of the fact that none of my appointees were Ole Miss alumni.

Because many college students had to drop out before they completed their degree programs, as my father had done, I encouraged the establishment of new degree-granting centers at Jackson, Meridian, Tupelo and Southaven. These centers would make it possible for non-traditional students to go back to college and finish their degrees while they were working full-time and raising their families.

Although I devoted much of my administration to higher education, we spent even more time on the public school system. After many discussions with Dr. Baxter, who had a comprehensive knowledge of the entire educational system in Mississippi, we realized that the general public was not fully aware of the serious deficiencies in the school system. In order to inform the public of the critical need for improving public education we held a Governor's Conference on Education each year during my four-year term. These annual meetings were attended by a broad spectrum of the population including legislators, teachers and administrators, parents, PTA officials, and others who had a genuine interest in public education. We were surprised but pleased to see 1,500 to 2,000 people in attendance at all of these meetings. In addition to the annual conferences, we also sponsored sixty-eight local seminars around the state. These smaller seminars usually attracted thirty to thirty-five participants.

One of the reasons I wanted to encourage public involvement in education was to create public support for new legislation. At the annual seminars we discussed the need for public kindergartens, sixteenth-section land reform, compulsory education, children's advocacy programs, the Manpower Training Program, and a master's degree incentive plan for teachers. All of the forums were open for general discussion and many other subjects were discussed. Many of these meetings were covered by the press, and the public was made aware of the changes that were needed.

The general public did not realize that some cities had incorporated sixteenth-section land inside the city limits, on which industrial and residential improvements had been made. We secured the introduction of several bills to transfer control of sixteenth-section land from the board of supervisors to the county superintendent and school board, but none of them were enacted. As district attorney, I knew of many cases of sixteenth-section abuses. One case involved a Hinds County indictment of a county supervisor who received a $16,000 bonus for an oil and gas lease of sixteenth-section land in Jasper County.

The "good old boy" management system of sixteenth-section lands has cost the school children hundreds of thousands of dollars over the years. Even though we were not able to pass the legislation that was needed to correct these abuses, we believed that our efforts would lead to changes later on.

Because the Governor's Conferences on Education were so successful, I initiated a series of meetings around the state that I called "Move the Capitol." The directors of various boards and agencies, members of my staff, and I held public meetings in various towns and cities around the state. We invited the public to meet with us and ask questions and make recommendations on how the government could better serve them. I made a promise during my campaign to reconnect the government with the people, and by taking the government to the people I fulfilled that pledge.

Some of the agency heads and elected officials were initially reluctant to participate in the forums, but the "Move the Capitol" project became so popular that they soon clamored to get on board. Sometimes we had to use four airplanes to fly state officials to those "Move the Capitol" locations. Carroll usually went with me and she was especially popular in the small towns and cities.

Everybody likes to meet and shake hands with the governor even if they did not vote for him, and most ordinary citizens would never admit to a sitting governor that they did not vote for him. The enthusiastic reception we got at those meetings made all the effort and expense worthwhile. As I met with the local citizens and engaged in good-natured conversation, I would sometimes ask them if they were members of the "Capitol Street Gang" or the "court house gang." After the initial shock of the question wore off, they would laugh and say something like, "Oh, no sir, not me, I'm on your side."

I learned from these local forums that ordinary citizens, if given the opportunity, would take a more active role in public affairs. I also realized that they could influence their representatives in the legislature. Consequently, in the last two years of my administration I held several public meetings and urged the citizens to ask their representatives to support my agenda. More than five thousand people attended a forum I held at the fairgrounds in Jackson, and I am certain that those rallies were instrumental in the success we had in the last two years of my administration.

My legislative program at the beginning of my third year in office included several of my earlier recommendations that had not been enacted. Joseph Bonney of the Associated Press wrote that I had "shattered" a long-standing tradition, and that none of the old timers around the Capitol could ever remember a governor presenting a major legislative agenda in the third and fourth year of his term. Most of my predecessors had fought for the first two years and then coasted during the last two. It was just not my nature to coast, and there was too much that I had not accomplished to let up.

During the last two years of my term the three educational study committees I had appointed completed their work. The Public Education Study Committee, the Quality Education Committee, and the Select Committee on Higher Education published their studies and made several recommendations. From those published reports I formulated a legislative agenda during the last two years of my administration, which included the following recommendations:

- an elected state superintendent of education
- an appointed state board of education
- a compulsory school attendance law
- establishment of public kindergartens
- attendance counselors in every school
- reduction of the student/teacher ratio in grades 1-3
- equalization of property tax assessments
- reorganization and standardization of school districts
- expansion of vocational and technical education
- establishment of an accountability procedure
- establishment of an annual school evaluation mechanism
- withhold accreditation if all teachers are not certified in their teaching areas
- salary increments based on years of experience
- financial aid to needy college students at public and private universities
- reduce the twelve-year tenure for the College Board
- increase the professional staff at the College Board
- place the R&D Center under the authority of the College Board

Although the legislature did not enact most of these recommendations until many years later, we were able to achieve many good things for public education. Money is not everything in education, but all other things being equal, money makes the difference.

During my administration the appropriations for public schools increased 64%. Allocations for higher education increased 80% and 100% for junior colleges. In my last year in office I signed the largest public school appropriation and the highest teacher pay raise in the state's history. The record appropriation was $241 million and the annual salary increase was $1,000.

CHAPTER 14

The Mansion Project

"Join with me in saving and restoring this
historic home of our heritage."

—CARROLL WALLER

The restoration of the Governor's Mansion and its designation as a National Historic Landmark was one of the proudest achievements of my administration. As First Lady, Carroll dedicated most of her time and energy to the project, fulfilling a commitment she had made during the campaign. With the cooperation of Dr. Richard A. McLemore, Director of the Mississippi Department of Archives and History, his successor Elbert Hilliard, and Charlotte Capers, the chief executor of the Mansion project at the Department of Archives, Carroll coordinated the efforts of many agencies and individuals. Among those contributing to the restoration of the Mansion were members of the legislature, the Building Commission, the restorationists retained by the Archives, interior decorators, contractors, artisans, craftsmen, technicians, and landscape architects.

Late in the 1971 campaign the condition of Mississippi's ante-bellum Governor's Mansion was a topic of controversy as it had often been in the past. Early in his administration Governor Ross Barnett undertook a $300,000 renovation of the executive residence. The disclosure that one of the guest bathrooms was remodeled at a cost $10,000, and included gold-plated fixtures, prompted both criticism and ridicule in the Jackson press. The Jackson *State Times,* a newspaper that Dumas Milner established as an alternative to the Hederman press, was especially critical and referred to the "facility" as Governor Barnett's "$10,000 gold bathroom." At the height of the controversy Governor Barnett said to a group of reporters, "I wish you fellows would quit saying it is my bathroom."

In January 1968 when Governor John Bell Williams moved into the Mansion, which is located on a busy thoroughfare in downtown Jackson, he was naturally concerned about the safety of his family. His decision to build a security fence provoked even more controversy than Governor Barnett's gold bathroom. The completion of the white brick fence, which even its severest critics later admitted was an attractive addition, was followed by a surprise announcement. On July 15, 1971, the State Building Commission declared the Mansion unsafe due to the extensive structural damage of the antebellum building. A few days after that announcement Governor Williams and his family moved out of the Mansion.

The Governor's Mansion included an historic section, which was designed by William Nichols and constructed in 1842, and a family annex that was added in 1908. Nichols was one of the premier public architects in antebellum America. He also designed Mississippi's Old Capitol, the Lyceum Building at Ole Miss, the president's home at the University of Alabama, and several Mississippi courthouses.

Before the Civil War the governor and his family lived in the original Mansion. Shortly after the war a small family cottage was built on the north lawn. During a major renovation in 1908 the family cottage was replaced by a two story family annex that was equal in shape and size to the historic section. By 1971 both the family annex and the historic section of the Mansion were considered unsafe.

During the 1971 campaign Carroll and I often discussed the Governor's Mansion, and we decided if I were elected governor we would do whatever was necessary to save one of Mississippi's oldest and most revered landmarks. In speeches around the state Carroll discussed the history of the Mansion and asked the women of Mississippi to help save and restore this "historic home of our heritage." Carroll and Bill, Jr., had a long-standing interest in Mississippi history and understood the importance of restoring this antebellum structure.

A month after the 1971 general election Governor Williams and I met with the Building Commission to decide the fate of the Mansion. Following a lengthy discussion we agreed to seek legislative approval for a complete restoration of the historic section and the replacement of the 1908 family annex with a new town house addition. After we reached agreement on the Mansion's future, I suggested an immediate inventory of the furnishings and art work. There had been times in the past, especially during heated political campaigns, when governors were accused of taking state property from the the executive residence when they left office. To avoid any future controversy, I also suggested that the legislature place the Mansion and its historical furnishings under the administration of the Mississippi Department of Archives and History. This would ensure continuity in the management of the Mansion and preserve its contents.

When the legislature convened in January 1972, Senators Don Strider of Charleston and John Paul Moore of Starkville co-sponsored an initial $1,000,000 appropriation for the repair and renovation of the Mansion. With funds for the restoration now virtually assured, the Building Commission retained Joseph T. Ware, A.I.A, and Edwin R. Lewis, N.S.P.E., to conduct a preliminary evaluation of the building and to prepare a detailed cost estimate for a complete restoration. After studying their preliminary report, which they filed on February 7, 1972, the Building Commission appointed Ware and Lewis chief architects for the restoration of the Mansion and authorized them to prepare full-scale specifications for the project.

In the spring of 1972 the Mansion's furnishings were inventoried and removed to a storage facility for safekeeping. With the Mansion cleared, more detailed evaluations were made.

Carroll's ultimate objective for the $3 million dollar project was not just to repair the structural damage of the building and make it livable, but to restore the historic section of the Governor's Mansion to the period of its construction, and as nearly as possible to William Nichols' original design.

To conduct the architectural excavations of the building and determine its original design, which had been modified several times during its long history, the Building Commission appointed Charles Peterson, an internationally renowned restorationist. Working with a small group of skilled craftsmen and relying on Miss Capers' special knowledge of the Mansion's history and interior design, Peterson removed the outer layers of paint and wall paper to locate doors, passages, stairwells, and other original construction details that had been altered over the years, especially during the extensive renovation of 1908.

Peterson solved many of the mysteries of the Mansion's original design. Perhaps his most significant discovery was the location of the original grand staircase that led from the vestibule at the Mansion's main entrance to the second story. The staircase had been removed in 1908, but the integrity of the original stairway was reestablished during the 1975 restoration.

When Carroll began collecting historical information that would be useful in the restoration of the Mansion, she was surprised to learn that no scholarly history of the Mansion had been written. Her interest in a history of the Mansion was heightened in the fall of 1974 by Judge J.P. Coleman's article in a Jackson newspaper. A former governor and resident of the Mansion, Judge

Coleman sketched the long and interesting history of the Mansion and suggested that it was time for someone to write a complete history of the Mansion. Carroll clipped the article and as we were flying to the Gulf Coast for a "Move the Capitol" day she showed it to me.

We talked about a history of the Mansion several times over the next few weeks and she discussed the matter with Dr. McLemore. He agreed that a scholarly history should be written and on his recommendation I contacted Professor David Sansing, a member of the history department at The University of Mississippi. He agreed to write a history of the Governor's Mansion, and at his suggestion Carroll co-authored the book with him. Most of the information in this chapter is derived from their book, *A History of the Mississippi Governor's Mansion*, which the University Press of Mississippi published in 1977.

While Carroll was meeting with architects and structural engineers, she was also interviewing former first ladies, reading old manuscripts and newspaper articles, and compiling information that would be used in writing the history of America's second oldest governor's residence that was still in use.

During its colorful history the Mansion has survived several narrow escapes. Jackson was called "Chimneyville" after the Civil War because so many of its buildings were burned during the assault and occupation of Jackson. The Mansion survived because General William T. Sherman used it as his headquarters and Union soldiers bivouacked on its spacious lawns.

When the Democratic Party regained control of state government after Reconstruction, L.Q.C. Lamar considered the Mansion a waste of the state's precious resources, recommended that the building be sold, and said the governor should live in a plain house like everyone else. Governor James K. Vardaman also recommended the sale of the Mansion after his election in 1903. This uncertainty about the Mansion's future discouraged the appropriation of the necessary funds for its proper maintenance.

By 1908 the sixty-seven year old Mansion was in such poor

condition that Governor Edmund F. Noel initially refused to occupy the building. But after Jackson merchants recommended demolishing the building and making the property available for commercial development, Governor Noel and First Lady Alice Tye Neilson moved into the Mansion. Governor Noel then persuaded the legislature to authorize a major repair and remodeling.

Between the remodeling in 1908 and the restoration in 1975, general neglect caused the Mansion to deteriorate and eventually forced Governor Williams to vacate the building.

Because the ultimate objective of the Mansion project was to restore the historic section to the period of its construction and its original design, Carroll and the Archives staff began a search for draperies, chandeliers, floor coverings, and other furnishings dating from the 1840s. Most of the furniture in the Mansion in 1975 was not suitable for use in the historic section. But the Bilbo bed and a few other items were retained because of their value as memorabilia. Among those items were parts of Ross Barnett's "gold bathroom."

To direct the search for period furnishings and to design the decor throughout the Mansion, the Building Commission obtained the services of Edward Jones, one of America's outstanding restorationists. His career included the restoration of several rooms in the White House. After joining the Mansion project, Jones literally went around the world—from England to India—collecting items for the Governor's Mansion. Jones worked closely with Jackson interior designer Berle Smith and James Wooldridge, the curator of historical properties at the Department of Archives.

While these delicate pieces of the massive project were coming together, Carroll launched an extensive speaking tour throughout the state to raise $100,000 to restore the Mansion grounds. To keep the people informed about the progress of the restoration she wrote an article, "News From the Mansion," that appeared in newspapers across the state. She also wanted to involve Mississippi school children in the restoration project and introduced a program called "Dimes for the Mansion." She visited schools around the state and invited the children to donate dimes to the Mansion project.

From the funds generated by Carroll's various endeavors Bill Garbo, a landscape architect with the Mississippi R&D Center, designed a neo-classical garden featuring Mississippi flora that was popular during the period of the Mansion's construction. Garbo was a native of Jones County and gave a most concerted effort to make the Mansion grounds authentic to the historical period of its construction. He even included oyster shell walkways.

When a magnolia tree that Mrs. James K. Vardaman and her son planted in 1905 was removed during the 1975 restoration, Carroll suggested that a desk for the governor's study be built from the stock of the seventy-year old tree. When she was told that the stock was not large enough, she arranged for a smaller desk that would be suitable for the first lady's study. Bill Garbo designed the desk and Bob Brooks of Jackson built it.

During the long restoration project Carroll and the Department of Archives, with the cooperation of Ed Lewis, the architect, and Terrell Wise, the general contractor, conducted a campaign to achieve a special distinction for the Mansion. Their goal was to have the Mansion designated a National Historic Landmark. In February 1975 officials from the United States Park Service spent several days in Jackson touring the Mansion and consulting with Carroll, Ed Lewis, Terrell Wise, Elbert Hilliard, Charlotte Capers, and James Wooldridge.

The Park Service officials agreed that the Mansion warranted the special designation and presented a recommendation to the Department of the Interior, which would make the final decision. After several anxious weeks of waiting, Carroll was informed that the Secretary of the Interior had approved the recommendation to name the Mississippi Governor's Mansion a National Historic Landmark. The restored Governor's Mansion is an invaluable asset to our state and its heritage. And the state is deeply indebted to all those individuals who dedicated themselves to that sometime tedious three-year project.

My family finally moved into the Governor's Mansion on May 19, 1975. A few weeks later we held a grand ceremony on June 8, 1975, celebrating the reopening of the Mansion. At that ceremony Carroll received the official document designating the Mansion a National Landmark. More than 2,000 visitors attended the reopening ceremony and toured the Mansion.

Carroll literally threw open the doors of the Mansion in the summer of 1975. It was her way of thanking the people of Mississippi for helping her save "the home of our heritage." Two weeks after the grand reopening Carroll and I held a reception for my colonels and their wives and our long-time friends and supporters. More than 8,000 visitors attended that reception. The next day we held another open house for state employees and public officials. More than 4,000 toured the Mansion on that day. During the six months from June through the Christmas holidays, 60,000 visitors from forty-six states and several foreign countries toured Mississippi's antebellum Governor's Mansion.

Our Christmas in the Mansion was really special. Carroll decorated almost every room, both in the family quarters and in the historic section. On December 10, to commemorate Mississippi's admission to statehood, we held a tree-lighting ceremony on the front lawn. The Christmas tree in the Mansion's main hallway was a double balsam grown in Yazoo County and donated by Mrs. W.M. Link. The donation was arranged by K.K. Hill, a Mississippi College student and a friend of our daughter Joy.

New Year's Eve in Jackson was traditionally celebrated by revelers cruising Capitol Street shooting firecrackers and all sorts of fireworks from moving vehicles. Somehow, New Year's Eve 1975 got involved with the reopening of the Mansion, and the crowd around the Mansion and the traffic jam on Capitol Street was enormous. Members of the First Family and our guests were interested spectators from inside the Mansion grounds.

Although Carroll and I and our five children lived in the Mansion only about six months, it was an experience and an honor that none of us will ever forget. In early January 1976, Carroll and I began preparing to vacate the Mansion so Governor-elect Cliff Finch and his family could move in before his inauguration.

On Tuesday January 13, I delivered my farewell address to a joint session of the Mississippi legislature. [See Appendix C]

With former governors soon after my inauguration: (left to right), J. P. Coleman, Ross Barnett, Paul Johnson, Jr., John Bell Williams

With four former governors during Ray Mabus' administration: (left to right), Governor Mabus, William Winter, J. P. Coleman, Bill Allain, and me

After speaking at the 2005 Neshoba County Fair four former governors (left to right), William Winter, Ray Mabus, Ronnie Musgrove, and I posed with Governor Haley Barbour

My son Bob and I had a good catch

Here is a picture of the one that didn't get away—
it was close to the state record

Taking it easy on Lake Bill Waller

One of the youth fishing rodeos I sponsored around the state

Having my picture taken with school children in the Capitol

Carroll and I have enjoyed the time we have spent with our children and
grandchildren through the years

Family celebrating my 80th birthday at the Governor's Mansion
on October 23, 2006

Several members of my staff helped me celebrate my 80th birthday at the Governor's Mansion: (left to right), Ron Little, Major General Harold Cross, Charles McKellar, Dr. Robert Robinson, Commissioner of Insurance George Dale and Dr. Milton Baxter. Not pictured is Wayne Edwards, who was also in attendance

Other pictures of the Birthday Celebration at the Governor's Mansion

CHAPTER 15

My Last Campaign

"Since the mid-1960s, the state has changed more than it did in a whole century after the . . . War Between the States."
—RUDY ABRAMSON, WASHINGTON POST, 1978

A lmost three months before my term expired, a *Clarion-Ledger* reporter asked me if I intended to run for the U.S. Senate. He was not talking about 1978. He was asking me if I was going to run against Senator John C. Stennis in 1976. Senator Stennis was seventy-five years old and there were rumors that he might retire. He was elected in 1947 to fill the unexpired term of Senator Theodore Bilbo who had died in office. Although Senator Stennis had been in the Senate for twenty-eight years he was still the state's junior senator.

Senator Stennis put an end to the speculation about his retirement when he announced on December 8, 1975, that he would seek a sixth term. Several weeks before the qualifying deadline, Senator James Eastland personally called on me at my law office in the Trustmark Bank Building, and asked me not to run against

Senator Stennis. I assured him that the rumors were false and that I would not be a candidate. Although Senator Eastland did not tell me that he would not seek another term, he intimated that there might be an open seat in 1978. Senator Stennis did not pay me a visit when rumors were circulating that I might run against Senator Eastland in 1978. Senator Stennis may have believed, as many others did, that Senator Eastland would not seek reelection.

I did not seriously consider running against Stennis, and I might not have run even if the seat had been open. I had two children in college and three teenage boys at home and had not spent much time with them during the last four years. I was also tired and was looking forward to going fishing and to a less hectic schedule. Carroll was willing but not anxious to undertake another high-stakes campaign and did not encourage me to make the race. At the press conference when I announced that I would not be a candidate, a reporter asked Carroll if she advised me not to run. She said no wife with good sense would encourage her husband to run for public office.

Senator Stennis was reelected in 1976 without opposition in either the Democratic primary or the general election, and he still got 544,433 votes. As soon as Senator Stennis was reelected, attention quickly shifted to the 1978 Senate campaign and to speculation about whether Senator Eastland would seek another term.

At the Medgar Evers Homecoming Celebration at Fayette on June 12, 1977, Mayor Charles Evers introduced me as "my governor and always will be" and added, "I'll support Bill Waller no matter what he runs for." You can imagine how that whetted the curiosity of the Mississippi press corps, and I was bombarded with questions about the upcoming Senate race.

Like Stennis, Eastland was in his seventies and had been in the Senate since the 1940s. If he had run in 1978, he would have been seeking a seventh term. Senator Eastland was a powerful and busy man in Washington. He was president *pro tempore* of the

United States Senate, which placed him fourth in the line of presidential succession. He was also chairman of the Senate Judiciary Committee, and many of his friends urged him to run again because Senator Ted Kennedy was in line to be the next chairman of the committee. But Senator Eastland personally liked Senator Kennedy, and he did not think that Kennedy's elevation to the chairmanship would be that bad. He had supported President John Kennedy in 1960 and their father, Joseph Kennedy, had been an old friend.

Senator Eastland was not in good health, and the recent death of his long-time friend Senator John L. McClellan of Arkansas caused his family some concern for the senator. Many of his closest supporters, including Martin Fraley and Thurston Little of Corinth, and D.A. Biglane of Natchez, confided in me that the stress of being a high-ranking senator with complex duties was weighing on his health and they, along with others, were urging him to retire. Some members of his family, and some of his oldest and closest friends, encouraged the senator not to make another race.

Even in 1972 Senator Eastland had made it clear to Deloss Walker, who was managing his campaign, that he did not want to make a lot of speeches at political rallies and service clubs. As an alternative to the traditional campaign of nonstop speeches and meetings, Walker designed a method for getting the senator before large crowds without a grinding schedule. Rather than making campaign speeches, the senator would be featured at "Eastland Appreciation Dinners" around the state. That strategy worked well except for the occasion when Senator Eastland visited the new Gulfport banana terminal. As he left the building he walked by a large group of longshoremen. They naturally wanted to shake hands with their famous senator, and he spent nearly an hour in the hot sun shaking hands. After that sweaty episode Senator Eastland told his press secretary Larry Speakes not to let that happen again.

As early as 1976 some political observers were predicting that

Senator Eastland would not run again. On February 29, 1976, the *Delta Democrat-Times* wrote that the "old days of permanent incumbency" were coming to an end and that "all evidence points to the conclusion that [Eastland] will not seek reelection." Bill Minor wrote on March 10, 1977, "The word is evidently out: Jim Eastland is definitely not going to run for re-election next year." On October 8, 1977, the *Commercial Appeal* announced that "Sen. James O. Eastland (D-Miss.), the central figure in Mississippi's political guessing game, is now within a few weeks of announcing his final decision."

Long before I announced that I would run, some of the senator's inner circle who had supported me in 1971 told me that Senator Eastland was not going to run. Bill Minor wrote that Eastland would not seek reelection and would probably support me because I did not run, at Eastland's request, against Senator Stennis in 1976. According to Edwin Pittman, who later served as attorney general and chief justice of the Mississippi Supreme Court, Senator Eastland let it be known that he would not seek a seventh term and that he would support me if I ran for the seat. I was not surprised by this, and I contacted some of my major contributors to begin laying the groundwork for a Senate race in 1978.

Then something happened that I still do not fully understand. In November 1977 the word was out that Senator Eastland had changed his mind and that he would announce for reelection. When I learned that the senator may have changed his mind, I drove to Doddsville to talk to Eastland. The senator told me that he was going to run, but I got the distinct impression that he would run only if he had no opposition.

Senator Eastland was really undecided about running again, and he just did not want to go through another grueling campaign. He told his Washington colleagues that he could not fulfill his responsibilities in the Senate if he had to conduct a long campaign against a strong opponent.

In addition to the talk that I might run, there was also speculation that Governor Cliff Finch would run if he could not get a succession amendment through the legislature, and that he was already lining up support for a Senate race.

Apparently, some of the senator's old friends and supporters who stood to lose their clout in Washington if he gave up the seat persuaded him to announce that he would seek another term. Local politicians enjoyed their hometown reputation as "Eastland's man," and they did not want to relinquish that exalted position.

I was convinced that the senator would not run even with token opposition, so I announced my candidacy on March 20, 1978. On March 21 Senator Eastland withdrew from the race, and the next day Governor Finch announced that he would be a candidate.

Eastland's announcement that he would not run left many of his strongest and closest supporters in "a state of shock." Many of them wrote letters and sent petitions to the senator urging him to reconsider.

The day after Senator Eastland announced that he would not seek reelection Senator Bill Burgin of Columbus told a *Clarion-Ledger* reporter, "I think it is a sad day for Mississippi when a political tadpole like Bill Waller can cause a statesman of Senator Eastland's stature to withdraw." Representative A.C. "Butch" Lambert of Tupelo said that Eastland "should not have been forced to conduct a statewide campaign." Senator Robert Crook of Ruleville added that Senator Eastland "was entitled to be re-elected without opposition."

The caption above the *Clarion-Ledger* article announcing my candidacy read, "Waller to Run Against Tradition." It was this very tradition of entitlement to public office, this "permanent incumbency," that I had been running against since the 1950s. I did not believe that members of the legislature or Senator Eastland or anyone else was entitled to office. I was convinced that I could defeat Senator Eastland if he ran, and I think that is why he withdrew.

A couple of weeks after I announced that I would run for the

Senate, my official portrait in the Hall of Governors in the Capitol mysteriously disappeared. Shortly after its disappearance Secretary of State Heber Ladner called Elbert Hilliard, the Director of the Department of Archives and History, and told him about the missing portrait. Secretary Ladner informed Hilliard that a Capitol policeman had seen Senator Bill Burgin remove the painting. My portrait was next to the main elevator and, evidently, Burgin, who was not overly fond of me, got tired of looking at me every day when he came into the Capitol. Secretary Ladner cautioned Hilliard to move carefully because the salary bill for executive officials was then before the legislature, and Senator Burgin was chairman of the Senate Appropriations Committee. Hilliard subsequently met with Attorney General A.F. Summer and explained the situation. Attorney General Summer assured Hilliard that he would take care of it. A few days later, after Summer had a friendly conversation with Senator Burgin, the portrait was found behind a stairwell and the episode was soon forgotten.

After Senator Eastland withdrew, thirteen candidates eventually announced for the office, nine Democrats, two Republicans, two Independents, twelve men and one woman, ten whites and three blacks. There was so much speculation about who might announce their candidacy that some prominent Democrats, including William Winter, Edwin Pittman, Congressman David Bowen, and Brad Dye, felt obliged to declare that they would not run for Senator Eastland's seat.

The other eight Democratic candidates were Governor Cliff Finch, Charles Sullivan, Maurice Dantin of Columbia, Dr. Robert Robinson of Jackson and my appointee to the A&I Board, State Senator Richard "Sonny" Tedford of Marks, Helen M. Williams of Jackson. Two Democrats, R.S. Broome of Sumrall and Andrew Sullivan of Macon, announced but eventually dropped out of the race.

The two Republican candidates were State Senator Charles Pickering and Fourth District Congressman Thad Cochran.

Mayor Charles Evers and Henry Kirksey of Jackson were the two Independents. Evers, Kirksey and Mrs. Williams were the black candidates.

The 1978 senatorial election was a low-key campaign and almost all the Democratic candidates held similar views on the major issues. One issue that I raised throughout the campaign was the need for a long-term national energy policy. I thought we had to increase domestic exploration and production of oil and gas as a means of freeing the country from dependency on Middle Eastern oil. I also favored a stronger enforcement of the FCC decency guidelines for limiting sex and violence on television, and I supported a thirty percent cut in federal income taxes.

The biggest issue in the campaign, at least among the Democrats, was my role in Senator Eastland's decision not to seek reelection. His longtime supporters bitterly resented me because they believed my decision to run forced his retirement. Most of Senator Easltand's supporters who lined up with me in 1971 to defeat Charles Sullivan, lined up with Maurice Dantin in 1978 to defeat me.

Maurice Dantin led the ticket in the first primary and faced Cliff Finch in the Democratic runoff. During the second primary Eastland's forces, with few exceptions, openly supported Dantin, who defeated Governor Finch.

In the general election Dantin faced the two independents, Charles Evers and Henry Kirksey, and Thad Cochran, who had defeated Charles Pickering in the Republican primary.

After the party primaries Senator Eastland announced that he would remain neutral and would not endorse either Dantin or Cochran. In the November general election Cochran led with 263,089 votes, Dantin got 185,454, Evers received 133,640 votes, and Henry Kirksey received 1,747 votes.

Thad Cochran was the first Republican elected to a statewide office since Reconstruction, and there was some discussion about a deal between Charles Evers and the Mississippi Republican Party. If Evers had not run, most of his supporters would probably have voted for the Democratic candidate, and that would have given Dantin enough votes to defeat Cochran.

Some of his old allies in the Loyalists faction of the Democratic Party accused Evers of selling out to the highest bidder. Evers responded to those accusations by pointing out that fifty thousand Democrats who voted for Dantin in the second primary switched to Cochran in the general election. Charles Evers eventually left the Democratic Party and became a Republican.

In February 1978, a month before I formally announced my candidacy, Bert Case and Paula Pittman interviewed Charles Evers on a Jackson television station. Evers had not entered the Senate race, and during that interview he gave no indication that he would. He did say, however, that he would like to see Bill Waller run against Senator Eastland. Charles Evers did not formally announce his candidacy or file with the secretary of state's office until after I was eliminated in the first Democratic primary.

Charles McKellar, who was on my Senate campaign staff and had been with me since the 1967 governor's race, became Charles Evers' political consultant in the general election. Charles Evers told Charles McKellar that he would not have run for the Senate in 1978 if Bill Waller had been the Democratic nominee.

We probably will not know if any deals were made until the historians have time to sort it all out.

However, there was a contemporary analysis of the Senate race that I found particularly interesting. *Washington Post* reporter Rudy Abramson said the 1978 Senate campaign, which included men and women, blacks and whites, Democrats, Republicans, and Independents, was an illustration of the sweeping changes that had produced what he called a "New Mississippi." Even though I lost the Senate election, I took some satisfaction in knowing that I had helped bring about the progress that Abramson described.

After the votes were in, and it was evident that I did not make the runoff, Jo Ann Klein and David Bates of the *Clarion-Ledger* cited my defeat as the latest example of the Mississippi political tradition "that former governors are finished politically when they leave office."

Nine years later when I announced that I was running for governor in 1987, Wayne Weidie reminded me that I was "bucking the ex-governors losing streak"and that "being governor is a political stepping stone to nowhere." Wayne Weidie was editor of the *Ocean Springs Record* and a syndicated columnist. Along with Bill Minor, he was one of Mississippi's most astute political observers.

At the time I made my third run for governor in 1987 only two former governors in the twentieth century, James Vardaman and Theodore Bilbo, had been elected to the U.S. Senate, and only two former governors, Hugh White and Bilbo, had been elected to a second term.

But I was not worried about jinxes. I thought the political climate had changed over the last decade and that people would not be affected by those old traditions. Besides, the early polls showed that I had low negatives.

By the late spring of 1987 eight Democrats and two Republicans had filed with the secretary of state's office. The other Democrats were Gilbert Fountain, a pipe fitter from Biloxi; H.R. Toney, a Byhalia businessman; Attorney General Ed Pittman of Hattiesburg; State Auditor Ray Mabus of Ackerman; Mike Sturdivant of Glendora; John Arthur Eaves, a Jackson attorney; and Maurice Dantin. The two Republicans were businessman Jack Reed of Tupelo and Doug Leman, a financial planner from Jackson.

Five of the Democratic candidates—Eaves, Pittman, Dantin, Sturdivant, and I—had run for governor before. Republican Jack Reed and Ray Mabus were making their first run for governor, but Mabus had been elected state auditor four years earlier.

Sturdivant, Mabus, and Reed were affluent, at least by Mississippi standards, and the 1987 race was an expensive campaign. As a measure of just how important money was becoming in Mississippi politics, until 1970 candidates in the party primar-

ies were limited to $50,000 for all campaign expenses. In the
1987 campaign several candidates spent more than a million dollars trying to get elected to a job that paid $63,000 a year. The
amount of money some candidates were spending became an
issue in the campaign, but the high cost of campaigning was a
political reality and there was not much that anyone could do to
keep it down.

Other than the increasing influence of money in politics, the
major issues of the 1987 campaign had been around since 1967.
Dan Davis, a *Clarion-Ledger* reporter, wrote that I might be able
to beat the "one-term-and-you're-out syndrome" because I was
conducting a "back to the future campaign." He noted that the
major issues of the campaign—governmental reorganization,
constitutional reform, the county unit system, economic development, and a teacher pay raise—were the same issues that I had
advanced many years earlier.

Although I pushed for the consolidation of Mississippi's agencies and commissions during my administration, in 1987 there
were still ten different agencies involved in economic development. Turf battles and squabbles between rival agencies had
impeded economic development, and Mississippi had a 12%
unemployment rate in 1987. In some counties it was even higher. The unemployment rate in Sharkey County was over 40%.
Almost two thirds of the unemployed were high school dropouts
with few skills and little training.

I always thought of Corinth and Alcorn County as economi-
cally solid, and was shocked when I learned of its 13% unemployment rate. This prompted me to call some of my Alcorn County
supporters to determine the problem. The basic answer was that
the unemployment rate among those actively seeking jobs was
about 3%. The other 10% were people who had never worked
and did not want to work.

For the school dropouts who wanted to work but had no skills,
I recommended tuition grants for vocational and technical training at the state's junior colleges. The strict enforcement of the

compulsory school law was also part of my plan to upgrade the skill level of Mississippi's general population. Because of the growing use of illegal drugs among unemployed and uneducated young people, I also recommended a state strike force to assist county and local officials in combating drug-related violence.

Mississippi's population was living longer, and many of our elderly citizens had little or no retirement income. Nothing is more traumatic for senior citizens than the fear that they will have nowhere to go in their last years. I recommended an intermediate care program for those who could not live alone but did not need to be in nursing homes. I pointed out that we were spending $25,000 a year housing criminals at Parchman, and I thought the state should find a way to assist its elderly citizens. As the need for health care has evolved over the years, many potential nursing home patients are assisted with home care, making the individuals happy to remain at home and reducing the cost of nursing home care. It was my belief in 1987 that about half of the nursing home patients could live at home with part-time home care.

Another prominent issue in the 1987 campaign was constitutional reform. Governor Bill Allain had appointed a three hundred member commission headed by former Governor J.P. Coleman to study the need for a new a new state constitution. The Commission made several recommendations, including a state convention to draft a new constitution. But the legislature did not adopt any of its recommendations. I had supported the commission's major recommendations and pledged to reestablish the commission if I were elected.

After my campaign got underway, I felt good about my chances. Mike Frazier, my campaign manager, along with Deloss Walker and Wayne Edwards, had organized a fine campaign staff and put me in a position to get into the second primary. I was confident that I could win the election if I got in the runoff.

I had a much better relationship with the press during the 1987 campaign than I had during my administration, or even in the 1978 Senate race. I think the press realized that there had been some major achievements during my administration, and they were willing to give me credit for that. I also came to realize that the press just wanted politicians to be open and honest with them and not try to use them for your own purposes. But they did love a good controversy.

One of the most significant aspects of the 1987 campaign was the high number of voters who were undecided late in the first primary. I think one of the reasons there were so many undecided voters was the large number of viable candidates, six of whom had previously conducted statewide campaigns. One lady told the *Clarion-Ledger* that she could not make up her mind because there is "so many of them."

In an editorial shortly before the first primary the *Clarion-Ledger* said the Democratic Party offered "one of the best slates of candidates Mississippians could have asked for." The editorial concluded that Mabus, Sturdivant, Dantin, or Waller would all serve the state well. The *Clarion-Ledger* also singled out Republican Jack Reed as well-qualified to serve as governor.

Another reason for the large number of undecided voters was Ray Mabus' age. He was a likeable candidate with good ideas and had been a successful state auditor, but he was only thirty-eight years old. Although he was the clear frontrunner, many voters were concerned about his age and wondered if he was old enough for the job. The age factor did not prove to be a negative for Mabus, and he was the youngest governor ever elected in Mississippi. During his term he was the youngest incumbent governor in the nation.

Just before the first primary vote, the *Clarion-Ledger* reported that the latest polls had Mabus in the lead with Sturdivant and Waller in a virtual dead heat for second place. But in the last few days of the first primary John Arthur Eaves was "propelled" into fourth place by the popularity of his pledge for a $10 car tag. Eaves' proposal brought to mind that twenty years earlier I had pledged to exempt the family car, like the family home, from ad valorem taxes. He could never have gotten his ten-dollar tag through the legislature, but it was an enormously popular idea with the voters. Eaves' late surge probably kept me out of the run-off.

When the final votes were counted Mabus led with 304,559, Sturdivant had 131,180, I was third with 105,056, Eaves came in fourth with 98,517, Dantin was a surprising fifth with 86,603, and Pittman received 73,667 votes.

Ray Mabus defeated Sturdivant in the runoff. Jack Reed defeated Doug Leman in the Republican primary, and then lost to Ray Mabus in the general election.

If there was any doubt about how much Mississippi had changed since the early 1960s, the election of a thirty-eight year old Harvard graduate in his first run for governor was convincing evidence of the progress Mississippi had made. The disappointing results of my last campaign were ameliorated by the sense of pride I felt in having helped Mississippi start moving straight ahead.

CHAPTER 16

Life After Politics

*"God does not subtract from a man's allotted time
the hours he spends fishing"*

A PROVERB

Since 1976 I have enjoyed many benefits and blessings from having served as governor. These dividends are not financial. Comparing the beginning with the end of the term, governors are probably worse off financially when they leave office. During my term as governor I was paid $60,000 annually. After federal and state taxes and retirement deductions, my take home pay was $1,800 per month. Former governors or their widows receive no special pensions or additional financial benefits from the state. Senator Howard Dyer of Greenville, who was aware that some widows of former governors had experienced financial hardships, introduced several bills to provide small pensions to former first ladies. But year after year the legislature did not pass those bills.

The enduring benefits from having served as governor are the relationships with friends and supporters throughout the state.

Nothing could be more endearing or beneficial than having a statewide network of loyal friends. Over the last three decades wherever Carroll and I have gone people have reminded us of our acquaintance and recited some important event that affected their families. I always had my picture taken with children who visited the Capitol or were involved in ceremonies and meetings with me. Those now grownup children often say to me something like, "I had my picture taken with you when I was in the third grade and visiting the Capitol." These priceless encounters remain a part of our daily interactions with people.

On many occasions a person will approach me and say, "I've never met you before, but my granddaddy knew you, and I'm really proud to have the opportunity to meet you." Hearing these comments over the last thirty years makes you feel that your efforts in politics were worthwhile.

My service as governor also had a beneficial impact on my family, including even distant relatives beyond the third degree of kinship. Starting with my own immediate family, it gave Carroll and our five children an opportunity to make contributions as members of Mississippi's "First Family." Their campaign appearances and speeches helped them become good communicators, and they gained invaluable experience in dealing with people from all walks of life. The campaigns were the equivalent of a graduate degree in public relations, and to that extent it greatly benefitted all family members who participated in the campaigns, going back to 1955.

After my term expired I did not go into lobbying or expand my corporate clientele because experience had taught me that that type of activity, in some cases, demeaned the office of governor. Many of my loyal supporters began coming to me with their legal problems when I set up a one man law office in the Trustmark Bank building in 1976. My motivation was to have a "people's problem solving" law practice representing individuals and small businessmen, which was the same type of practice I maintained before 1972

I also planned to have a law practice that Bill, Jr., could join when he graduated from law school. At the time I opened my Capitol Street office in 1976, Bill, Jr., had graduated from Mississippi State and was enrolled in the Ole Miss law school. He joined me after graduating, and we created the law firm of Waller & Waller in 1977. Bill, Jr., remained with the firm until January 1998 when he began his service on the state supreme court.

Bob is also one of my partners and has been with the firm for the past twenty years. We are fortunate to have a great legal team that has been together for many years, including Stephanie Vest, and valuable staff members including Susan Rozina, CLA, and our general manager Terry Whittington. If my present good health remains I plan to "keep on keeping on."

I would urge young men and women to be careful that the occupation or profession they choose will be engaging and fulfill-ing. If you choose something that you like to do, and enjoy the work and the work product, then your life will be successful, happy, and rewarding. I have known scores of men and women who got trapped into something that they did not like to do, and agonized every work day until retirement.

The law is a great career, and I have never regretted my deci-sion to practice law. No two days during my long career have been the same or have been boring. Every day that a lawyer goes to his office there is something new and different to deal with. I have had the honor of representing people in probably forty of Mississippi's eighty-two counties, and when I attend court in those counties I have the pleasure of renewing old acquaintances that were made during my statewide campaigns.

In some of the local courts I often come in contact with former highway patrolmen or former law enforcement officials that I had some association with in years gone by. Recently, at the U.S. District Court in Hattiesburg, I met three former highway patrol-men who were in charge of security at the courthouse. They thanked me profusely for the pay raises that highway patrolmen received in each of the four years of my governorship.

Another enjoyable aspect of life after politics has been the opportunity to participate in elections involving my family and others. After several years in law practice, Bill, Jr., informed us of his intention to run for a judgeship. He first ran for chancery judge in Hinds County, and was narrowly defeated. When a vacancy occurred in the central district of the Mississippi Supreme Court in 1996, Carroll and I, and his wife Charlotte, encouraged him to enter the race for the vacant seat. We actively supported his candidacy, and he won the seat over seven opponents, all of whom were prominent lawyers or judges. In 2004 he was reelected, having only one opponent.

My other political endeavors have included backing various candidates, some successful and some unsuccessful. Early in 1991, when Kirk Fordice of Vicksburg started making rounds in Jackson, I committed to support him. I was among his very first Hinds County supporters and participated in fund raising and other activities.

Many people, especially Carroll, complain about me being a workaholic, and there is evidence to support this moniker. However, I do have several entertaining and recreating hobbies. As I mentioned in an earlier chapter, I grew up fishing on Clear Creek and at the Sardis Reservoir. I have relentlessly pursued the sport on local lakes and the Barnett Reservoir. My close friends Red Hancock of Bentonia and Raymond Bonner taught me how to fish on Eagle Lake and the borrow pits and flood waters of the Mississippi River. My friends Bill Allen, Bobby Kinchen, and former law partner Bob Pritchard and I have made many fishing trips to Mexico and offshore in Louisiana and the Mississippi Gulf Coast. We even made a week long fishing expedition to Cuba.

Beginning in 1995 I started improving several small lakes on the property known as "Camp Kickapoo." The lakes and adjoining cabins are frequently used for family recreational activities, as well as church and Boy Scout outings. I jokingly brag that I stocked the Kickapoo lakes with fish, grew the fish, caught the fish, cleaned, cooked, and ate the fish. I have mounted large mouth bass weighing in excess of eleven pounds and honestly feel that I will catch the state record in the very near future. Frequent visits to Camp Kickapoo may be my equivalent to a dose of hadachol.

When I told that delegation of powerful legislators who visited me in my office early in my administration that I would not be a ceremonial governor, that did not mean that I would not cut any ribbons. Actually, I cut many ribbons and attended many ceremonies. One of the ceremonies that I especially enjoyed was the dedication of Lake Bill Waller.

Working closely with Avery Wood, the Director of the Game and Fish Commission, we secured private and state funds to build a two-hundred acre lake on the Hugh White Game and Fish Reserve near Columbia in Marion County. The good people of Marion County named the lake in my honor.

The dedication of this recreational facility was accompanied with much fanfare. Competition in bow and arrow and rifle marksmanship, was followed by Marion County horsemen riding across the earthen dam carrying flags to the ceremonial platform. Marvin Polk introduced Supreme Court Justice Vernon Broom who first paid tribute to Gordon Strickland, area manager for the Game and Fish Reserve, and Shelby Davis, assistant manager, and than introduced me. The two thousand people attending the ceremony gave me a rousing welcome.

I began my remarks by thanking the press for their fine coverage of this event, especially the *Hattiesburg American*. During my brief speech I commended Columbia Mayor George F. Newman, Senator Emerson Stringer, and Representatives Vasco Singley and Neil Smith for their support and determination toward the completion of Lake Bill Waller. At the conclusion of my remarks Gordon Strickland presented me a rod and reel on behalf of the citizens of Marion County. I then emptied the first container of the ten thousand channel catfish and the two hundred thousand bream and redears that stocked the lake. After the ceremony, "Sandwiches, deviled eggs, fried chicken and cokes were served to all just above the dam on a shady bluff."

Over the last thirty years there is no telling how many boys and girls have learned to swim and fish in Lake Bill Waller, as I did in Clear Creek and Maybelle's Lake. Lake Bill Waller is temporarily closed while undergoing a substantial renovation, and is scheduled to reopen in 2007.

Carroll and I have remained active in church and civic affairs. Our entire family, all four sons, our daughters-in-law and grandchildren, are active members of the First Baptist Church. All four of my sons and I are active deacons, and Bill, Jr., is currently the chairman of our Board of Deacons.

I have long had a keen interest in both college and professional football. Carroll sometimes scolds me for watching too much football. One of my all-time favorite college games is the 1947 Ole Miss-Tennessee game at Crump Stadium in Memphis. I was a student at Memphis State and saw Ole Miss defeat Tennessee for the first since the series began in 1902. Charley Conerly led the Ole Miss Rebels to an easy 43-13 victory.

And I will never forget when I hosted the Republican Governor's Conference for the Ole Miss-Tennessee game in Jackson in 1973. Governor Winfield Dunn, who was a 1950 Ole Miss graduate and the Republican governor of Tennessee, called and asked me if I could arrange for his colleagues who were in Nashville for the national Republican Governor's Conference to attend the game. I made the arrangements and Governor Ronald Reagan of California, Governor Christopher Bond of Missouri, Governor Jack Williams of Arizona, and Governor Dunn attended the afternoon game in Memorial Stadium. Ole Miss upset Tennessee in a televised game 28-18. Little did I realize that the number of Republican governors would increase dramatically over the next few years and that Governor Reagan would become president.

When I am not working or watching football, I do a lot of basic cooking – veggies, fish, meat and related "men's foods." I also do a little gardening, mainly tomatoes.

To say that all that has happened through 2006 has been good and happy would be incorrect, because we have also known sadness and grief in the loss of our daughter Joy in 1981, coupled with the deaths of my father in 1981 and Carroll's mother, Edith Overton, in 1981; my sister, Mildred Waller Burtschell in 1997; and our beloved stepmother, Mrs. Emma Waller, in 2002 at the age of ninety-six.

Life goes on, and we have managed our grief by focusing on our four children, our ten granddaughters and four grandsons. We have endeavored to give them as many opportunities as possible to bond with their grandparents. At this writing, all fourteen grandchildren still have all four grandparents, with whom they are constantly associated. The oldest grandchild and my namesake, William Lowe Waller, III, is a physician and his sister, Jeannie, is a graduate student at Ole Miss. The other twelve are still in grade school, and we are looking forward to their future growth and development with the help of all the Waller family.

Carroll and I have been blessed throughout our lives by family and friends. As we approach our fifty-sixth wedding anniversary, we look back and ahead with happiness and will continue to devote our time and efforts for the benefit of our family, friends, clients, and the good old State of Mississippi.

Inaugural Address

WILLIAM LOWE WALLER
January 18, 1972

Judge Brady, Governor Williams, Lieutenant Governor Winter, Mr. Speaker, Mr. President, distinguished members of the Legislature, Justices of the Mississippi Supreme Court, Members of our Congressional Delegation, former Governors of Mississippi, Members of the Consular Corps–my fellow Mississippians:

We have come a long way together.

How can I express adequately–the gratitude in my heart and in the heart of my wife, Carroll, and our children–for having placed in my care and keeping the high office of Governor–the highest honor the people of this fine state can bestow?

The answer to this question will be resolved by applying the creed of my campaign and its valiant workers–often repeated, we said: "Waller Works." I shall thank the people for this confidence and trust given me by working hard, honestly, and with all my strength, to serve all our people.

I am honored to have a staff of Colonels made up of the finest men in this state. The advice and counsel of these men will be sought and used throughout my term.

With divine guidance and your help, I intend to make this the most successful administration in the 155 year history of this state. Never before has a new Governor had so many advantages–a cooperative public basically at peace with each other; elected state officials offering unlimited help; and legislative leaders willing to work hard for progress. Many other advantages arise from the progress of former administrations. It is proper then that we pause–briefly–to signal the accomplishments of our living past Governors. I want the people here today and those who may see this program today or later to know that all of the two million people of this state are grateful to these great men who sacrificed so much for a better way of life for all of us–I will now recognize the Governors from 1956 to 1972 –Honorable James P. Coleman, –Honorable Ross Barnett, –Honorable Paul B. Johnson, Jr. –and our present Governor, The Honorable John Bell Williams. Gentlemen–please stand that we might extend a warm thanks for your contribution to our growth.

As the 56th Governor I pledge to you a progressive administration for economic and cultural growth. At the end of the next four years all Mississippians and the nation can point with pride to the fact that our state stands equal to and as well respected as all other states.

I shall take only a few minutes today to summarize my feelings about Mississippi. Later my program will be fully described in my state of the state messages to the House and Senate.

I am proud of the cooperation, friendship and team spirit which has already been demonstrated in conferences with 174 members of the House and Senate. I can assure you that we are working together and that this teamwork effort will extend throughout this administration.

Our citizens are peaceful and law abiding. We plan to keep it that way.

I promise you that state government will be responsive to the needs of our people. There will be no graft or irregularities in state departments. Our aim–a full measure of services for each tax dollar. I pledge to treat your tax dollars with the same care and caution that you treat your own money.

I have made two state-wide campaigns covering a total of four separate elections in the last four and one-half years. I have visited with you in every walk of life. I have gained a personal and valuable knowledge of your spirit, attitude and beliefs. Your outlook is unbelievably positive and optimistic, and so much so, that

I am convinced that this state stands right on the threshold of monumental economic and cultural growth.

I will not stand aside and idly observe the God-given talents of one single Mississippian wasted. Every adult illiterate, every school drop-out, and every untrained retarded child is an indict-ment of us all. We cannot continue paying this terrible human and financial price for such failures. It is time to end this waste. The examples established for us in some states and foreign coun-tries by eliminating this waste is a challenge to all Mississippians.

My partners in our new Mississippi growth—the members of the Senate and House—are not here by accident or mere chance—we are all here because we accepted the challenge as a candidate and received a mandate for progress from the people. I see this as meaning a full development of human and natural resources. This we will do.

Looking affirmatively at this challenge I would like to briefly outline two areas needing change through legislative action, namely, economic development and efficient operation of state government. We are losing some of our best and most productive Mississippians from every age group. I believe these ambitious career-minded people want to stay. They will not leave if state government is creative and progressive. Moreover, some who have left will return for the same reason.

One major change for the better will be a small business devel-opment bureau in our Agricultural and Industrial Board, thereby giving every person a chance to have a part of the growth oppor-tunities offered by the free enterprise system. This change will make further use of the services of our Research and Development Center created in the Governor Johnson adminis-tration. By these and other changes, we plan an industrial expan-sion rate superior to even that enjoyed during the Barnett admin-istration. Such investments will allow us to say to ambitious peo-ple of all ages, particularly the young, come get involved with us—NOW!

The fastest growing industries in this nation are tourism and outdoor recreation. In natural beauty, in natural resources, in ante-bellum homes and in ante-bellum history, this state has outstanding opportunities to gain its fair share of this industry. Thousands upon thousands of Americans will come to see our scenic beauty and historical sites—Vicksburg, where military strategy and tactics were more complexly scored than at Gettysburg; the Choctaw Indian nation; the beautiful Gulf Coast; and countless other unique attractions of interest, education and history. We will get our fair share of the tourist under a creative new program to develop these sites along with our state parks. By restoring your Mansion to its 1839 glory, all Mississippians and tourists will be able to visit this historical shrine. Moreover, we will gain the same great investment return as that now being received from the Old Capitol, which was restored during the administration of Governor Coleman—this facility will be used later today for the official State Reception. We will build major tourist and convention facilities on our Gulf Coast sufficient to attract conventions having membership in all 50 states. These dollars will come fast—they will help every Mississippian.

I know many of our citizens are handicapped personally and the economic growth generally is stymied because of an inadequate highway network. This administration, with legislative teamwork, will seek passage of a major highway construction program. Considerable advance work of broad application has already been done by my highway committee. I want to thank this committee of unselfish and professional men of vision who are serving without pay.

Transportation is another field vital to the growth of this state, namely, that of our rivers, streams and gulf ports. These facilities should be expanded and promoted to handle interstate shipping as well as foreign trade. Your state is ideally situated to be a major port state in the near future.

Involvement of all our people will be a major theme of this administration. We will have separate executive councils composed of youth, labor, and retired citizens. This will open new vistas of communication with state government.

One clear need communicated to most all political leaders is an enforceable absentee voter law for students and others who are now unavoidably away from home on election day. An involvement with the ballot is essential for good government.

Much has been said about waste and inefficiency in our state government. I compliment Governor Williams for using the talents of the business and professional community in gaining the benefit of an exhaustive plan for reorganization. Our people cannot afford waste of tax money in any form, and I propose that we attack this problem now and initiate modern management practices in state government. The problem is too complex to handle in one limited annual session. Although I am the first Governor that will operate an initial program through a legislative session limited to 125 days, I remain optimistic that a large part of these laws can be passed before May 8, our adjournment date.

Much of the nation does not know how great this state really is. Through visionary operation of state government and the implementation of modern public relations concepts, it is my goal that Mississippi will be as popular and respected as any state at the end of these four years.

I am the product of a rural educational system. I know what a superior education can do for our young people. Therefore, I am committed to the proposition of a superior public educational system, and at the same time, to those practices in adult education and training that will accommodate increasingly higher pay, and the demands of the future.

The nagging problems related to drugs continue to concern all parents and well-meaning Mississippians alike. Can your state government do anything? Yes, and now. I have already made arrangements to start a drug treatment center at our state mental hospitals. Initially, we will concern ourselves with evaluation, screening, and rehabilitation to aid the courts and law enforcement agencies in determining how to save that wayward teenager on a first offense. I believe this program will lend comfort to concerned parents and give us a major step forward in solving this blight on our society.

You are concerned about the rising number of traffic deaths and injuries. We are working hard on a broader concept in the Department of Public Safety and are in the process of initiating new plans on highway safety and traffic control. I have already sent a representative to Tennessee to learn how our guest today, Governor Winfield Dunn, a native of Meridian, accomplished the major feat of reducing highway accidents by 60% while having highway patrol travel reduced by 500,000 miles. I can assure you that we will continue to exchange information between our sister states on major problems such as this.

A balanced budget, that is, spending less than you collect has been traditional with our Governors in recent history including those present here today. I want to personally commend Governor Williams for leaving this administration with a surplus. I pledge careful management of the tax dollar so that Mississippi can retain its high ranking as one of the few states that is not operating with a deficit.

When I ran for Governor no organization asked me to run and no machine sponsored my candidacy. I won with the help of the people who were not directed or controlled by organized political groups. My victory, the victory of the people, is an expression of a form of democracy superior to any existing today. Mississippi is a truly democratic state. It must have a state party representing all two million people. We have issued a call for help, and I renew this plea for help here today, namely, that you go to your precinct at 10:00 a.m. on January 22 and help us have great public support for the organization of our state Democratic Party for 1972 through 1975. Every Mississippian is invited to participate. These precinct conventions, followed by county and district conventions, will determine the leadership of your party for the next four years. Continuing good federal relations demands that you participate in the leadership of your party for a proper voice in national affairs. Remember this—that 600,000 voters identified with this party in November—a number unequaled in the history of this state—and this vote, I believe, represents the true political spirit of today.

Shortly, we will depart from this solemn and meaningful occasion for further ceremonial activities. Before we leave, I want to again humbly and sincerely ask every Mississippian to remember that the men and women of the Mississippi Legislature, joined by other state officials, cannot alone solve the vast problems of economic growth, state government reorganization, education, injustices, crime, pollution, and highways. This control rests in your hands, the people of Mississippi.

I have talked to you today in a positive and optimistic manner for I believe this to be the mood of the people. This mood arises from a belief by our people that Mississippi is at the very beginning of a bright and prosperous new era. I know this belief is shared by the young and old alike—and that destiny is ours. But, I agree with William Jennings Bryan who said, "Destiny is not a matter of chance, it is a matter of choice. Destiny is not a thing to be waited for, it is a thing to be achieved." Our destiny awaits us—with hard work—it is ours.

I pledge that your Governor will work hard, and I promise you my best. I ask you for your best and for your prayers.

State of the State Address

WILLIAM LOWE WALLER
January 25, 1972

I want sincerely to thank you for allowing me to appear before you on this occasion to outline my thoughts regarding a legislative program for this year.

As I stated last Tuesday, I am grateful for your unusual demonstration of cooperation. I repeat that I am working hard to be a member of the team formed between the governor and the legislature for creative legislation leading to a faster economic growth for our state. I assure you that it is my desire to work with you in moving this state forward.

If my addition is correct, we have only 103 days left in this legislative session. Therefore, I think it imperative that we commence from this point on to work hard to accomplish our joint legislative goals.

I want to assure each of you most sincerely that it is not my purpose here today to dictate or to otherwise interfere with legislative prerogatives. I am here simply to pass on the sense of what I believe is a public mandate for legislative achievement.

You have already introduced or you are now working on new laws covering the subjects which I will outline as follows:

1. HIGHWAYS. I believe an adequate highway network to facilitate economic growth and to reduce the high accident and fatality rate on our highways is a high priority among your personal legislative goals. Today, I have the advantage of passing on to you the results of long hours of study by my Highway committee which has been working now for several weeks.

I do not believe that the 300 million dollar highway program passed by the legislature in 1969 is moving fast enough to produce results. We can expedite the expenditure of the remaining portion of this program by two changes, viz: (1) The amendment of our eminent domain law to permit the Highway Department to commence construction while litigation proceeds over the value of the land;

And (2) the removal of the interest ceiling of 6 percent per annum on bonds authorized for sale under this program. I understand that bonds totaling 200 million dollars have not been sold and the economical sale of such bonds can be facilitated by the removal of the interest ceiling.

With the changes which I have suggested, construction can be let to contract some time during the fiscal year 1973 which ends on June 30, 1974.

An analysis of the use of the 300 million dollar program indicates now that approximately 100 million has already been committed to contract for the purpose of widening and overlaying. This leaves 150 million dollars available now for new construction.

Approximately 350 miles of 4 lane facilities in congested areas and hazardous rural sections can be constructed with this remaining 150 million dollars. As you know, most all of our highway dollars are matched with equal federal funds giving us a program of approximately 300 million dollars yet to be spent on new construction.

I believe the legislature would want to look carefully at the method of expenditure of this remaining portion of the 1969 authorization.

Although my imagination is staggered by the thought of spending a total of 300 million dollars in the immediate future for new 4-lane construction, I am advised by my highway committee that this will fall far short of providing a complete network of safe highways for economic growth. Therefore, I believe you will want to look at an additional funding program of a long range nature covering an additional 10 to 12 years beyond that to be covered by existing funding.

We need an additional 600 million dollars to complete this highway network. As you probably know, it takes 5 years from engineering to ribbon cutting for the construction of the type of highways needed. Therefore, it is essential that the legislature look at the long range solution now so as to give proper authorization for planning, right of way acquisition, and construction.

I too, am hesitant to pass on to the people another tax increase for highways, however, our own economic well being and personal safety may demand that we act now.

Assuming that we need additional revenue to pay the principal and interest on additional highway revenue bonds, I want to assure you that I have no precise answer as to the amount needed or the source for such revenues at this time. My Highway committee has some suggestions which they will pass on to you if requested.

The Highway committee further recommends that some type of formula be designed by the legislature for creating priorities for solving the most critical needs for highways in an orderly fashion. The Highway committee, together with its full time executive director, stands ready to continue rendering such service as requested by the respective committees of the legislature.

The Highway committee may not have the solution, but I want all of you to know that they have made a sacrifice attempting to solve this most complex problem and urgent need of our people.

The individual members of the committee as well as its executive director will be available to consult with the committees or with individual legislators to study the underlying facts leading to these recommendations. I sincerely hope that we can meet this major problem head-on and arrive at a decision before the end of this session.

2.   **INDUSTRIAL DEVELOPMENT.**   All of us hope to increase our per capita income. To this end, I believe that we

need two essential and productive state agencies to create new impetus in the field of industrial and business expansion.

I think it is time that we considered restructuring the operation of our Agricultural and Industrial Board and our Research and Development Center. We need to remove overlapping functions and to recreate the exact mission of each agency. There is sentiment, and I concur, to allow the R&D Council rather than the Board of Trustees, to control the R&D Center's operation. This would allow direct input into our industrial development as opposed to a quasi industrial, educational, and civic mission.

We need the direct aid of each agency as a coordinated and unified function. We cannot afford to have competing and overlapping agencies. A new name for the A&I Board, such as "Mississippi Industrial and Tourist Board" would correctly reflect the mission of this vital agency and eliminate confusion.

I hope you will favorably consider a bureau of Small Business Administration within this agency so as to work closely with new Mississippi businesses and give adequate response to the increasing demands for development of home grown industries. As we expand industrially, there is an increasing need for support industries locally owned and operated. A bill will be introduced creating a fund to guarantee bank loans for necessary working capital for small Mississippi owned enterprises.

In a new concept to renew our efforts to get our fair share of the tourist industry and all other types of economic expansion. I will create a Council for Economic Development by executive order, composed of businessmen to coordinate the activities of the private industrial development organizations with that of state government. I hope you will lend local support to this council as I believe it will be a new creative arm of state government.

I encourage your support to help create more interest from the private business and banking community to form private development corporations now authorized under our state laws. These private development corporations can be used for both debt and equity capital investments. In all of these efforts, the main thrust will be directed toward helping to develop new opportunities for our people—new opportunities which will give the people of Mississippi a higher standard of living, a better way of life.

3. TOURISM AND STATE PARKS. On February 1 we will initiate a new law which I believe will be helpful in the administration of our state park system. However, many of you who use these state parks will agree that we are substantially behind our sister states in capital improvements.

I hope you will look favorably at some new plan to bring our state parks to a level where we can compete for the recreational dollars spent by Mississippians as well as travelers. Also, we must move rapidly to take advantage of our historical sites and natural attractions. I am looking forward to working with you on new programs, including an effort being made by several areas of the state to have coliseum accommodations for public affairs as well as conventions.

4. ABSENTEE VOTER LAW. Many of us found our supporters unable to vote and we must now pass a law giving our college students, out of state workers, and others an opportunity to vote in all elections. As you consider this amendment, I urge you to also consider rigid penalties for abuse of the absentee voting right.

5. STATE GOVERNMENT REORGANIZATION. Many of you agree that we need to change certain functions of state government by eliminating overlapping agencies and creating more efficiency and economy in the operation of state government. The entire proposition of reorganization is too complex to consider in this session, however, I believe that we can and should consider three changes, namely, a new Department of Administration, an expanded Department of Revenue, and an expanded function of the Department of Public Safety.

6. DEPARTMENT OF ADMINISTRATION. It is my understanding that the work product of the former administration is now being converted to a bill covering this new department.

It is my belief that the creation of this department will greatly benefit the people of Mississippi through a more efficient handling of public funds and with much less confusion and uncertainty when new duties are imposed upon state government. I favor uniting the commission of budget and accounting; the state purchasing department; the surplus property procurement commission; clearing house for federal state funding; the classification commission; the building commission; and the capital commission into one major division of government to be known as the department of administration.

Many of you have expressed sentiment that we need more post audit functions and I suggest that this new department will give the legislature the authority which it needs to assure that the executive branch of government is operating in accordance with legislative intent.

7. DEPARTMENT OF REVENUE. It is my understanding that a bill has been prepared and will be introduced which will create a Department of Revenue through the transfer of tax collecting duties of the Motor Vehicle Comptroller's functions to the State Tax Commission and the transfer of the duties of the premium tax collection from the Insurance Department to the State Tax Commission.

The bill, as I understand it, contains provisions for transferring law enforcement from the Motor Vehicle Comptroller to the Department of Public Safety. This new department would efficiently handle all tax collecting duties of state government. It would be able to use modern techniques of data processing to insure the collection of all money due the state.

8. DEPARTMENT OF PUBLIC SAFETY. An expanded concept in this agency would include the transfer of the Bureau of Drug and Narcotic Enforcement from the State Board of

Health; a bureau of vehicles to cover the enforcement of our laws covering tags, titles, licenses, and safety inspection; and technical compilation of other functions of state government as related to law enforcement.

9. PUBLIC RELATIONS AND INFORMATION. In an effort to rapidly sell and promote the economic development of our state both to Mississippians and to the citizens of the other 49 states, I believe it would be wise to change the name of the State Sovereignty Commission and to allow this agency to undertake a broad mission in the field of public relations and information, thereby giving us a professional approach to this vital field.

10. VETERANS FARM AND HOME BOARD. I believe you will want to support an amendment to include the eligibility of National Guardsmen in this program and to increase the amount of loans from 16,000 to 20,000 dollars.

11 EDUCATION. Within the limits of our general budget, I urge you to support enabling legislation to allow more degree granting facilities in areas of Mississippi now handicapped because of the location of the nearest degree granting facility.

12 PROPERTY ASSESSMENT EQUALIZATION. Court decisions in other states make it mandatory that we face this problem at an early date. I hope you will conduct studies in this session which will lead to the introduction of fair and equitable legislation.

In conclusion, I want to again thank you for your unusual and outstanding cooperation and friendship. I believe the people of our state are proud of the progress that we have made thus far and are complimentary of our efforts toward a teamwork concept in this administration. Each of you have a standing invitation to visit with me on any subject at any time of the day or night. I believe this will be the most productive session of the legislature in the history of the state.

State of the State Address

WILLIAM LOWE WALLER
January 13, 1976

L ieutenant Governor, Lieutenant Governor-Elect, Speaker of the House, members of the Mississippi Legislature, former Legislators, elected officials:

Section 122 of the Constitution requires the outgoing Governor to report on the condition of the state government. This responsibility today presents me an opportunity to reflect upon major accomplishments during the four years of this administration.

Hundreds of people have stood with me to make the accomplishments of this administration possible. I offer my grateful thanks for the support which I have received both within state government and from scores of private citizens.

On January 18, 1972, when I made by inaugural pledge, I said, "working hard, honestly and with all my strength to serve all of our people" — I believe this is a good creed and one that has made possible certain accomplishments.

The people owe a debt of gratitude to the present and former members of the Senate and House that served these past four years – including the fact that this is the first administration since 1890 to have four complicated and involved, annual sessions of the Legislature. Many of the Legislators agreed with me some of the time, and some of the Legislators agreed with me on a few issues – none of the Legislators serving these four years agreed with me on every issue. This is good, and this is healthy for government, because the Constitution mandates, and the nature of government requires, that there be a certain advocacy between the branches of government and that, when necessary, this advocacy becomes adversary. The two branches of government cannot be, and should not be, wholly compatible on all issues.

Carroll Waller and I have actively traveled throughout the state, and have visited many of the smaller communities and all of the 82 counties. This has afforded me an opportunity to learn more about our state – the ideology and the philosophy of all of our people. The knowledge which I gained from this extended dialogue with the people leads me to conclude that our state is united for progress and has an aggressive spirit that can lead to great things in the immediate future.

I hope you have a copy of our published administration report entitled "The Challenge to Change." This is a compilation of the activities of all of the significant functions of state government. I hope you will read the report – a reflection upon all the major happenings in state government, including legislative changes. I refer you to the report to review many items of legislation studied and reviewed by legislative committees and special study commissions. I hope that the work product in the development of these legislative changes will not be lost, and that you will consider the propriety of carrying forward many of the proposals of the past four years.

Speaking of work effort, I would like to remind the people that the 1972-1976 legislature has been the hardest working legislature in our history – having considered 9,653 bills filed, which was an increase of 50% over the previous four year administration, which had 6,663 bills to consider.

I have asked you to reflect carefully upon the numerous commissions and study groups which have functioned throughout these four years and to use the work product of funds expended and expert advice obtained to write new legislative proposals in the future.

As recently as thirty days ago, I met with a number of Legislators on a task force to consider means and methods of developing our numerous inland ports on rivers and waterways in this state. This is but an example of the ongoing projects which should be continued, and which will produce results for our state's economic growth opportunities.

One other interim study commission that I call to your attention for emphasis, and as an example of the outstanding efforts of senators and house members, is that of the tourism study commission, which has spent endless hours considering the need in this state for a major tourist attraction – defined as a destination point for travelers. Whatever the recommendations of this commission might be in the future – I respectfully urge that the resources of these longstanding study-groups not be lost and that they be carried forward actively.

All state employees seem to me to have a renewed dedication and professional performance of their duties. Many outstanding agency directors that were in office prior to my administration and those that were appointed by me have demonstrated a level of excellence that is probably without precedent in this region.

Today, I pay tribute to the loyal and devoted state employees and to those county and city officials who have magnanimously cooperated with federal projects and state programs. This is the reason why Mississippi is the fastest growing state in the nation, and the reason why our multi-national industrial companies are now turning in increasing numbers to Mississippi.

Our economic development programs are being cited nationally. We have seen awards for our efforts in small and minority business assistance and in promoting the concept of the free enterprise system in our state. Recently, the Congressional Joint Economic Committee listed Mississippi's economic development programs as among the most innovative and effective in the nation.

We have successfully opened dependable foreign markets for our agricultural commodities and manufactured goods – the food and fiber center established by the legislature in 1973 is now receiving international attention for the role it is playing in the development of new food products for sale and distribution to the underfed millions of the world.

These and other efforts have required the coordination of

many public and private sectors. By working together we have made unprecedented progress in the development of our human resources.

In education we were able to increase funding for grades 1 to 12 by 64% – we increased funding for our universities by 80% and for the junior colleges by 100%. No other state can claim these advances in the support for education.

Our new dental school, I am told, is now rated as potentially the finest in the nation, having been adequately planned and adequately funded by the Mississippi Legislature.

The establishment of new areas of study such as the schools of Veterinary Science and Architecture have given young Mississippians enthusiasm and identification with our state and its future.

We were able to put together the largest public works program in the history of our state – A $600 million highway program. In the field of outdoor recreation, we have made new state parks available throughout the state; have created more resources in the Game and Fish Commission; and have adopted the wildlife heritage project of acquiring 40,000 acres of the most beautiful land in the world.

Again, Mississippi excels according to national authorities in preserving our wildlife heritage and in offering outdoor recreational opportunities for every citizen.

The largest building program in the history of our state was augmented in this administration, including the expenditure for capital improvements at our state institutions of more than $260 million. Our newly restored Governor's Mansion has brought national attention and prestige to our state.

All of us together have fought hard to improve Mississippi's national reputation and image. There is substantial evidence for you to believe today that Mississippi has emerged as a state with a new perspective and a new plan for development.

In fact, Mississippi is regarded by both public and private leadership nationally as a state on the move with an accelerated growth pattern and with great opportunities for economic expansion.

I believe our rate of growth, which cannot be measured minutely from week to week is exceptionally high and that this momentum will continue to increase under the next administration.

These are exciting times for Mississippi. Our best years are right now and immediately in the future.

Mississippi's unemployment rate has consistently been in the area of 3% below the national average and our personal income has increased at a rate 15% higher than the rate of national increase.

In the last quarter of 1975 we saw significant signs of improvement in our state's economy. At the end of December, our tax collections were 7% higher than the previous year and total collections exceeded the estimated amount of revenue.

The National Industrial Development Research Council – a professional organization of developers who select new plant sites for the nation's leading companies – has given Mississippi a perfect 100% rating. We were one of only ten states to receive this rating which is one way of saying that the people who make the big decision rate Mississippi at the top.

A recent report of the National Planners Association predicted that Mississippi will lead the nation in creating new industrial jobs in the next decade. In a recent report in *INDUSTRY WEEK Magazine*, this group predicted that manufacturing jobs in Mississippi will rise 23.6% between now and 1985.

Our state government will have an ending cash balance on June 30, 1976, of at least $25 million. The state's credit remains unimpaired, and we have suffered less in the last 24 months than most any other state in the union. For example, some 25 states have either increased taxes or reduced services, and there are many others now operating with huge deficits. I congratulate this legislature and the administrators of the departments and agencies for having been careful and businesslike in the operation of state government. With careful management and a short delay, Mississippians should look forward to receiving all of the services

of state government which are needed, whether it is in transportation, health care, education or whatever.

I predict that the federal government will not maintain the
level of spending in this state. The president has assured all the
governors that federal revenue sharing will continue. However,
with the mounting problems facing congress, I do not see how we
can expect to receive the same number of dollars in the next four
years that we received in the past four years.

In closing, let me say to you very candidly, that I feel that I
received better support from the people and from the legislature
than any governor in recent history, and I say this in spite of the
fact that certain members of the Mississippi news media enjoyed
those small spats between the governor and the legislature.

The people of Mississippi truly deserve the best possible form
of government that we can give – and I challenge you to throw
aside personalities or political choice, and to be behind Governor
Finch and Lieutenant Governor Gandy, and create a faster
growth rate for our state. The future is bright, and I hope that I
will be invited back here one day to share with you the great
achievements of this, the new administration.

Achievements of the Waller Administration

1972-1976

A. ECONOMIC ADVANCEMENT

1. Created trade missions to the Middle East, Far East, Europe, and South America and opened new markets for Mississippi products which helped to create additional jobs in the state.

2. Created the Food and Fiber Center at Mississippi State University which developed new ways to process and market raw materials and increase the value of the gross state product.

3. Capital investment in new and expanded industries at $3 billion as compared to a total of $2.5 billion in new and expanded industries over the previous 27 years.

4. Created more than 54,000 new jobs in the four years of the administration.

5. Increased gross state product by 55 percent.

6. Increased Mississippi per capita income by 43 percent.

7. Created Mississippi Film Commission to promote the state as a leader in the motion picture industry. In 1975, Mississippi ranked second only to California in movie production.

8. Created Mississippi Economic Development Corporation to advance economic growth.

9. Created the Office of Minority Business Enterprise, the first such economic development agency in the nation.

10. Organized a state Small Business Administration to assist with loans to owners of small businesses.

11. Attracted to the state such blue chip industries as General Motors, Dupont, and National Geographic.

B. EDUCATION

1. Increased funding for public education, grades 1-12, by 64 percent.

2. Increased per pupil expenditures in public schools by 48 percent, to that point the largest increase in the state's history.

3. Created Governor's Office of Education and Training.

5. Created model program for drug education, placing drug education specialists in classrooms.

6. Created schools of dentistry, veterinary science, and architecture within the state's Institutions of Higher Learning.

7. Elevated five state colleges to university statues — Alcorn State University, Delta State University, Jackson State University, Mississippi University for Women, and Mississippi Valley State University.

8. Increased appropriations to state universities by 80 percent.

9. Increased funding for junior colleges by 100 percent.

10. Completed Mississippi's educational television network with the network receiving national awards for excellence for programming.

11. Largest annual teacher pay increase in the state's history.

12. Conducted annual seminars on the needs of public school system

C. TRANSPORTATION AND HIGHWAYS

1. Initiated $600 million highway construction program, to that time the largest public works program in the state's history.

2. Completed work on Interstate Highways 55 and 20.

3. Completed work on a $300 million highway construction program that had been started in 1969.

4. Initiated four laning of State Highway 6 from I-55 in Batesville to Oxford, the home of the University of Mississippi, and on to Tupelo, the industrial center for Northeast Mississippi.

5. Opened hospitality centers on two interstate highways.

6. Completed or placed under contract 235 miles of four-lane and two-lane corridor highways.

7. Expanded the Port of Gulfport.

8. Authorized development of the Port of Rosedale in Bolivar County, a Mississippi River port.

9. Began actual construction on the federal Tennessee-Tombigbee Waterway development.

D. CRIMINAL JUSTICE

1. Created model drug rehabilitation program.

2. Led the nation in state reduction of traffic fatalities.

3. Reinstated death penalty for capital crimes in Mississippi.

4. Enacted uniform jury selection laws.

5. Appointed first professional prison administrator in the state's history and created a nationally recognized training program for prison employees.

6. Created first regional prison facilities.

7. Established the Mississippi Department of Youth Services.

8. Introduced work release program under an expanded Probation and Parole Board.

E. GOVERNMENT SERVICES

1. Enacted open meetings law and established policy of openness in all phases of state government for the first time in state history.

2. Launched "Move the Capitol" program in which the Governor and his administration leaders scheduled open "cabinet" meetings in communities throughout the state.

3. Created a Minority Council which met monthly with the Governor to address issues related to minority populations.

4. Appointed minorities and women to major state boards and agencies.

5. Created a state Department of Mental Health.

6. The state's industries for the blind, for the first time, became self supporting.

F. TOURISM AND HERITAGE

1. Gained approval of a $25 million bond issue for revitalizing the state park system and created five new state parks.

2. Funded and constructed the Coast Coliseum in Biloxi.

3. Restored the Governor's Mansion, and succeeded in having

it designated as a National Historic Landmark, only the second governor's residence in the nation to be so designated.

4. Sponsored the first Governor's Conference on the Arts.

G. HUNTING, FISHING, AND RECREATION

1. Developed four water parks in South Mississippi through the Pat Harrison Waterway District.

2. Constructed nine water parks in Central Mississippi through the Pearl River Basin Development District.

3. Created four recreational parks in North Mississippi through the Tombigbee River Valley Management District.

4. Acquired and/or increased acreage of five wildlife management areas.

5. Created annual Governor's Youth Fishing Rodeo.

6. Developed state-owned Lyman Fisher Station, a fish hatchery, resulting in placing of six million fish of various species in public waters.

7. Acquired 32,000 acres in the Pascagoula River basin in Jackson and George counties, recognized as the world's largest hardwood bottoms, deeded to the state under the Wildlife Heritage Act.
   Undisturbed by man, the area filled with game, wildlife, fauna and flora, is a "Nature World" for Mississippi.

H. HEALTH CARE AND SOCIAL SERVICES

1. Created Governor's Select Committee on Health

2. Developed statewide plan for health care.

3. Expanded family planning services.

4. Reorganized State Board of Health and mental health agencies.

5. Created nutrition programs for the elderly, the first such programs in the nation.

6. Expanded community-based programs for care for the elderly.

7. Created Mississippi Department of Youth Services.

8. Expanded Probation and Parole Board and created work release programs under the Board.

I.   TAXPAYERS AND CONSUMERS RELIEF

1. Reduced state income taxes by $19 million.

2. Eliminated taxes on prescription drugs and farm supplies.

3. Doubled homestead exemption for elderly citizens.

4. Created Consumer Protection Agency.

5. Reduced interest rates allowable on small loans.

6. Revised laws for home owner and farm owner insurance resulting in consumer savings.

J. FISCAL INTEGRITY

1. Ended the Waller Administration with a $134 million surplus.

Colonels and Aides de Camp of Governor William Lowe Waller

1972-1976

J. C. "SONNY" MCDONALD, CHIEF OF STAFF

ADAMS COUNTY:
Robert A. Barrett
D.A. Biglane
James M. Biglane
Dr. Charles S. Borum
Alphonse Buttross
Peter Buttross, Jr.
Peter, Buttross, Sr.
B.C. Callon
Forrest Ralph Colebank,
     Jr.
Forrest Ralph Colebank,
     Sr.
James Rutherford Cox,
     Jr.
Sammy Dossett
Edward Ellis
Harvey E. Fitzpatrick
Dean L. Fortenberry
Norman Germany
Prentiss H. Graves
Gordon W. Gulmon
Robert B. Haltom
W.B. Hargett
M.M. (Slim) Hedglin
Dr. J. L. Henderson
Dr. G. Swink Hicks
Edward Hinson
Charles R. Hodge
Edward M. Hudson
E.T. (Pete) Jackson
Homer C. King

Dempse McMullen
Orrick Melcalfe
Monroe J. Moody
Robert A. Nobile
John J. Nosser
Leslie Reed
William F. Riley
Whit E. Robinson
Paul Schilling
M. T. Seale
Barnett S. Serio, Jr.
R.B. Sharp
Burnon D. Smith
John V. Whitt
Fernie Wood, Jr.
Clarence N. Young
John R. Young, Jr., M.D.
Joseph S. Zuccaro

ALCORN COUNTY:
J. Hal Anderson
Rodger Bain
E. S. Briggs
Bobby Bumpas
Troy Bumpas
Jesse L. Clifton
Thomas E. Cooper
Ray Crow
Hull Davis
John P. Davis
H. L. Denton
Bobby Elam

Mark Fraley
Joe Franks
L. D. Furtick
Gerry Godwin
Leroy Green
Johnny Henson
John Hopkins
William C. Hussey
Max Johnson
Wilford (Bud) Johnson
Robert G. Krohn
Bobby Little
Leland Martin
D. C. (Duke) Mathis
J. Richard Milam
Know Mills
Jerry Moore
Lynn Nash
Aaron Parsons
Bill Phillips
R. L. (Bobby) Phillips
O. W. Pittman
James E. Price
Roy Savage
Truitt Stockton
Dick Walden
Sanford Whitehurst
Maury Whitfield
A. J. Wigginton
John T. Wilbanks
Ronald Windsor
Hank Worsham, III

AMITE COUNTY:
Jesse L. Adams, Jr.
Benoyd H. Bell
Melvin Blalock
W. L. Crawford
Willie Joe Cruise
E. H. Hurst
Charles L. Kinabrew
Ray Lee, M.D.
John M. Mabry
Gerald Miller
Clifton A. Terrell
N. B. Travis, Jr.
Milton H. Walker

ATTALA COUNTY:
James W. Atwood
Charles Billie Brashier
Lonnie Braswell
Elmo H. Breazeale
Frank Cornelius Burch
John Moody Burge, Jr.
Wayne Carrol Burkett
Robert P. Cummings
David Eubanks Dodd
Edward Marcell Duke
Donald Laney Edwards
Robert Clarence Ellard
Ezra Daniel Ellis
G. M. (Mac) Gallaspy
Dr. R. Neaves Gilliland,
    Sr.
Willie Doyle Goss
Louis Lamar Gowan
Ernest Matt Graham
Don Bryce Hayes
Willie Clark Howell
Horace G. Hutchinson
J. Marlin Ivey
Chatwin M. Jackson, Jr.
Bill Jordan
Herbert Cannon King
George Allen
    McDonald
W. A. Monroe
Ernest Myrick
John Swanson Niles

Harold Benard
    Nowell, Jr.
E. Felix Parrott
Bernice Ray Pearson, Sr.
Hugh Swinton Potts, Jr.
Thomas Coleman Potts
Harold Ross Sides
Thomas Julian Swafford
George Judson Thorton
James D. Watts

BENTON COUNTY:
David H. Bennett
S. P. (Sonny) Childers
George G. Gray
Bryant C. Hines
Howard Johnson
Bobby J. Leak
J. K. McGaughy
Marlin B. Pulliam
J. C. Ray
Neil J. Stroupe
Wyatt Thomas

BOLIVAR COUNTY:
J. E. Baskin
Homer B. Benton
Earnest M. Boling, Jr.
William S. Boswell, Jr.
Bryn Bright
J. B. Bruce
J. W. Busby
A. B. Caston
Stanley Child
Jimmy Ervin
Rudolph Griffin
Clarence Pate
William Allen Pepper,
    Jr.
Garland Pope
Phillip Rizzo
P. Nevin Sledge
Douglas B. Taylor
Clayton West
John D. Williams

**CALHOUN
COUNTY:**
Ed Alexander
Jimmy Earl Aaron
M. W. Arrington
Dr. W. J. Aycock
Rodney Beckett
Wilburn William
    Beckett
Ulon Bowles
William Dunbar Brand
William Howard
    Brasher
Hugh Brower
J. S. Bryant
Billy Keith Burnham
R. B. Chandler
Charles Chrestman
Gwin Cox
Dr. Charles H. Crocker
Ottis B. Crocker, Jr.
William J. Crutchfield
Vernon Davis
James A Harrelson
Danny Hawkins
F. H. Hawkins
Gary L. Hawkins
H. L. Hawkins
Charles H. Holcomb
R. R. Inman
W. B. Kimzey
J. W. Knight
Paul M. Lowe, Jr.
Rex Marshall
William Earl Morgan
J. M. Mounger
Henry Joe Patterson
Jerry Plunk
T. W. Plunk
James E. Snyder
Dr. Ray Teas
Van B. Todd
Dr. Thomas P. Waits
Harry E. Waller
Stanley Williams
J. C. Willis

CARROLL COUNTY:

Mack L. Boykin
B. H. (Bilbo) Brown
H. P. Bryan, Jr.
Rev. Norris I. Corley
Dr. M. S. Costilow
Luther S. Gilmer
G. A. Sanders
Donald Shelton
George W. Tuberville, Jr.
W. B. Vance
T. A. Watson

CHICKASAW COUNTY:

Theodore E. Casey
R. Kenneth Coleman
C. Webb Collums, Jr.
Edward E. Davis
Brandon Gann
James H. Hardin
James J. Hill
Mack Hinton
Gordon Huffman
Leon Marin
Robin H. Mathis
C. P. McKinnis
Walter M. O'Barr
T. M. Parks
Harry G. Robinson
William C. Stewart
William C. Stewart, Jr.
W. F. Thomas
William E. Walker, Sr.

CHOCTAW COUNTY:

Oliver Benton Anderson, Sr.
Alvin Coleman
James Cecil Lancaster
Arnold McHan
Paul James McIntyre
J. Al Owen
Rev. Dan Thompson
David A. Winfield

Bruce Lavell Worrell, Sr.

CLAIBORNE COUNTY:

Col. Jake L. Abraham
Lee h. Abraham
A. Alford Batton
Nicholas M. Ellis
Wiley H. Hatcher
James Hudson
Robert E. Lee
Wade H. Lowe
Henry S. Marx
Clyde L. Nelson, Jr.
James W. Person, Jr.
John W. Salter
Elvyn P. Spencer

CLARKE COUNTY:

Harold Edward Akins
Monroe Allen
Ardell Covington
Clifford Moore (Buddy) Davis
Van Edward Dees
Carroll Dudley Donald
Wallace Franklin Eddins
Clifford T. Farrar
Henry Lewis Flowers
Billy Harris
Rev. Harold Boyd Harris, Jr.
James Monroe Haywood
A. L. (Buddy) Irby
Thomas Jasper Nichols
Larry Lavon Redmond
Lavon Redmond
Glynn Robinson
Clarence Sellers
Franklin Linton Slay
Fred Edwin Stanley
James W. Watts
Larry Eugene Yarbrough

CLAY COUNTY:

James O. Bishop
J. T. Brand

Robert F. Brand
George W. Bryan
James D. Bryan
John F. Bryan, Jr.
Harvey S. Buck
Eugene F. Cater
Jabe H. Christopher
D. Earl Clark
J. D. Denton
Kenneth D. Dill
William E. Doughty
L. A. Duke
Thomas A. Duke
Robert D. Harrell
Ernest E. Hicks
R. Barnes Marshall
Jeff L. Montroy
Evan E. Tumlinson
G. Larry White
Wayne White
Noel M. Wright

COAHOMA COUNTY:

Francis Marion Brewer
Ralph Campbell, Jr.
Melton S. Cauthen
J. W. Corley
George Pat Davis
Joseph F. Ellis, Jr.
Lester (Buddy) Ellis
James Thomas Ervin
Fitzgerald Farris
James E. Furr, Jr.
Ralph Gaddy
Sam Godbold
Travis Gorrell
J. C. Hawes
William S. Heaton, Jr.
J. O. Hitchcock
H. B. Hood
Lonnie B. Lowe
James N. Maclin
Wilburn Meredith
Ralph G. Metcalfe
William Edward Metcalfe
Joseph David Nosef, Jr.

J. H. O'Briant
Chester L. Owens
T. J. (Jack) Perry
Harvey T. Ross
David Sandige
W. J. (Red) Shepard
Vito J. Sharvati
Douglas Tynes
Tom Ware, Jr.
Jerry Williams
Joel R. Williams
Walter H. Williams
William Edmund Young,
Jr.

COPIAH COUNTY:
John T. Armstrong, Jr.
Robert A. Ashley
D. W. Blakeney
Carey V. Bolls
A. Dan Breland, Jr.
Cecil R. Burnham
Frank Carney, Jr.
Frank A. Carney, Sr.
E. Forrest Case, Jr.
Hollis Cowan, Sr.
Ben C. Daughtry
Edwin H. Dennis
Dale Drummonds
Hubert Gallman
Walter Doug Garland,
Jr.
Harold Graham
Howard Graham
R. E. Harper
William D. Hawthorn
Joe Hennington
Frank Higdon
Norman N. Jackson
Herbert H. Johnson
Dr. John H. Long
E. R. Lowery
Sells T. Newman
William Lewis Reno, Jr.
H. C. Rose
Harold W. Scott
Dr. James R. Stingily

**COVINGTON
COUNTY:**
Bobby Boleware
R. Eddie Blackwell
William S. Cliburn
Kenneth Crawford
Jackie Dickson
Bobby Joe Dykes
Roscoe Fairchild
Dr. E. D. French
J. S. Gatewood
Rudolph R. Gibson
F. M. (Speck) Graham
Lawrence Hemiter
Guycell Hughes
William (Boots) Hughes
Hubert S. Lott
Allison Mooney
Norman G. Stevens, Jr.
Marvin C. Taylor
Douglas J. Tyrone
Joe L. White

DESOTO COUNTY:
Kenneth Abele
Barry Wilson
Bridgeforth
Dudley Black
Bridgeforth, Jr.
Donald M. Brown
William M. Cole
John H. Coughran
Robert Stuart Acree
Curbo
William Edward Davis
N. C. Furguson
Charles Irby Ford, Sr.
Ross L. Franks
Bob Goodman
Bob Gray
William F. Hagan, Jr.
Carl B. Hamilton
Boyd Hardin
Ora Walker Hardin
William Douglas Hardin
Arthur E. Huggins
R. Stamps Jarratt
Bob S. Jones

Thomas Worthington
Jones
Dud Lewis, Jr.
J. H. McCracken, Jr.
Ronald Leon Moody
James Barry Morgan
Erlend R. Nichols
Harry Rasco
Floyd S. Robertson
Clarence E. Sutton
James Owen Thompson
David Hoover
Vandenburg
Dr. Henry M.
Wadsworth, Jr.
L. R. White
Paul Dean Whitfield,
Sr.
Joe Lex Wooton

FORREST COUNTY:
Dorrance Aultman
Peter J. Baricev
Edward E. Beasley
J. C. Bell
Stephen H. Blair, Jr.
W. H. Boteler
Raymond C. Brandle
Wilson Brandon
M. L. Bruce, Jr.
Walter P. Cartier
B. L. Chain
Gary Chamblee
J. B. Culpepper
George C. Curry
Clyde Dearman
Raymond M. Dearman
O. H. Delchamps, Jr.
Frank Dement
John Efird
Wiley Fairchild
James Finch
Charles Finnegan
Joe Dale Fortinberry, Sr.
Jugh P. Garraway, Jr.
Van Grady
R. A. Gray, Jr.
Morgan W. Guess

Royce C. Hamilton
W. A. Hanberry
George Hays
William M. Headrick
William M. Headrick, II
Roland W. Heidelberg, Jr.
David K. Hemeter
Steve L. Henderson
Edwin B. Henson
Willie Hines
Charles W. Holt
H. C. Hudson
Horace O. Hughes
Paul B. Johnson, III
Jerry Lynn Johnson
Rex K. Jones
Donald Kelly
Joe R. King
Richard Lancaster
Emmitt Landry
N. Jack Lee
Norman Lovitt
Louis E. Mapp
John W. McArthur
J. L. McCaffrey
J. Warren McClesky, Jr.
Michael E. McElroy
J. F. McFatter
Rev. Monsignor James McGough
James F. McKenzie
Bob E. Mixon
Alfred Moore
H. R. Morgan
Josh Morris
Chester S. Moulder, Jr.
Cecil Ray Mullins
Leslie Newcomb
Louis E. Norman, Jr.
R. L. O'Neal
Maxwell Pace
Clarence T. Pearson
Norman J. Petro
Claude F. Pittman, Jr.
Claude F. Pittman, III
Jack H. Pittman
Reid Pittman

E. A. Pledger, Jr.
Homer J. Poore
Peter Potter
Thomas F. Puckett, M.D.
Ernie F. Ray
James B. Reed
Sam Rees
Ernest Rhodes
H. T. Richardson
M. M. Roberts
Shelby Rogers
James C. Rowell
Kaiser Runnels
T. F. Schrader, Jr.
Irvin E. Sellers
Bernard R. Shamp
Herschell Shattles
Mike Shelton
Paul T. Shows
O. L. Sims
Charles H. Smith
Johnnie Lee Stevens
D. Gary Sutherland
John R. Tadlock
Frank Tatum, Jr.
Joe F. Tatum
John F. Tatum
John D. Thomas
Louis U. Thompson, Jr.
Ted Tibbett
J. Louis Tonore
John Tullos
William F. (Tripp) Turman
J. Ed Turner
Thad (Pie) Vann
Joe P. Venus
Jon Mark Weathers
Stoney Williamson, M.D.
Joe R. Winstead
C. W. Woods, Jr.
Obie Yonce

FRANKLIN COUNTY:
Buford Ashley

Wilson Buckley
Billy Chapman
Buford Davis
Joe Frost
Wayne Hutto
Wayne Kent
Dr. William Larkin
W. M. Scarbrough
Jack S. Stanley
Allen Watts

GEORGE COUNTY:
K. M. Brannon
Joe L. Cochran
Woodrow John Cochran
Anthony S. DiBenedetto
Roy E. Dunnam
Alfred L. Eubanks
Perry L. Eubanks
Clayton Evans
Edward E. Evans
Reginald J. Green
Robert A. (Pete) Hall
Author F. Holcombe
Ray Hunter
Darryl A. Hurt
Harold L. Landrum
Maurice L. Malone
Reverend John Merk
Herman Roberts
T. A. Wilder, Jr.
Hulett Upton

GRENADA COUNTY:
Robert Harl Alexander
William T. Brewer, Jr.
Filo Coats
Clinton U. Collins
E. J. Embry
Phil Embry
Dr. Ben P. Evans
George Garner, Jr.
O. W. Geeslin
Burton Hankins
Lebeth Huggins
Max Juchheim

Ed Lewis
John Little
Harry Lott
Joe Love
Mitchell M. Lundy
Billy W. Majure
James O. Marchbanks
Paul McElroy
Wayne Russell Miley
Phil Poovey, Jr.
Nick Potera
Robert E. Ratliff
Robert Earl Ratliff
Jack Richardson
J. M. Robertson
George Scarberry
William O. Semmes
Robert Lewis Smith
John Tedford
Henry Joseph Theis
Dr. Walter D. Vick

GREEN COUNTY:
Richard G. Byrd
Billy G. Cooper
Donald L. Crocker
Lamar Green
T. D. (Pig) Green
Ford C. Hodges
Ogden J. Miller
Hyatt Platt
Wayne Pulliam
James V. Reynolds
T. C. Rounsaville

HANCOCK COUNTY:
Roy Baxter, Jr.
Ray James Bordages
Louis J. Breaux
Egan Norwood Carroll
Charles E. Carter
Elus E. Depreo, Sr.
Wayne Phillip Ducomb
Sam L. Favre, Jr.
Robert L. Genin, Jr.
Percy Franklin Gibson
Joseph Ruble Friffin

Ronald L. Guilbeau
Alton A. Kellar
E. G. (Jim) Kelley
Jerry L. Ladner
James Ausbon Rester
Clifton Gilbert Roberts
J. D. (Big John)
    Rutherford
Dr. John D. Rutherford,
    III
Billy Dale Sills
Hildin Shaw
Johnson S. Shaw
Herbert L. Stieffel
James N. Travirca
Paul White

HARRISON COUNTY:
Jesse D. Adcock
T. H. Anderson
Alphonso L. Babin, Sr.
Scofield C. Berthelot,
    Sr.
Earl B. Blessey
Ermon Bond
Sonny L. Broadus
Neville J. Broussard
Charles F. Burkitt
Adrian D. Burns
O. H. Burns
Larry Q. Cantrell
Donald D. Caudill
Ernest Cook
J. B. Cooper, Sr.
Dr. Thomas H. Cooper
Glen Cothern
Joe L. Creel
James A. Crosland
Floyd Davis
Joe S. Dickson
Bennie E. Dollar
Douglas W. Dubuisson
William F. Dukes
Jerry J. Ellis
Joseph A. Ellis
David J. Faulk
J. R. Fayard

E. D. Flanagan
John M. Foretich, Sr.
Paul M. Franke, Jr.
Paul M. Franke, Sr.
Lawson E. Gallotte, Jr.
Lawson E. Gallotte, Sr.
C. E. Glindmeyer
Russell M. Godard, Jr.
Bob Irving Golden
Bob Irving Golden, II
Houston C. Gollott
Dominic
    Gospodinovich
Frank Graham
Brown Graves
Peter Halat
Edmond M. Haley
Thomas V. Haley
Earl D. Hammond
Phillip W. Hawk
Harry P. Hewes
Boyce Holleman
Alben N. Hopkins
Reverend L. M. Hudson
Moody B. Irby
Robert W. Kelly
Edgar L. Kinner
Paul F. Kovacevich
Jim Landrum
Russell E. Lee
Oliver K. Lion
Sherwood Manuel
Jerry B. Massey
Raymond Mathers
Homer (Louis)
    McKnight
R. B. Meadows, Jr.
David W. Mills
Albert Joseph Misko
George A. Misko
Donn Ronlad Mitchell
Sam Sterling Mitchell
A. Jake Mladinich
Leonard (Luke) Moore
Maurice Morgan
Thomas Morgan
Sam Morse
Bobby G. O'Barr

Joe M. Petro
Ralph Pietrangelo
Dr. Stephen Pitalo
Lester M. Porter, Jr.
Benjamin Franklin
   Prichard
Charles Proffer
Laz Quave
Andrew Laughlin
   Rainey
Clifton Curtis Randall
J. N. Randall, Sr.
William Ashton
   Randall
Richard R. Rosetti
Henry C. Rushing
Calvin Ryan
William A Saucier
John K. Savell
Gerald E. Scharr
George Schloegel
Lawrence Shrmetta
Frank Slaughter
Rafield L. Slay
D. C. Stanbro
N. L. Stanbro
Norman Arthur
   Stanbro, II
Edwin A. Stebbins
Gus Stevens
W. Adron Swango
Glen L. Swetman
Gill N. Switzer
Edward C. Thompson
Anthony Tonerey, Sr.
Howard O. Towry
F. Walker Tucei
Charles A. Webb, Jr.
Charles E. Weems, Sr.
Laddie Weems
Armand E. Weilbacher
James E. Weir
J. E. Wentzell
Gibran Bernard Weby
Liddle White
George L. Wright, Jr.
George L. Wright, Sr.
Norman Yandell

V. W. Yeager, Sr.

HINDS COUNTY:
J. M. Abraham
Fred Adams
Paul Adams
W. W. (Bill) Adams
Eddie R. Adkins
S. C. Agnew
John L. Albritton, Jr.
John E. Aldridge
Robert C. Alexander
Walter H. Alexander
William A. Allain
John L. Allegrezza
Charles Allen
Earl H. Allen
H. T. (Tom) Allen
W. H. (Bill) Allen
Joel L. Alvis, M.D.
Dale E. Anderson
James D. Anderson
Johnny F. Anderson
Thomas (Luke) Andries
H. H. Annison
Paul N. Apostle
Gene Arledge
M. V. Arledge
Ed Arnold
Thomas Edward
   Arrington
William Arrington
D. B. Arthur
Douglas B. Arthur, Jr.
Albert Wells (Jack)
   Ashford
Y. W. Atkison
B. Galloway Austin
W. E. Austin, Jr.
W. G. Avery
George C. Bailey
Woodrow W. Bailey
Owen W. Baldwin
Dr. George Ball
C. D. Barland
Charles Clarence
   Barlow
M. S. Barnett

Ross Barnett, Jr.
William R. Barnett
Steve E. Barter, Jr.
Jack E. Bass
A. E. Beall
Fred Beemon
James C. Bennett
John W. Bennett
Grover U. Berry
Herbert Berryhill
James Allen Berryhill
Earl L. Bezard
A. B. Biggs, Sr.
Melvin Bishop
J. L. (Jim) Black
T. G. Blackwell
J. D. Blaine
Charles Gilmore Blass
Henry E. Bodet, Jr.
Raymond D. Bonner
R. K. Bonslagel
Dr. Richard E. Boronow
Dan Bottrell
Jim Bourne
Francis S. Bowling
Thurman L. Boykin, Jr.
Ray T. Bracken
Charles R. Brady, Jr.
Dan Hill Brady
Judge Thomas Pickens
   Brady
George W. Brannon
Tom Bratcher, Jr.
Tommy L. Breazeale
Alvin E. Brent, Sr.
Herschel Brickell
Jack C. Brock
Clarence L. Brooks
James H. Brooks
Algie Broome
James L. Brown
Marion J. Brown
Tom C. Brown
Dr. Clyde C. Bryan
John R. Bryan
John Howard Buford
Thomas Doyle Buford
Delos H. Burks

Harold W. Busching
C. Buck Bush
O. P. (Jack) Byars
Charles F. Byrd
John M. Byrd
Breck Cabell, Sr.
Frank Cabell, Sr.
Gary Cahill
Bryan Campbell
Ray R. Cannada
Gerald B. Carmichael
J. D. Carmichael
H. C. (Boo) Carroll
Charles King
   Castleberry, Jr.
Ed L. Cates
John W. Causey
John A. Chamblee
Bartlett Buford Clark
Julian L. Clark
John Clingen, III
Curtis E. Coker
William J. Cole, III
Ben C. Collier
W. Donald Colmer
William H. Cooke, Jr.
Jerry L. Corvin
Henry B. Covington
Dr. Sam A. Cox
A. D. Craft
Billy Stewart Craft
Lanny M. Craft
Larry Craft
E. E. Craig
Boston Criswell
John Crocker
Clark W. Cross
James L. Cummings
Sanford M. Cummings
Kelly Currie
Jack D. Curry
Claudie L. Dallas
Raymond Dallas
Dr. Ralph Daniel
Rank Dantoni
Barney L. Davis, Jr.
James Davis
Colonel James L. Davis

Murl O. Davis
Ralph Davis Day
Russell C. Davis
Joe T. Dehmer
Joe T. Dehmer, Jr.
Douglas G. Dendy
Nicholas John Dennery
F. Lee Dickson
Dr. Arthur H.
   Dohlstrom
Ralph Dorris
Warren Dorsey
W. Edsel Dotson
Nelson L. Douglass
Fred Drinkwater
Kenneth Drummonds
John DuBose
Daniel R. Dugger
Percy E. Dumas
Richard B. Durgin
A. L. East, III
William Eastland
Woods Eastland
David S. Edmonds
N. Frank Edmonds, Jr.
Carl Edwards
Larry Edwards
James A. Elliot
James Elwin Etheridge
Don Evans
Edsel Evans
George W. Evans
Dr. S. R. Evans, Jr.
W. J. (Jack) Evans
William J. Everitt
George K. Farr, Jr.
R. E. Farr
Robert E. Farr
E. E. Farrow
Lawrence A. Feduccia
Carl Ferguson
William W. (Bill)
   Ferguson
Albert Charles Ferrell
Henry Michael Fischer
Doxey Fisher
Alvin P. Flannes
Wayne Flannigan

David F. Flemming
Curtis Flowers
Lewis R. Floyd
Dr. Marshall
   Fortenberry
D. G. Fountain
John H. Fox
T. E. Franklin
Cresco Frazier
Jack Freedman
Pete H. Friersson
Dr. Earl Fyke, Jr.
King F. Ganner
Jackie Gardner
Leslie Gardner
Marshall L. Gardner
Randall M. Gardner
Denby Garrison
Raymond Gartin
Alex Owen Gatewood
Dr. Hiram A. Gatewood
Earl C. Gharst
Bill Giardina
Farris C. Gibbs
Jack Giddens
Normer Gill
George B. Gilmore
W. K. Goff
E. Frank Goodman
John E. Gore, Jr.
William A. Gowan
William A. Gowan, Jr.
C. M. Grantham
Steve Grantham
P. A. Greenwell
Gus Gregory
Owen F. Gregory
Lamont Griffith
Ray C. Guidry
Charles C. Hairston
Alan Halliburton
O. W. Hamblin
Roy E. Hamblin
Robert B Hamilton
Harvey J. Hanks
John L. Hannon
Hack Hardin, Jr.
James W. Harris

Stanley M. Hart
John L. Harvey
Jack A. Hatcher
Thad Hawkins
Judge George William
  Haynes
E. F. Hederi
Fred C. Henderson
R. M. Hendrick
J. O. Hendrix
Wayne Herbert
Bill Herm
Dr. J. R. Herrington
William C. Hewitt
L. B. Hilburn
L. Breland Hilburn
Richard A. Hill
Ken Hilton
Sam J. Hodges, Sr.
Alex A Hogan
David E. Holderfield
Jim M. Holiman
W. J. Holy
Thomas A. Holliday
L. Wendell Hollis, Jr.
Edward H. Holmes
Warren A. Hood
Durward L. Hopkins
Bryant Horner, Jr.
Homer Lee Howie
Charles A. Hubbard
John Hubbard, Jr.
Austin Hudson
Charles Hughes
Dr. Calvin T. Hull
John Hulsebosch
Charles L. Hunt
Joe Jack Hurst
Frank Hutton, Sr.
Ronald C. Hux
R. W. Hyde, Jr.
E. P. Jackson
Harry Jacobs
Allison James
David B. Jenkins
F. L. Jenkins, Sr.
Dr. Marvin H. Jeter, Jr.
R. B. Johnson, Jr.

Russ M. Johnson
Dr. Sidney Johnson
Hal Johnston
J. T. Johnston
E. Grady Jolly
Dr. C. Edmondson
  Jones, Jr.
Everarde E. Jones
Walker W. Jones, Jr.
William J. Jones
Robert W. Karlak
James R. Keenan
Sam Keith
Tom B. Kelly
William Kelly
Howard Kennedy
Horace L. Kerr
Frank Kimbrell
Reverend Charles King
Paul B. King
E. G. Kirby
Joe Kirkland
Roy A. Kitchins
E. A. Knight
James P. Knight, Jr.
George G. Lack
Don Lacy
Dr. Floyd E. Lagerson,
  III
E. E. Laird, Jr.
Dr. C. H. Lake
Clifton Landrum
Alex William Langley
Edward H. Larkins
Carl A. Lee
L. J. Lee
Robert E. Lee
Vincent Lee
Horace B. Lester, Sr.
Edwin R. Lewis
Roland C. Lewis
Dick Liddell
William J. Liles, Jr.
R. W. Little
E. C. Lloyd, Jr.
Joe P. Loftin
Winfred B. Lott
Guy C. Lowe

Jay Clinton Lowe, Jr.
Will Lowery
W. B. Lucy
O. M. Luke
Francis J. Lundy
Dr. J. C. Luter
Dr. Paul W. Lycette
Nick J. Lymberis
Robert A. Mahaffey
James Toby Majure
Richard H. Malone
Edward Charles
  Maloney
John P. Maloney
Emmett Malvaney
Robert G. Marchetti
Dr. Charles Martin
Curtis L. Martin
Henry O. Martin
Jim L. Martin
Mike Martinson
Cecil B. Matheny
James H. Matthews
Calvin May
Charles Mayfield, Jr.
Preston R. Maxson
Harold R. Mayer
Frank H. Mayo
William E. Mays, Sr.
J. D. McAdory
John C. McBeath
James M. McCain
W. B. McCarty, Jr.
Billy J. McCool
Dr. J. T. McCullough
J. C. (Sonny)
  McDonald
J. L. (Pete) McGee
J. B. McGehee
Judge M. M. McGowan
A. H. McGuffee, Jr.
John S. McIntyre, jr.
Alex McKeigney
Gene McKey
Ben M. McKibbens
Ernest W. McLaurin
B. L. (Ben) McLemore
Charles McMullen

David McMullan
Joe K. McPhail
Richard D. McRae
Sam P. McRay
Sidney D. Meadows
James H. Means
Birl B. Miller
Harold D. Miller, Sr.
J. A. Miller
John E. Miller
Scott F. Miller
William A. Miller, Jr.
Sam Irvin Milner
Sammy Milner
Albert Mitchell
Carey Moak
Henry Andy Moak
John M. Mobley
W. H. (Sonny)
   Montgomery
Dr. James B. Moore
Lloyd Pat Moreland
A. D. Morgan
L. T. Morgan, Sr.
William Richard
   Morgan
William Morgan, Jr.
Jerry Morphis
Dan Morse
John E. Moses
Walter Anthony Moses,
   Jr.
Ernest C. Moss, Jr.
H. D. Mulholland
Earl Mullen
Tom Murley
John M. Murphy
Dr. John W. Murphy
Charley Myers
Dewey Myers
Emile Nassar
J. T. Naugher
Hugo Newcomb, Sr.
Paul N. Nielson, Jr.
Charles D. Noble
Dr. Lewis Nobles
Dr. Edward R. North, Jr.
George Nuzzo

Louie Odom
William P. O'Leary
Delbert Oliver
Willard Oliver
Emmett H. Owens
Dr. Terry S. Ozier
Thomas D. Pace, Sr.

Thomas Dredzell Pace,
   Jr.
Thomas Dredzell Pace,
   III
Larry G. Painter
Richard T. Parker
A. Tom Patterson, Jr.
Thomas Bell Patterson
Costas E. Pavlou
Alex S. Payne, Jr.
James A. Peden, Jr.
Randolph Peets
Carey E. Pennebaker
James Mike Peters
Grady L. Pettigrew
Don Pettit
Logan Phillips
Rubel Phillips
Thomas Hal Phillips
M. S. Pierce
William Leslie Polk
Amos A. Ponder
Barry H. Powell
Robert I. Prichard
Robert A. Pritchard
Ralph L. Priester, Jr.
Paul J. Pryer
Ben Puckett
Arnold L. Pyle
Van D. Quick
J. I. Rankin
P. M. Ratcliff
R. P. Redd
James C. Reddoch
Seab Reynolds
William T. Richardson
Sam Riddell
John Rider
John W. Roberts
Nolle T. Roberts

Bill Robertson
Dr. Douglas Robertson
James F. (Jack)
   Robinson
Robert Robinson
Sidney A. Robinson, Jr.
Bill R. Robinson
Jack Roell
Leroy Roell
D. S. Rosen
Dr. William H.
   Rosenblatt
William Rumbavage, Jr.,
   D.V.M.
Dr. James V. Russell
C. D. (Pat) Russum
Ernest E. Saik
James R. Sanders, Jr.
Rae Sanders
Dr. Sam Sanders
Woodrow Saway
Clarence R. Scales
J. W. Schimpf
Seymour Schwartz
William H. Scott
C. Pat Seabrook, Jr.
L. E. Sellers
L. M. Sepaugh
Charles H. Sewell
Kenneth B. Shearer
Thomas B. Shelton
Dan C. Shepartd, Jr.
J. E. (Buddy) Sheppard
H. B. Shirley
Dr. Alex C. Shotts, Jr.
Leon Shulmeister
Dean S. Shuttleworth
Dr. Eugene F. Simmons
Dr. Heber Simmons
W. D. Sims
C. E. Smith
Hebert Smith
James Pat Smith, Jr.
Jarmon Ford Smith
John P. Smith, Jr.
John. T. Smith
J. W. Smith
J. W. (Red) Smith

Ravon M. Smith
Robert G. Smith
Robert W. Smith
W. Hugh Smith
Ralph Sowell, Jr.
James. M. Spain, Jr.
Joe L. Speed
William L. Speed, Sr.
Dr. James P. Spell
Jack E. Spence
Thomas H. Spencer
Robert L. Stainton, Jr.
Charles T. Stark
G. C. (Jack) Starkey, Sr.
E. W. Stennett
C. K. Stephenson
James J. Stewart, Jr.
Robert N. Stockett, Jr.
Robert N. Stockett, Sr.
John E. Stone
H. G. street
Roger Stribling, Sr.
Udell Stubbs
Billy Louis Sullivan
Floyd M. Sulser
Dr. Bruce Sutton
John L. Swindle
Thomas M. Tann, Jr.
Hillarie (Boots) Tanner
Jerry Q. Tanner
Anthony A. Tattis
Bob Taylor
Larry L. Taylor
Dr. R. L. Taylor
Denny A. Terry
John H. Thames, Jr.
John Mack Thames
Bob Thomas
Leon S. Thomas
Wayne Thomas
Wayne Edward Thomas
E. Lloyd Thornton
Johnnie Thornton, Jr.
Glenn E. Thurmond
Kenneth P. Toler
B. H. (Bill) Toney
Herbert H. Touchton
Robert N. Touchstone

Wm. O. Townsend
Bob Travis
Jack A Travis, Jr.
Joe P. Tubb
Robert E. Turcotte
William H. Underwood
Paul Ussery
Donald O. Vaughn
E. Howard Vickers
Phillip Wade
W. Ralph Wadlington
Jack B. Wakeland
Charles E. Wallace
William L. (Bill)
    Waller, Jr.
Charles Walsh
Willie Ray Walsh
James C. Walton
O. B. Walton
Will B. Walton
Erwin C. Ward
Lincoln E. Warren
Sam W. Warren
Joseph M. Warwick
Ralph L. Waters
A. C. Watkins
Edward F. Watkins, Jr.
Homer W. Watkins, Jr.
Malcolm Dent Watson
Malcolm Dent Watson,
    Jr.
Dr. Robert L. Watson
William V. Watson
J. C. Weaver
Daniel Weber
Robert S. Weir
Bernard Weiss
Jacques Leon Weiss
James M. Wellborn, Sr.
Lee M. West, Jr.
Jack L. Westbrook
E. D. White
Harold R. White
Dick Whitehurst
Yandell Wideman
James A. Wilcox
Cecil D. Wilkinson
Gene A. Wilkinson

George A Wilkinson
Leslie L. Wilkinson
Louis Wilkinson
A. H. Williams
Edwin Cale Williams
John Perry Williams
Merton E. Williams
Morris Williams
Johnnie H. Williamson
C. R. Wilson
Howard A. Wilson
John P. Wilson
T. E. Wilson, III, M.D.
Terrell Wise
Charles R. Wood
James A. Wood
George Woodliff
Charles A. Word
Thomas B. Worley
Dr. Charles N. Wright
T. E. Wright
Charles S. Yeager
George W. Yeates
Harold P. Young

HOLMES COUNTY:
D. C. Conn
Tom A. Cothran
Homer L. Daniel
Charles P. Durham
Charles P. Durham, III
R. K. Farmer
James Joe Ferguson
William (Tom) Garrett
J. R. (Bob) Gilfoy
Dr. H. L. Gowan
Joe Guess
E. W. Hooker, Jr.
W. B. Johnson
J. C. Lever
Anthony B. Mansoor
C. W. (Billy) Martin
Paul F. McCain
William Henry
    McKenzie, Jr.
Calvin A. Moore
Calvin A. Moore, Jr.
Nolan H. O'Reilly

Malcolm E. Phillips
J. R. (Sonny) Sanford
Robert C. Thompson
Charley C. Wade
William D. Wilson
Robert M. Young

HUMPHREYS COUNTY:
Thomas J. Barkley, M.D.
Robert W. Bearden
R. O. (Buddy) Bridgers
Charles E. Daley, Jr.
Carol Dupuy
James L. Estes
J. W. Gardner
R. P. Hairston
Dr. James L. Houston
J. Drue Lundy
Ollie Mohamed
Mitchell R. Pearson
Bill Perkins
James W. Sandifer
T. M. Simmons, Jr.
James D. Sudduth
Irby Turner, Jr.
Irby Turner, Sr.
O. J. Turner, III
Thomas Newell Turner, Jr.
Thomas Newell Turner, Sr.
Reverend Joseph A. Warner

ISSAQUENA COUNTY:
Henry Bobbs, III
Arthur Lawler
James T. Mabus, Jr.
James T. Mabus, Sr.
Harper R. Myres

ITAWAMBA COUNTY:
Billy Wayne Brewer
Johnny Crane
Bobby Gene Davidson

Doyle Davis
Mackey T. Dozier
Nathaniel Dulaney
Otto P. Forrest, Jr.
Glenn Franks
Tommy R. Gann
Billy Gilliland
Delmus C. Harden
Larry E. Homan
William L. Kilpatrick, Jr.
Boyce McNeece
Woodrow W. Mears
M. Hubert Miles
Dan W. Moore
Truman Shields
Charles Allen Spencer
Eugene O. Spencer
Malcolm Stubblefield
Bon Gene Thornton
Ray Thornton
Charles Thurmond
Frank Turner

JACKSON COUNTY:
Fred Broom
Cicle E. Byrd
Norman A. Cannady
Harold R. Comello
Donald W. Cumbest
George R. Dale
William H. Davis, Sr.
Wallace M. Easley
Marcus B. Garrett, Sr.
Joseph B. Gatewood
J. C. Gay
Edwin W. Gladney
Jack Godsey
Gary Gollott
Tyrone Gollott
Roger A. Goodwin
W. C. Gryder, III
Russell F. Harris
Harold M. Harwell
Phillip W. Hawk
Raymond J. Hudachek
Naif Jordan
Earl L. Koskela

Bernard H. Krebs
Harry L. Krebs
Peter J. Kuluz
Lewis M. Langlinais
Wayne Lee
Ray S. Lightsey
Raymon A. Marro
Jack T. May
Jolly McCarty
Robert T. "Bob" McCoy
Gentry F. Miller, Jr.
Roy Miller
W. S. Moore
James C. Page
Thomas Ray Palmer
James C. Parks
Richie E. Perkins
Frank T. Pickel
Arnold E. Pierce
Ted D. Prevost
William T. Roberts
Henry Rushin
Don B. Simpson
Samuel Smolcich
Richard D. Tanner
Alton L. Thompson
Aaron Versiga
James Kell Walker
John F. Walker, Jr.
W. C. Weatherby, Jr.
Charles J. Weeks
Johnny Whitehead
Fielding L. Wright
Charles W. Wynn

JASPER COUNTY:
Robert L. Abney, Jr.
Thomas W. Bass
E. L. Bishop
Jimmie B. Davis
Lee Harrison, Jr.
J. I. Jenkins
Don Jones
Kenneth Lewis
Cleo McCormick
Elton R. Montogomery
Opie Moss
Gary W. Sauls

Bill R. Stringer
George E. Suchy
James A. Sumrall
Sam T. Weir
Neil W. Windham

JEFFERSON COUNTY:
John Seton Allred, Jr.
Leon Goodson
Albert S. Lehmann
Charles Russell
  McPhate
Ed Davis Noble, Jr.
R. T. Pritchard
Robert N. Prospere
Lester Kenneth
  Tanksley

JEFFERSON DAVIS COUNTY:
James E. Baxter
James Carraway
Dr. David B. Dale
Daniel R. Deen
Donald Ray Dukes
Samuel Lee Dyess
Thomas Victor
  Garraway, Jr.
Kermit Hathorn
Jessie Scott Hatton
Gary Jones
Truett McNease
John C. Reardon
George Eddie Schultz,
  Jr.
Robert C. Speights, Jr.
Lloyd S. Steverson
Thomas Sutton
W. M. Warren
Frank C. Wilson

JONES COUNTY:
Bill Agin
C. C. Caldwell
William M. Caldwell
Ron L. Carroll
Leonard Caves

L. A. Connerly
Arthur A. Cox, Jr.
Wilmer O. Dillard
Gerald Donald
J. E. Dubose
W. Harold Elliott
John T. Ferguson
Sonny Fisher
William Daniel Hall
Dr. C. A. Hollingshead
John W. Hunt
Dale B. Jefcoat
H. S. D. Jordan, Sr.
Robert M. Keith
James C. Kelley
George D. Maxey
Carlos R. McDaniel
H. D. McDaniel
J. Sneed McInvale
Alpheus H. McRae, Jr.
Brent Meador
Joe N. Nester
Paul B. Newton
Billy R. Ousley
E. U. Parker, Jr.
R. E. Parker
Curtis Powell
Ralph Powers
J. N. Pryor
James Reeves
Dr. Fred Lindsey Risher
Don T. Scoggin
Cleo Shows
Herman Shows
James W. Smith
N. C. Smith, Jr.
Lowell W. Tew
T. Maury Thames
H. Wayne Trayler
Thomas M. Waldrup
Guy M. Walker
Bobby Walters
David Walters
J. Larry Walters
Ronald Estes
  Whitehead
W. A. Wilby
Charles E. Williams

KEMPER COUNTY:
T. L. Clay
Charles M. Cross
H. Murray Hailey
L. D. McDade
William L. Pilgrim
Roy Rigdon
Lamar Sledge
George Smith

LAFAYETTE COUNTY:
Robert M. Alexander
Milton Baxter
Eldridge D. Bonds
C. A. Briscoe
T. E. Briscoe
Billy Ross Brown
Fred U. Byars
Phillips W. Carpenter
Jeptha Clark Clemens
Paul Coleman
Omar D. Craig
Jack Cullen
Sidney E. Doyle
J. W. Ford
Dr. Porter L. Fortune, Jr.
Gerald A. Gafford
Albert A. Grantham
W. Glenn Griffin
Pat W. Haley
Gayle Hewlett
Garner L. Hickman
Joe Jim Hogan
Dr. Robert L. Holly, Jr.
Dr. M. B. Howorth, Jr.
Robert W. King
John Dale Landreth
W. W. Lee
M. F. Lynch
Judge T. H. McElroy
Karl Metts
Ben Arthur Mistilis
J. W. Mitchell, Jr.
W. I. Oakes
Edgar Harold Overstreet
Joe W. Overstreet
Charles T. Ozier

Leenard Ragland
Basil Richmond
Charles Bramlett
 Roberts
Homer L. Samuels
Fred W. Smith
H. E. Upchurch
Coach John H. Vaught
Earnest W. Walker
Andreth H. Waller
Charles L. Waller
Don Waller
E. Nolan Waller
M. H. Waller
P. A. Waller
Samuel Wayne Waller,
 Jr.
Bill Webb
Robert Whitten
Parham H. Williams
Bob Williford
James A. Wilson
Reverend William T.
 Wright

LAMAR COUNTY:
Reverend George D.
 Berger
Preston Bond
Denny J. Bonner
Otis Bounds
Ronald Breland
J. Robert Buntyn
Herschel Cameron
S. F. Carlisle, Jr.
Dorman Davis, Jr.
William Elkins
Michael R. Eubanks
P. T. Eubanks
Durel Foles
Porter Hudson, Jr.
R. L. Keith
W. E. Lott
William Clyde Lott, Sr.
J. P. Miles
Leroy Miles
Miller Myatt
Carl Roberts

Ira D. Russell
Curtis Wilson

**LAUDERDALE
COUNTY:**
Garlon Paul Acker
Leon M. Bailey
N. D. Brookshire, Jr.
Henry D. Burns
Don Chamblin
Dan Coit
John Leland Culpepper
Marty Davidson
Phil W. Davis
Robert Charles Dickson
M. D. Ellis
W. H. Entrekin
Dr. M. L. Flynt, Jr.
Lix J. Fruge'
Withers Gavin
M. E. (Buck) Greene
Tommy Smith Gunn
T. Michie Hill
James G. Hobgood
John William Hodge
Austin James
Richard L. Johnson
Virgil Jones
Walter I. Jones
Thomas Usry Lawrence
Charles Leroy Lewis
Irvin Leroy Martin, Jr.
Ransom N. McElroy
Robert W. Miles
Clarence L. Milling
Thomas Young
 Minniece
E. J. Mitchell, Jr.
John Mitchell
Ray Carl Mollett
Chad Y. Morgan
Paul M. Neville
Lyndon P. Parker
William E. (Bill) Ready
William M. Renovick
Eugene Reynolds
Melton E. Thodes
Jesse Dee Riddell

Dr. Clarence W. Roberts
Ham E. Sanders
R. E. Scruggs
Elmer Sharp
D. J. Sharron
Herbert Shirley
James T. Singley
Eddie D. Smith
James d. Stodard
Phil Swartzfager
Jetson Perry Tatum,
 M.D.
Frank Abe Taylor
Hillman Taylor
H. D. Temple
Lamar Temple
James C. Wilbourn

**LAWRENCE
COUNTY:**
Mims Berry, Jr.
Mims Berry, Sr.
E. C. Brister
Jimmy Brooks
James Ernest Clinton
Leslie J. Johnson
Donnie W. Lambert
H. Ted Lambert
Frank Malta
Hubert Rutland
Marvin Simmons
Judge E. A. (Beby)
 Turnage
Robert Glynn Turnage
J. Hilton Wall
John W. Waller

LEAKE COUNTY:
Robert Allen Adcock
David Crawley Alford
Joseph H. Denson
Darrell F. Dickens
James (Pete) Eason
Billie Glen Ellis
Samuel Clarence Ellis
Lee L. Fisher
Jack Hardage
Norris Harrell

Haywood Herrington
Rex D. Ingram
Reverend Max Jones
Cary L. Lewis
Dr. James Mayfield
Urvin McRae
Billy Minshew
Robert L. Moss
Rufus Nazary
Willie Fred Nazary
Bobby T. Oliphant
Willie Mack Osborn
Eugene Power
Wallace Day Sanders
Otis E. Sikes
James Edwin Smith, Jr.
James Edwin Smith, Sr.
Lafayette William
  Smith
Dr. Andrew Lamar
  Thaggard
Reverend Adin Adair
  Ward
Billy Tom Ward
Leon Watkins
Laston L Webb
Thomas Kermit Wilcher
Grover C. Williams
Milton C. Winfield
Philip Taylor Young

LEE COUNTY:
J. Sidney Abernathy
Harold Altom
George Beam
Roger Bean
W. M. Beasley
Paul Kent Bramlett
Charles D. Brewer
Dr. Harvey M.
  Campbell
Albert Creeley
Glen H. Davidson
Thomas S. Edwards
Lucian Filgo
Dr. Houston Franks
Royce H. Franks, Jr.
Woody W. Gardner

Chauncy R. Godwin, Sr.
Hebert L. Green
Paul Haynes, Jr.
Ralph C. Harsin, Jr.
Aubry L. Hays
Robert Earl Herndon
Charles (Bozy)
  Hutcheson
James A. Jackson
Guy Jenkins, Jr.
Tommy Jones
Cleo Keith
Hollis Kinsey
Elmo E. Lyle
James A. Marlin
J. W. Martin
W. A. Mayfield
Dr. Tom Morgan
Paul Murphy
J. R. Parker
George Partlow
Buddy Payne
John M. Pearce
Sidney L. Pipkin, Jr.
Sidney L. Pipkin, Sr.
Carlyle S. Poole
Martis D. Ramage
James E. Raspberry
James W. Roberts
Dudley M. Segars
Reese Senter
Troy K. Short
Grady A. Smith
Arlon D. Spencer
Jim A. Spencer
Ferrell Spicer
James M. Stephens
John Bunyan Stone
Dr. W. L. Stroup, Jr.
Bobby Taylor
Charlie Watson
Robert O. Watson
Otis Webb, Sr.
Otis Cecil Webb, Jr.
Henry M. Whitfield
Richmond Morgan
  Whitfield
Kenneth R. Wilburn

LEFLORE COUNTY:
Doyle Baker
Mike J. Ballas
Emmitte Barrett
Johnny Barrett
O. E. Bogart, Jr.
David Brewer
J. R. Brown
Willis Burch Brumfield
Larry Chittom
J. F. (Boja) Clarke
John F. Clarke
Wade Corley
Reverend Jimmy W.
  Dukes
Charles H. Dunn
Melvin Farrish
Johnny Favarra
David D. (Bill)
  Ferguson
J. J. Ferguson
Orlando Fratesi
E. C. Gosa
T. R. Gregory
Tom Ed Guest
Danny Hardin
George L. Haynie, Jr.
R. W. (Dick) Hickman
James Higginbotham
Robert (Bunky)
  Huggins
Edward J. Iskra
Ray W. Joe
Morris E. Johnson
Wesley Kersey
L. B. (Jack) Killebrew
Gordon Lackey
James R. Love
William K. Lusk
Alex Malouf, Jr.
James E. McAdams
Thorn McIntyre
Don McPherson
Donald McShan
R. A. Montgomery
Charles P. Morel
James K. Murphy
B. F. Peeples

W. W. Philley
Marsh Pickett
Jess Pond
Z. A. Prewitt
Joe Pugh
Raymond Riston
C. H. Robinett
Charles T. Rose
D. T. Sayle, Jr.
H. Lawrence Stacy
Ray Tibble
Frank Utroska
Robert Utroska
James Whatley
Rufus Wier
John Winstead
Fred Witty
O. Avery Wood

LINCOLN COUNTY:
Dallas V. Anding
Leon Bardwell
Daniel F. Barrett
Ferdinand Francis
   Becker, II
Bruce H. Brady
Sam J. Bramlette, Jr.
James Wesley Case
Lamar M. Case
Claude (Bill) Diamond
Louis Monroe Durr
James Hilton Furr
Dr. Billy F. Gerald
Irby Goss
W. Morris Henderson
Walton Morris Jones
Ben Laird
Roy P. Malta
Versie Collins Nations,
   Jr.
Malcolm T. Nelson
James F. Noble, Jr.
V. Vincent Panzica
Fred A. Ratcliff
Gordon Redd
Joe Edward Reynolds
Gene Simmons
J. W. Slay

Jimmy Lee Smith
Oddee Smith
Steve J. Smith
R. M. Staurd
Dr. David H. Strong
J. Rex Touchstone, St.
James E. Tramel
Roland B. Wall, Jr.
Will Roy Watts
Lucien S. Whittington
Truman R. Williams

**LOWNDES
COUNTY:**
B. A. Atkins
William M. (Bill)
   Brigham
Eddie Byars
Dudley H. Carter
A. E. Cline
Woodrow Dowdle
Lentz d. Gatlin
W. N. Haggard
James Harpole
James G. Hawkins
Hoyt T. Holland, Jr.
George Leo James
Hugh Kinard
O. C. Logan
Glen Lollar
John Mitchener
J. Douglas Parkerson
John E. (Eddie) Perkins
John R. Perkins
Dr. Perrin Smith
S. A. (Bill) Smith
Emil Spencer
R. Penn Taylor
James B. Thompson
V. W. (Pinky)
   Thompson
Henry K. VanEvery
Thomas F. Woolford, II
Tom Younger

**MADISON
COUNTY:**
David M. Adams

Dr. George D. Allard
R. J. Arnold
Billy S. Beasley
Dudley Bozeman
P. W. Bozeman
Chris Brady
W. B. Brannan
James A. Butchart
David Buttross
Edward Buttross
Ernest L. Buttross
S. R. Cain, Jr.
W. S. Cain
W. G. Clark
Walter M. Denny, Jr.
Hugh Dickson
Fred Estes
General Leslie L. Evans
J. R. Fancher
Joe R. Fancher, Jr.
Robert A. Filgo
R. L. Goza
Rob Griffin
Sam Hailey
Gordon W. Hart
Linn Hart
Edward Hayes
Eugene Hinton
Millard Holcomb
Joe Hutchison
Coy Irvin
Coy Irvin, Jr.
Joe Lupe
Lewis Henry Johnson
Charlie M. Jones
Hermit A. Jones
Joe Kirby, Jr.
W. H. Ledbetter
Ben P. Lewis
Pat H. Luckett, Jr.
M. C. (Fish) Mansell
John Martin, Sr.
R. L. May
Horace McMurphy
Ott Noble
Kline Ozborn, Jr.
Jeff D. Pace
Marion D. Pace

Charles (Chuck) Penn
L. A. Penn, Sr.
Lester A. Penn, Jr.
Donald J. Powell
Robert H. Powell
Bill Presley
Jim Quinn
J. D. Rankin
J. D. Raspberry
S. C. Richardson
Tom H. Riddell, Sr.
Tom H. Riddell, Jr.
Tom H. Riddell, III
H. C. Roberts
W. T. (Bill) Robinson
Frank Simpson, Jr.
Frank D. Simpson, Sr.
Marion C. Smith
William Hugh Smith,
  Sr.
Dr. E. G. Spivey
John B. Stephenson
J. N. Stewart, Jr.
James A. Stewart, Sr.
Reverend Morris A.
  Taylor
A. Thomas Taylor
Wardell Thomas
Ray Thompson
Don Leo Varner
Joe Watts
D. R. Yandell

MARION COUNTY:
Charles Shelton Ball, Jr.
Robert A. Bass
L. D. Bennett
Otis B. Broome, Jr.
George D. Byrd
Billy W. Carter
Dr. J. B. Conerly
W. T. Cooper
David Edwin Fite
Frank A. Fortenberry
Lester Haddox
Robert F. Haddox
Norton B. Hahn

William R. Houston
Thad B. Lampton, Jr.
C. C. Mabry
Billy Ray McKenzie
Boyd McKenzie
Burley Moree
Byron Fleet Morris
Roy Newson
Robert J. Pace
Bill Pachmayr
Lee Anthony Polk
Harry L. Rankin, Jr.
Harry L. Rankin, Sr.
Ben Rawls
Sedgie F. Reid, Jr.
Thomas L. Riley
Craig Robbins
Laverne Robbins
Charles E. Robertson
Shelby Simmons
Willie W. Simmons
John G. Sowell
Charles M. Thomas
Dwight L. Wesley, Jr

**MARSHALL
COUNTY:**
J. M. (Flick) Ash
George M. Buchanan
Wayburn Callicutt
Dennis C. Carlisle
C. D. Collins
Joe Cooper
Charles N. Dean
Robert P. Dent
J. K. Hurdle, Jr.
Joe H. Hurdle
T. D. Hurdle
Egbert w. Jones
Alfred E. Loftin
Jack McClatchy
Johnny Taylor
James C. Totten
Morris Valentine
Dudley Walker
Odell J. Wilson
G. Hamlet Yarbrough

MONROE COUNTY:
Larry Brazil
Dr. Robert Eugene
  Coghlan
Sterling B. Crawford
Charner Willette
  Duckworth
Jim C. Dye
J. C. Dyson
David G. Hodo
Albert I. Langford
Walter Henley Lann, Jr.
Steve Frederick Martin
Clarence R. Maxcy
Jerry Maxcy
Charles Wesley
  Montgomery
William T. Oakes, M.D.
Casey F. Randle
Jerry A. Reese
Robert Nelson Stockton
Sherrell R. Sturdivant
Jesse Vander Turnage
John David Turnage
Dr. John Neil Turnage
Smith McRae Turnage
William Stevens Turner
Wade Weatherbee
John Wright

**MONTGOMERY
COUNTY:**
Charlie Howard
  Aldridge
W. A. Austin, Jr.
Paul G. Beck
Wayne Braswell
Milton Brister
William P. Dodson
J. V. Ferguson
T. D. (Bill) Golding
Billy E. Graves, Jr.
E. F. Henderson
Paul Hood
Bobby B. Howell
James E. Kennedy
Billy D. Lancaster
William Liston

Larry McClellan
Earl A. Moore, Jr.
Lenis Pearson
Mal S. Riddell, Jr., M.D.

**NESHOBA
COUNTY:**
Tim Allen
Reverend T. E.
    Anderson
W. Uriah Banks
Dr. Jim Barfoot
W. T. Blackwell
Glenwood Breland
Olen Burrage
Robert J. Coghlan
Stanley Dearman
L. L. Flint
T. V. Gamblin
Robert Huck Graham
Earl W. Gray
Morgan Hardy
Hubert Hodgins
Terry Jordan
Jerrell (Pete) Ladd
Curtis McDonald
Eric Mioton
C. V. Mitchell
Richard Molpus
Claude Peebles, Jr.
Wendell Perry
John Risher
W. Tingle Savell
George Saxon
Ray O. Smith
Alvis C. Thaggard
Laurel G. Weir

NEWTON COUNTY:
Dr. L. Bernell Adkins
Jack W. Brand
RobertW. Carleton
Edwin H. Johnson
Dr. H. L. May
J. E. McMullan
Milton McMullan
O. C. McNair

J. R. Pace
Judge L. B. Porter
W. K. Prince
Hansell Reeves
Bert Sellers
Billy Thames
Robert R. (Bob)
    Tillman
Wade H. Turnage, Jr.
M. E. Wade
James Dale Wakham,
    M.D.
Bennett C. Ware
Robert Weir, Jr.

**NOXUBEE
COUNTY:**
Ernest L. Brown
Robert Crespino
Dr. Pat Gill
John Lamb
Dr. John A. Nicholas

**OKTIBBEHA
COUNTY:**
Bobby Briscoe
Donald Joe Bryant
John A. Crawford, Jr.
Thomas H. Fondren
Ivan L. Hand
Joe Dale Hartness
Ralph Hewlett
Dr. James E. Long
Raymond Love
Paul G. Milsaps
Bob V. Moulder
F. Warren Oakley
W. E. Phillips
R. Tom Sawyer
Dr. Dempsey Strange
J. Wilmot Thomson
Larry Turnipseed
Thomas O. Wakeman
D. D. Waldrop
Dudley Waldrop
Will E. Ward
Floyd Williams

PANOLA COUNTY:
Jesse Mike Amis
Francis Oren Banks
A. L. Brock
William R. Buntin
Hugh C. Clayton
William Wingfield
    Dugger, Jr.
C. Bennett Ellzey
Larry Wayne Fisher
David Robert Garner
James Hollis Johnson
Russell Franklin Koonce
Calvin P. Land, Jr.
Reverend John B. Laney
Richard Wesley
    Matthews
Miles C. Mitchell
James Hal Moore
Tommie Lee Murphy
Tom Sawyer
Milton Cline Wardlaw
William L. Watt

**PEARL RIVER
COUNTY:**
Robert W. Applewhite
James Branch
Grady Brown
Richard Buckley
Michael H. Burks
Joe H. Fortenberry
William J. Guarino, Jr.
Curtis Holston, Jr.
James Oliver Jones, II
R. Fred Moore
Darriell T. Pigott
Robert Ingram Prichard
Edward Lefferage
    Robbins
Ames Culpepper
    (Rusty) Russ
R. E. (Rusty) Smith
J. Monroe Spiers
Bill J. Stegall
Charles Horatio Stewart
James Urban Stewart
S. G. Thigpen, Jr.

J. P. Walker
Joe A. Wesley
John Laymon Wesley
Joe H. Whatley
R. Gordon Williams
John W. Wilson

PERRY COUNTY:
Adolph Johnson
  Alexander
Billy Ray Carey, Sr.
Charles Edward Carley
Dee Hammett
Herbert Hensarling
James Alvin Howard
Frank Harold Jones
Richard E. Lewis
Herbert Stuart
  McSwain
G. F. Mixon
D. O. Thoms, Sr.
Pettis D. Walley
Pettis Walley
James R. White

PIKE COUNTY:
Frank B. Alford
Gordon W. Banister
Dr. A. V. Beacham
James W. Bell
William L. Bierbaum
Carlis Blanton
C. R. Breeland
Pat H. Brumfield
Smithie E. Buie
Wayne C. Dowdy
Jesse M. Eisworth
Ralph H. Felder, Jr.
David G. Forrest
Jerry L. Fortenberry
Tom E. Hewitt
William T. Hewitt
Dr. Warren A. Hiatt
Horace Holmes
Dr. H. T. Huddleston
James S. King
E. E. Lawson
Paul McCullough

Harold B. McRaney
Willie A. Moak
Frank Oakes
Joe N. Pigott
Edmund E. Prestridge
Clyde Ratcliff
Milton L. Roach
Malcolm L. Roseberry
Clyde E. Simmons
Jewel G. Smith
Oscar A. Stovall
Dean B. Strickland
R. E. Turcotte, Jr.
Maurice H. Wall, Sr.
Mike Conner Williams
J. O. Wood

**PONTOTOC
COUNTY:**
G. H. Andrews
Troy Blevins
Lynn G. Browning
E. L. Carpenter
Marvin Clowers
Calvin Coleman
Bob Cook
W. L. Friday
James H. Grisham
Joel Hale
Tommie Hale
Burt Haney
C. J. Hardin, Jr.
Charlie Hicks
Wendell Hooker
Ladell Luther
J. W. Mitchell, Sr.
Buddy R. Montgomery
Frank Oswalt
J. G. Parrish
James D. Patterson
William Rex Patterson
G. Thompson Pound
Powell Prewitt
Larry Russell
D. O. Sneed
D. L. Ward
Robert B. Waters
Elvin Ellis Wilder

Dr. Paul W. Whiteside

**PRENTISS
COUNTY:**
William T. Armstrong
Johnny Arnold
James H. Bethay
Thirmon Bingham
Dewey Burcham
D. C. Cadle
Tommy D. Cadle
Emmitt Carr
Joe Carter
Eddie W. Caveness, Jr.
Willard Chaffin
Howard Davidson
Stanley Downs
Jack Dubard
Paul Ellzey
J. Robert Floyd
Donald Franks
M. D. Goff
M. Paul Haynes, Sr.
W. H. Holley
Jerry Hutchinson
Douglas Jumper
Thomas Keenum
Mike Kemp
Richard M. Kemp
Jimmy Moore
Hershel Perrigo
E. O. Poden
Harold Russell
Vernon Vandevender
John Vassar
Hal White
Harold T. White
C. M. (Mack)
  Whitaker, Jr.
B. F. Windham

**QUITMAN
COUNTY:**
J. T. Aldison, Jr.
Raymond Barker
Dow Rodger Bridges
Joe M. Brown
Jerry Caffey

Dean T. Champion
B. H. Cobb
David Kenneth Cobb
N. W. Faust
Emmet Lamar Gaston, Jr.
Charles Scott Grantham
Sidney Earl Guest
Quitman Elliott Harrison
Billy Harold Holcombe
Burt A. Jamison
Ottis Meredith
Robert Elmer Pinion, Jr.
Ben E. Pittman
Leroy Reid
D. B. Wilder
Herbert R. Wilson
Robert F. Workman, Jr.

RANKIN COUNTY:
Eugene Adcock
Leon Babin
Jerry E. Baker
L. D. Boling
Carlos N. Bradshaw
R. E. Broome
E. D. (Mike) Brown
Crawford M. Bryant
F. E. Burgess
M. H. Burnell, Jr.
C. B. Busby
Henry A. Busick
George Carter
S. N. Casey
Timothy E. Clarke
Billy D. Cook
Grady Rudolph Cook
Tom Coward, Jr.
J. R. Crutcher, Sr.
B. E. Dean
Milton L. Etheridge
Jerry R. Fulton
E. D. Gardner, Sr.
C. D. Gatewood
Dave P. Gayden, Jr.
James H. Gilmore

Xavier M. Gilmore
Reverend Ted Giordano
Thomas S. Giordano
John Pat Grubbs
Clyde P. Herrington
W. T. (Bill) Hogg, Jr.
Clarence E. Ivey, Jr.
Jerry T. Johnston
Johnny B. Jolley
Tommy Kennedy
Preston O. Lewis
George Dan Martin
Marcus Martin
Jimmy K. Mashburn
Albert D. Moore
John L. Morris
Hames E. Netherland
Roy C. Perdue
D. C. Phillips
William L. Polk, III
Bobby J. Raines
Andrew W. Rees
Alton J. Romero
Jack Root
Daniel M. Russell, Jr.
Ted Sanderson
Reverend H. Sellers
Dr. Buren S. Smith
Elbert Allen Smith
James W. Smith, Jr.
James W. Spears
James C. Stewart
Jackie D. Thompson
Francis J. Watkins
Hurst Webb
Joe P. White
W. L. Whittington
Jack Williams
Joe R. Wood
Thomas L. Zebert

SCOTT COUNTY:
Jack Armstrong, Jr.
Jim W. Armstrong
Lane E. Booker, Jr.
Thomas W. Colbert
Edwin M. Davis
W. M. Dearman

W. Earl Elliott
Edward M. Gaddis
Lamar W. Gatewood, Jr.
Richard H. Gatewood
Jack Holman
Dannye L. Hunter
Erle Johnston, Jr.
Dwight Lewis
Tiths Mapp
Jim D. Mashburn
Fred A. Moore
Ricky Phillips
Benny Clyde Rogers
Freddie B. Rogers
Robert (Bob) Sibley
Jerry L. Sistrunk
Jack L. Smith
Robert (Bob) Stringer
Jack Stuart
Jack N. Stuart, Jr.
Barry Tisdale
M. A. Turner, Jr.
Ebb F. (Buddy) Vines
Eugene Watkins
Donald Q. Weaver

SHARKEY COUNTY:
S. E. Boykin
Leon Davis
Ralph Ferrell
Roy Girrard
James B. Heidel
William J. Hunter
Maurice E. Phillips
Penly Sorrels

SIMPSON COUNTY:
Tom B. Alexander
Joe Harold Allen
William A. Allen
E. O. Berry
Larry Broadhead
John R. Busby
H. B. Floyd
Royce Foster
Preston O. Gordon
George B. Grubbs
Floyd Harrison

Bob R. Kidd
W. J. (Bill) King
Charles A. Massey
Eugene B. Polk
Bennie H. Prince
M. B. Puckett, Sr.
Vardaman J. Runnels
H. B. Smith
Siegfried Steinberger
L. A. Thames, Sr.
P. J. Turner
Roy Upton

SMITH COUNTY:
Charles Blakeney
John Locke Bryant
Joe R. Cook
Delton D. Craft
Wayne Currie
J. V. Dukes
Quenton E. Floyd
George A. Henderson
Joseph H. Houston
Joseph S. Howell
Dr. Robert E. Jennings
Hollis Jordan
Windell A. Kennedy
Alfred M. LaPrairie
Dr. Bobby Maddox
Charles McAlpin
Bobby Moore
Sellers Norris
Jerome W. Phillips
G. Stanley Roberts
Jimmie Smith
Billy N. Tadlock
Billy L. Therrell
Travis Thompson
Douglas Wayne
    Thornton
Eugene C. Tullos
Rupert H. Tullos, Jr.
Roy Wyatt

STONE COUNTY:
John A.. Altman
Cleston Barnes
Carl Wilson Boone

Richard V. Brooks
Conner Cain
Charles E. Davis
Thad H. Davis, Jr.
John C. Dees
Edward A. Evans
Polk Evans
Virgil Gordon
David Herchel Hall
Bill Holder
L. A. Krohn
Jimmy M. McDaniels
Durwood Stephens
Woodrow Stephens
James W. Street
Edward Robbins Taylor
Harold Wesson
James N. White
John White
Leroy Yeager

**SUNFLOWER
COUNTY:**
J. T. Allen
R. Julian Allen, III
Howard A. (Hal)
    Atkinson, III
R. N. (Dick) Barrett
Robert Bennett
Ted Borodofsky
Rodgers Brashier
Frank Brumfield
Joe M. Buchanan
John Burrell
D. L. Cole
Walter Crook
John T. Davis
Morris Downs
H. C. Eastland
James C. Evans, Jr.
Edward O. Fritts
W. A. Gatewood
Robert Golden
Larry Hall
John Haltom
J. B. (Bill) Hollowell
Wayne King
Sidney Levingston

Lake Lindsey
Paul Lott
Reverend Bob Lynch
Douglas Neil Magruder,
    Sr.
W. D. Marlow, III
Joseph W. (Bill) Maxey
Terry Maxwell
Charles E. Moak
Joseph A. (Bubba)
    Mohamed
Brewer Morgan
Henry Paris
John Sidney Parker
Travis E. (Red) Parker
W. D. Patterson
Will Green Poindexter
Hunter Pratt
R. M. Randall
Talmon Evon Russell
B. C. Ruth
Clyde Rutledge
Andrew W. Shurden
E. E. Shurden
E. T. Shurden
W. O. Shurden
George K. (Pat) Smith
Joel G. Sturdivant
Champ T. Terney
Pasquel Townsend, Jr.
Reverend James D.
    Watson
Jack K. Wood

**TALLAHATCHIE
COUNTY:**
Paul A. Adams
Andrew (Andy) Baker
Deward D. Bloodworth
C. Benford Brown
Thomas Bartlette
    Buford
Phillip Carnathan
C. C. Chandler
Larry Gene Cole
Freeman C. Coleman
Eugene C.. Fedric
Harvey Goad

Boyd Winford Griffin
James T. Henson
William Kimzey
Leslie Curtis Mabus
Larry Jess McCachren
Harold Moyer
Smith Murphey, IV
Joe Murphy
Durow A. Nelson
Roger Neilson Newton
Pleas Miller Norris
K. C. Peters
David Lafayette Rice
Morris E. (Buddy) Ross
George Henry
    Rounsaville
John Robert Sanders
Tommy Spinosa
Henry Clarence Strider,
    Jr.
Frank B. Swearengen
Joe L. Tennyson
H. D. Tubbs
Jack Criswell Webb
James Jackson Webb, III

TATE COUNTY:
J. Heber Aiken
John M. Dixon
Don Elliff
Carey Embrey
Earl Embrey
Hansel H. Fair
Herbert B. Grisham
Leon E. Hannaford
R. E. Houston
Doyne Hughes
John Jackson
Roy E. Johnson
Robert R. Latham, Sr.
James B. Petrea
C. R. Rials
W. F. Schneller
A. Cleo Sykes
Bobby J. Wardlaw
Billy Wells
John Whalen

TIPPAH COUNTY:
C. C. Bennett
Dewitt Braddock
J. W. Duncan, Jr.
Paul C. Gaddis
Raymond Gaillard
R. S. (Bob) Hardin
Arthur Johnson
Mack Johnson
J. Y. Keith
H. C. Locke
Ira McClusky
Lloyd H. McClusky
J. W. McMillin
John Lee Montgomery
Sam Moore
Billy Nails
Charles S. Pannell
Sperry Reaves, Jr.
Tommy Smith
W. L. Towlinson
Clayton Wammack

**TISHOMINGO
COUNTY:**
P. O. Beard
John H. Biggs
Woodrow Black
Russell Bonds
Herbert Clayton Bostick
Jackie L. Bryant
Howard Rayburn Byram
Richard O. Clark
C. W. Claunch
Frank Crossett
John L. Denson
Dr. Kenneth D. Draper
Herman Gann
Jack W. George
V. W. Grisham
Billy Haskel Hamilton
M. P. Haynes
William Alfred Holland
Bobby Keith Horn
Edward Hubbard
Joe Hussey
G. P. James

David O. Jourdan, Jr.
Millard W. Kent
Dr. Bobby F. King
Donald Glenn Landrum
J. C. Marlar
Kenneth E. Mayhall
E. L. McNatt
N. L. Phillips
Clyne Haskel Pounders
Alva P. Randle
Zoma Jack Rye
G. B. Sartain
Harold Collins Sparks
Myrl Tennyson
Jack Thorne
A. J. Waddle
Dan Young

TUNICA COUNTY:
James S. Branyon
Henry G. Lee
Dutch C. Parker
Billy Pegram
O'dell A. Sanders
W. E. (Billy) Watson, Jr.

UNION COUNTY:
William Henry (Bill)
    Barnett
Charles Coker
Robert Eugene Coltharp
Hugh Craig
Dr. David Bradley Ellis
Robert Vernon Embry
Herman R. Hendrix
Jim Hines
Arthur Audell Hobson
Darrell Leo Ivy
Walter Johnson
T. M. Moody
Houston Pannell
Everett Audie Randle
Dr. Paul King Shannon
O. Zack Stewart
Richard Tate
John Waldrop
James Lawrence West

WALTHALL COUNTY:
Roy Atchison
Harold D. Beckner
Cobert Blackwell
Bill Brent
Tommy Brumfield
Bobby J. Conerly
Jerry F. Connerly
Vernon Craft
Wendell Craft
Van Fairburn
Buck Felder
Earl Ginn
Willie J. Guy
Percy Johnson
H. V. Laird
William Lampton
Chance A. Morris
Al Pigott
Thomas J. Prisk
A. J. Rayborn, Jr.
E. L. Reeves
Otis Simmons
James Singleton
Joseph M. Stinson

WARREN COUNTY:
Edward J. Abraham
Ernest Abraham
Fred M. Abraham
T. F. (Tommy) Akers, Jr.
J. Ernie Albritton
Ben W. Allen, Jr.
Bobby L. Andrews
K. B. Brown
Nat W. Bullard
Percy L. Coleman
James R. Davis
Joe Dawsey
Glenn Dunn
Scott Dyson
Regional Ellis
Rbert Toy Evans
Mickey Farris
R. C. (Dick) Ferguson
Alex Gold
Boyd Golding

Shouphie Habeeb
Gerald Hasselman
Jess E. Hester
Frank Holifield
Philip H. Irwin, Jr.
Roy Johnson
Udelle T. Jones
Reverend Harold C.
    Jordan
L. C. Latham
Frank Maxwell
Crawford Mims
Ira L. Morgan
Milton J. Robichaux
Dr. Joe M. Ross
Walter J. Runyon
Lupious Sanders
H. B. Showman
George Tanous
Landman Teller, Jr.
James C. (Buddy)
    Terrell, Jr.
J. Stanford Terry
George Thomas
Russell Thomas
W. T. Walker
Raymond O. Wilson

WASHINGTON COUNTY:
Jimmy Azlin
Don Otho Baker
Jesse E. Brent
Hampton J. Collier, Jr.
J. Hampton Collier
John Allen Collier
William P. Condon
John W. Cope
F. D. Dawson
Anse Dees
John T. Gibson
Bennie F. Gresham
Dr. Nelson Hamilton
Thomas Wilson Hays
C. B. Hendricks
C. G. Hull, III, M.D.
Frank W. Hunger
Walter H. Kendall

Bob Leavell
J. B. Lee
Conrad Longfellow
J. T. Love
Paul Love
William E. McLellan,
    III
T. J. Meredith
Dr. Everett F. Mitchell
Mack Mooney
Robert L. Morgan
R. E. Nelms
Frederick E. New
J. C. (Hoss) Noble
J. A. Petty
Glenn Pool
Sam Provenza
C. D. Purser
Dr. William P. Reese
Reverend James
    Richardson
Bob Robinson
Bruce Rogers
W. A. Ross
Dr. T. E. Royal
Durwood Ruegger
Irwin G. Starr
G. A. (Archie) Sterling
Larry W. Suchy
L. O. Swint
Rob Thomas
Roby Thompson
Joe H. Ting
H. L. Wade
E. W. Waller
William A. Williamson,
    O.D.
Terrence O. (Terry)
    Young

WAYNE COUNTY:
Louie Bishop
Nolan Clark
James S. Cochran
Lamonte Cook
Ulysses Cooley
John G. Giles, Jr.
W. Ovett Hardy

Spencer Hudson
Grady H. Jones
T. O. Kelley
John T. Lomax
Wilbur J. (Bill) Martin,
    Jr.
Howard Mason, Jr.
Dr. T. O. Massey
Dr. L. O. Murphy, Jr.
Henry W. Odom
William A. Prather
Herbert Ramey, Jr.
Pete Reynolds
Troy H. Shirley
H. T. Strickland
Tradis West
Dr. Allen A. Williams

WEBSTER COUNTY:
J. H. Barton
Joe Bob Davis
A. D. (Dave) Davison
Arnold Duncan
V. W. Easley
James Travis England
Howard Griffin
Robert Griffin
Sam Hightower
Norman W. Hilliker
Boyce Jenning
Terry Landrum
Roger W. Mason
James Mike McCain, Sr.
John Harpole Patterson
John A. Savage
Ullin D. Schmitz
Alonza Skelton
John A. Stevens
W. E. Taylor
Jesse Weeks
Joe K. Wood
Bilbo Wright
Thomas H. Wright
W. H. Yates

**WILKINSON
COUNTY:**
Z. E. Bell

William Henry
    Catchings
Milton D'Aquilla
Dr. Warren H. Dye
Hillery Horn
Charles Inman
Marshall Lumpkin
W. B. McKey
Jessie Moore
Donnie Nutt
Lories Jennings Owens,
    M.D.
Steve Reed
Henry Rosso
Ronald J. Senko
Ernest Ray Smith
William H. Smith
Alonza Sturgeon
Charles Wesberry

**WINSTON
COUNTY:**
Bobby Van Bouchillon
Henry F. Brandt
Romeo Cecil Bridges
James Everett Calloway
Billy Wade Clark
Frank Deramus
Jerry Lavaughn Donald
William Delbert Estes
Joe Brooks Ezelle
Charles Marion Fancher
Therrell Dean Files
Dr. Felix Horton Giffin
Don Goodwin
Earl Hale, Jr.
Phillip Clyde Hill
Henry Bane Hudspeth
Hubert Johnson
W. T. Kemp, Jr.
William Kenneth
    Lawrence
William A. (Bill)
    Mitchell
Ernest Myatt
Sam Eugene Myatt
Robert Gerald Myers
George Shaner

Burris Olin Smith
Ken Statham
Giles Kenton Ward
James L. Warner
Jack Warner
Dwight Kimball Webb
James Vardaman Webb
Holland Ray Wright

**YALOBUSHA
COUNTY:**
Franklin L. Brown
William C. Callaway
Vernon B. Johnson
William R. Oliphant
Bennie C. Taylor
Daniel Waller
Thomas A. (Jack)
    Waller
Harold G. Williams
M. Binford Williams
J. S. Womack

YAZOO COUNTY:
Haley Barbour
Thomas Campbell, Jr.
William Carroll
Victor Cook
Henry Creel
Rayford Hancock
W. S. (Red) Hancock
Father Patrick Joseph
    Hannelly
A. D. Hearst
J. H. Hogue, Jr.
Jerry Johnson
Robert F. Jones
A. S. (Son) King
J. A. Lambert
James H. Neeld, III
Dan J. Nicholas, Jr.
Thomas C. Parry
Hollaman M. Raney
C. E. Savery
Herschel G. Turner

Index

Involvement begins with civil rights
   movement, 61
"It's Charlie's Time", 107–108, 120
"It's Time for a Change", 120

J

Jackson, Mississippi, 13, 28, 43, 59,
   61
Jackson Air Base, 34
Jackson Brace Company, 102
Jackson City Council, 160
Jackson Daily News, 65, 70, 101, 107
Jackson movement, 59–60
Jackson Police Department, 61, 62,
   72
Jackson State College, 161
Jackson *State Times*, 173
Jackson State University, 59, 137,
   160
Jackson's City Court, 59
Jaycees. *See* Junior Chamber of
   Commerce
Jeter, Betty, 97
Jeter, Marvin, Jr., 117
Jeter, Mrs. Marvin H., Jr., 117
Jobs held by Bill Waller, 21–22, 23,
   24, 25–26, 27
Jobs held by Carroll Waller, 39
Joe's Drive-In restaurant, 65
Johnson, A.L., 137
Johnson, Helman, 137
Johnson, Lyndon B., 86, 87, 95
Johnson, Mrs. Paul B., Jr., 86
Johnson, Paul B., Jr.
   campaign promise, 58
   Commission on the Status of
      Women report, 97
   commitment to law and order,
      92
   creation of Research and
      Development Center, 203
   former governor, 202
   inaugural parade of 1972, 130

Phillips 1963 loss to, 87
   race for Lt. Governor, 88
   Sullivan and Eastland ill will,
      121
   wife to run as surrogate candi-
      date, 86
Johnson, Paul B., Sr. (father), 121
Johnston, Earle, 107
Joint session of the legislature,
   143–144
Jones, Durley (cousin), 25
Jones, Edward, 177
Jones, Hermit, 117
Jones Junior College, 160
Joy Waller Art Gallery, 42
Junior Chamber of Commerce, 85,
   91, 96, 103, 117
Junior college presidents, 160–161
Junkin, John, 108
Jury selection process in Beckwith
   trial, 73
"Justice in Mississippi, Notes on the
   Beckwith Trial" (Herron), 73–74
J.W. Norris Funeral Home, 23

K

Kennedy, Carroll, 148
Kennedy, John (President)
   accusation regarding J.
      Meredith and Ole Miss, 58
   assassination attempt, 111
   Eastland support of, 121, 183
   U.S. Marshalls at Oxford, 60
   voting record of W. Winter, 95
Kennedy, Joseph (father), 183
Kennedy, Robert (Attorney
   General), 58, 95
Kennedy, Ted (Senator), 183
Kennington's Department Store
   (Jackson), 37
Kentucky Fried Chicken, 104
Key, Mary (Mrs. John Waller), 7
Kilpatrick, Max, 148